THE MANY LIVES OF THE BATMAN

Critical Approaches to a Superhero and his Media

EDITED BY ROBERTA E. PEARSON AND WILLIAM URICCHIO

ROUTLEDGE NEW YORK

🄱 **BFI PUBLISHING** LONDON

First published in 1991 by

Routledge an imprint of Routledge, Chapman and Hall, Inc.
29 West 35 Street
New York, NY 10001

Published in Great Britain by

BFI Publishing
21 Stephen Street
London W1P 1PL

Library of Congress Cataloging in Publication Data

The Many lives of the Batman : critical approaches to a superhero and
  his media / [edited by] Roberta E. Pearson and William Uricchio.
       p.   cm.
   ISBN 0-415-90346-7 (HB).—ISBN 0-415-90347-5 (SB)
   1. Batman (Comic strip)—History.   2. Comic books, strips, etc.—
United States—History and criticism.   3. United States—Popular
culture.   4. American literature—History and criticism.   5. Myth in
literature.   I. Pearson, Roberta E.   II. Uricchio, William.
PN6725.M36   1991
741.5'0973—dc20   90-49797

British Library Cataloguing in Publication Data

The Many lives of the Batman
  1. American strip cartoons
  I. Pearson, Roberta E.   II. Uricchio, William
  741.5973
  ISBN 0-85170-275-9
  ISBN 0-85170-276-7 pbk

Contents

Acknowledgments

Many people assisted us in various ways in the course of putting together this collection of essays. We owe Dennis O'Neil special thanks for taking the time to share the secrets of the batcave with us, for his generosity with his scripts and the bat-bible and for his interest in the project. Edward Buscombe of BFI Publishing has consistently provided trans-Atlantic editorial support, counsel and the occasional bat-clipping. We thank Tony Bennett for his encouragement, for struggling through some of the essays in very rough draft form in order to meet the deadline, and, perhaps most importantly, for investigating the ideological implications of the popular hero with his coauthor Janet Woollacott in *Bond and Beyond*. Richard Taylor, formerly of Warner Communications Inc. and now Palmer Professor of Telecommunications at the Pennsylvania State University, has helped us in our dealings with DC Comics, as well as provided insights into corporate structure and copyright and trademark issues. We thank William Germano for conceiving of the cover image and Peter Hine for doing the artwork.

Marion Dougherty and Jo Bergman of Warners kindly provided information and assistance about their roles in the Batman film and music video. Lisa Henderson, Scott Bukatman, Steven Ellworth and Tom Andrae deserve thanks for helpful discussions, critical readings and other aid. Our research assistant, Tom Schumacher, collected bat-material for us and gave insightful responses to some of the essays. Siegfried Zielinski kept us abreast of Batman in Berlin. Lois Seitz of the Liberal Arts Computing Center at the Pennsylvania State University reformated many of our contributors' disks into our word processing program. Ruthanne Long, Cindy Willson, and John Yingling patiently and efficiently responded to last minute requests for clerical assistance. The staffs of the Special Collections Division of the UCLA library and of the Library of Congress Serials Division, particularly Daniel Wisdom, facilitated access to the accumulated comic books of the past while Dianna Saiers, of Dianna's Comics in State College, did the same for the present. We must also express our gratitude to our contributors, without whom the book would not be possible.

The editors wish to acknowledge their debt to each other for a thoroughly equal collaboration. The realities of publication force one name to precede another on the cover of this volume as well as within it, but academic Realpolitik force us to state that the name sequence nowhere indicates "seniority." Throughout the editing of this volume, as well as the writing of the various pieces, we have collaborated to such an extent that we could not ourselves distinguish our "individual" contributions.

We regret the absence of illustrations, particularly since they would have, in many cases, helped to elucidate the argument. DC Comics refused to grant us the right to use images as they did not feel that this book was consistent with their vision of the Batman.

Holy Shifting Signifiers:
Foreword

In introducing *Batman: The Dark Knight Returns*, Alan Moore notes the degree to which Frank Miller is able to dramatically redefine Batman's character in spite of his fidelity to almost every aspect of that character's mythology:

> Yes, Batman is still Bruce Wayne, Alfred is still his butler and Commissioner Gordon is still chief of police, albeit just barely. There is still a young sidekick named Robin, along with a batmobile, a batcave and a utility belt. The Joker, Two-Face, and the Catwoman are still in evidence amongst the roster of villains. Everything is exactly the same, except for the fact that it's all totally different.

In outlining the changes wrought by Miller—the portrayal of Gotham City as an almost postapocalypse scene of urban decay, his foregrounding of the fascistic element in Batman's advocacy of vigilanticism beyond the law, the transmutation of Robin into a girl as a commentary on the repressed gay aspects of the Batman/Robin relationship—Moore counterposes these to what he describes as a tendency toward statis inscribed in the comic book. Inherently conservative in view of their conception as a juvenile medium, he argues, "comic books have largely had to plod along with the same old muscle-bound oafs spouting the same old muscle-bound platitudes while attempting to dismember each other."

Cast in this light, the Batman of the late 1980s—of Miller's graphic novel and of Moore's own *The Killing Joke*, and, of course, of *Batman: The Movie*—appears as if a sudden irruption into the field of signs, a moment in the popular hero's life that is without parallel or precedent. Clearly, the kinds of cultural and ideological remodeling of Batman that have prepared the way for and marked the passage of his fiftieth anniversary have been significantly new in many respects—and often

conflicting ones. If Batman has been figured forth in a new guise so
as to serve as a vehicle of social commentary, that same process of
redefinition has simultaneously served as a means of breathing new life
into, and organizing new circuits of distribution for, a commodity
which might have otherwise have been looking at a long shelf life. Yet,
while right to stress its importance, it is misleading to see this moment
in Batman's career as exceptional. Indeed, the anniversary publication
of various commemorative collections of Batman stories offers compelling evidence of the degree to which—in comic book format alone—
the figure of the Batman has been subject to a constant process of
redefinition.

For one whose "bat-teeth" were cut on the comics of the late 1950s
and the parodic TV series of the mid-1960s, it thus came as something
of a surprise, reading *The Greatest Batman Stories Ever Told*, to discover the strength of the Gothic associations of Bob Kane's first Batman
stories. And there have been many changes in between—some resulting
from new writers, others from changing publishing and marketing strategies, others in response to changing external circumstances like the
Comics Code of the 1950s—affecting not merely the character of Batman, (or as purists would insist, of the Batman) but his milieu, his
helpers and, of course, the villains he opposes.

It is these changes—the migrations of a shifting signifier—that Roberta Pearson, William Uricchio and their co-contributors have sought
to chart in this collection. In doing so, they have been commendably
pluralistic in their approach. In considering the changing textual conditions of Batman's existence—the conventions of genre, technical and
aesthetic developments affecting the graphic arts, the character system
of the Batman oeuvre—they have related these to changes in the economic conditions of the comic industry, its marketing strategies and
its relations to the film industry. And these considerations, in turn,
have been connected to the changing discourses—of crime, urbanism,
sexuality—to which, as either political conditions have required or as
a changing cultural environment has suggested, the figure of Batman
has been adjusted. The economic considerations affecting the many
and diverse forms of Batman's commodity circulation (Batman toys,
the licensing of the Batman logo, etc.) are also examined as are the
possible psychoanalytic bases of the caped avenger's appeal, while the
interviews with Frank Miller and Dennis O'Neil accord the creative
intentions of graphic artists' full and proper consideration. Nor, finally,
have the conditions of reading been neglected. Indeed, the attention
paid to the variable assumptions, values and intertextual coordinates
which have influenced the way Batman texts have been read by different
kinds of readers and audiences in different circumstances convincingly

demonstrates the degree to which, once a popular hero is taken up within a culture, it fulfills a range of signifying functions which, lacking the kinds of empirical and ethnographic evidence offered here, can often only be guessed at.

In concluding his introduction to *The Dark Knight Returns*, Moore suggests that Miller's most significant renovation of the Batman mythos was that of introducing time into the life of the hero. This is true, and not merely in the sense that Miller's Batman is cut free from the timeless eternity in which comic book heroes often live so as to age and thus confront the prospect of his own mortality. It is also true in the sense that Miller's Batman bears the impress of all of the previous guises in which the character—and his allies and opponents—have been incarnated. The early Gothic Batman, the Cold War Batman of the 1950s and his 1960s parodic successor: these are all there, like so many sedimented layers of plot, narrative and characterization which the text works with—or against—activating the reader's latent knowledge of these matters and, thereby, registering the significance of the remodeling of Batman which the text undertakes. The same is true, of course, of all of the major new forms in which Batman has been incarnated for his sesquicentenary celebrations: Batman 1989 was, above all, a self-consciously double-levelled Batman calling for a similarly double-levelled reading response.

It is too soon to say whether this shift will prove irreversible or not. Indeed—notwithstanding the likelihood of a sequel to *Batman: the Movie*—there is nothing to vouchsafe that Batman will have a future. For what is most clear from *The Many Lives of the Batman* is the heavy weight of circumstantial considerations in the careers of popular heroes. Some have dramatic deaths, others just fade away while a handful seem to go on forever. Whether Batman is destined for longevity or whether 1989 was, indeed, the twilight of the idol remains to be seen. In the meantime, however, the various perspectives on Batman collected here offer a resource which, in the light it throws on the past lives of Batman, also helps us to better understand the Batmania of the past few years. If the late 1980s saw the birth of a more complex Batman, the nuanced and probing forms of analysis developed in this study serve both to match and comprehend the complexity of their object.

Tony Bennett
Griffith University
Brisbane
January 1990

Contributors

Camille Bacon-Smith is currently visiting lecturer of writing and folklore at Temple University and the University of Pennsylvania.

Tony Bennett is an associate professor and director of the Institute for Cultural Policy Studies at Griffith University in Australia.

Bill Boichel is the owner and operator of BEM in Pittsburgh, which operates in several areas of the comic book industry including retail sales, comic book conventions and publishing.

Jim Collins is an assistant professor of communications at the University of Notre Dame.

Henry Jenkins is an assistant professor of literature at the Massachusetts Institute of Technology.

Andy Medhurst teaches media studies at the University of Sussex in the United Kingdom.

Eileen Meehan is an assistant professor of media arts at the University of Arizona.

Patrick Parsons is an assistant professor of mass communications at the Pennsylvania State University.

Roberta E. Pearson is an assistant professor of mass communications at the Pennsylvania State University.

Christopher Sharrett is an associate professor of communications at Seton Hall University.

Lynn Spigel is an assistant professor of communications at the University of Wisconsin (Madison).

William Uricchio is an associate professor of mass communications at the Pennsylvania State University.

Tyrone Yarbrough is a Ph.D candidate in folklore and folklife at the University of Pennsylvania.

Introduction

William Uricchio and Roberta E. Pearson

"Batman?" said many of our fellow academics incredulously upon hearing of this collection. True, it seemed a timely (and perhaps opportunistic) enterprise but couldn't we find more worthy topics of inquiry? Though many seemed willing to grant, albeit grudgingly, the legitimacy of studying music videos, romance novels and sixties television, lingering doubts remained about a comic book hero who dresses up in a funny costume to fight crime. Discussions of *Detective Comics* and toy batmobiles still seemed to elicit more snickers than serious reflection.

Yet, as many of our contributors point out, 1989 was the Year of the Batman, manifested in a plethora of corporately orchestrated expressions of a fifty year old popular hero. Sheer numbers alone should convince skeptics that this particular comic book hero, at least, has significant cultural impact: double platinum record sales for the Prince Batdance album; a box office take in the multi-millions of dollars; millions more in revenues from merchandising tie-ins and even sales of close to a million for *Legends of the Dark Knight* #1, the first solo Batman comic book title in five decades. These figures attest not only to corporate marketing savvy, but to public willingness to embrace the character on a number of levels.

While the ubiquitous Bat-hype of the summer of '89 brought the Batman (or Batman as non-purists call him) to the forefront of popular consciousness, the extensive intertextual background stemming from the fifty year, multimedia history of the character provided greater cultural resonance than was the case with other intensively marketed blockbuster movies such as *Star Wars*. The multiple "Batmen" of 1989 and the preceding five decades testify both to the institutional maintenance of the character and to the modulation of that character required to keep abreast of perceived market demands, leading to a distinctly identifiable commodity on the one hand and diverse expressions of that commodity on the other. The carefully coordinated production and circulation of bat-texts in 1989 originated from a powerful, multinational, profit-motivated media giant, but one cannot for this reason discount both producers' and audiences' negotiations of a complex synchronic and diachronic intertextual frame formed by the simultaneous presence of various comic book adventures (reprints, multiple story issues, graphic novels), the reruns of the sixties television series, the Batman film, the Prince video, the related commercials, and the over three hundred licensed, not to mention the hundreds more unlicensed, product tie-ins.

Why Batman, then? As the above suggests, the character constitutes a complex cultural phenomenon that unpacks on many levels. The Batman character can be used as a means for illuminating the production, circulation and reception of the media products that make up contemporary popular culture. The synchronic and diachronic richness of the character demands the application of a number of different and complementary theoretical paradigms which together represent the wide-ranging analytic perspectives of contemporary cultural studies and permit including the voices of both producers and audiences.

The first four contributions to the volume detail various aspects of the production process. Bill Boichel offers a useful historical overview of the Batman's fifty year plus history, locating the character's antecedents, chronicling additions to the character's mythos and charting the undulations in the character's persona. The interview with Batman editor Dennis O'Neil discusses his significant reconfiguration of the Batman, details the organization of labor within the comic industry and addresses the pivotal role of the fans. Christopher Sharrett's interview with Frank Miller focuses specifically on Miller's *The Dark Knight Returns*, the major Batman comic text of the last decade, considering the place of the superhero in fin-de-siècle America. Eileen Meehan's essay complements and complicates the views expressed by these voices from within the comics industry. Meehan uses a political economy paradigm to investigate Warner Communications Inc.'s use of Batman as a commercial text to multiply profits across media and product forms and maximize the exploitation of various markets.

Patrick Parson's essay takes an historical macro-view of comic book readership since the Batman's first appearance. Parsons uses the discourse of both the industry and its critics to map the contours of the audience over the years, discussing external pressures on the industry, the industry's own marketing strategies and the role of fandom. Camille Bacon-Smith, writing with Tyrone Yarborough, applies an ethnographic perspective to construct a micro-view of both comic fans' and general viewers' reactions to *Batman: The Movie*. The methodologies of these articles represent two very different approaches to that most vexed of issues in mass communications, audience reception, and begin to chart the diverse responses of various fan communities.

The next two articles deal more directly with distinct fan communities. Lynn Spigel and Henry Jenkins address issues of popular culture and popular memory, focusing on the *Batman* television series of the 1960s, seeking to understand how television shows function in viewers' lives. They first review the contemporary debates around the series' cultural status. They then use this historical background to situate the personal memories of interview subjects about the place of the *Batman* series in their lives then and now. Andy Medhurst's essay provides a British gay perspective on both the television series and other bat-texts. He speaks of a particular community's appropriation of Batman and Robin's relationship as well as of the camp aspects of the television series.

Drawing on recent developments in narrative theory, Jim Collins explores what he terms the "hybridization" of popular narrative in the post-modern age. Collins argues that texts such as *Batman: The Movie* and *The Dark Knight Returns* self-consciously evoke and playfully rework the intertextual encrustations that have become inseparable from the text.

William Uricchio and Roberta E. Pearson investigate the series character nature of the Batman, discussing tensions between character coherence and fragmentation engendered by market and authorship pressures. They argue that character maintenance depends upon the presence of five key components, which manifest themselves in the iterative events of crimefighting and bring with them certain ideological implications.

Together the essays provide a multifaceted perspective on one of the longest lived of American popular heroes, revealing the complexities of various aspects of the processes of production and reception in multiple media. The essays also represent many of the paradigms which constitute contemporary cultural studies. The diversity of subject and method makes this volume the first serious academic exploration of the many lives of the Batman.

1

Batman: Commodity as Myth

Bill Boichel

"And thus is born this weird figure of the dark . . . this avenger of evil . . . The Batman." Thus concluded "The Legend of Batman," a two-page introduction that led off *Batman* #1 (Spring 1940). Though this story appeared less than a year after Batman's introduction in the opening pages of *Detective Comics* #27 (May 1939), the character had already become a "legend," both a resonant signifier and a valuable property—the world's second superhero. The first superhero, Superman, represented a calculated response to the Nazi concept of the *Übermench:* an ideal, superior man who would lead the masses to victory. Created by two Jewish high-school buddies from Cleveland, Ohio, Jerry Siegal and Joe Shuster, Superman first appeared in June 1938 in *Action Comics* #1. A native of Krypton, Superman was a uniquely American *Übermench* with a social conscience. Discovering his superpowers, he "decided he must turn his titanic strength into channels that would benefit mankind, and so was created Superman! Champion of the oppressed, the physical marvel who had sworn to devote his existence to helping those in need!"

Superman's overnight smash success encouraged the character's owners, National Periodical Publications, to commission a similar character, Batman. The host of costumed superheroes following in the Batman's wake supplied clear evidence that the phenomenon of the superhero had arrived. But neither Superman nor Batman nor any of their super colleagues could have achieved national visibility had the comics industry not existed.

Initially intended as circulation boosters in the rivalry between newspaper publishing giants William Randolph Hearst and Joseph Pulitzer, newspaper comic strips first appeared in the last decade of the nineteenth century. The Yellow Kid, created in 1895 by Richard Outcault for Pulitzer's *New York World,* is the most notable character of this period. Acquired by Hearst for his *New York Journal*, the character's association with the Hearst paper's sensationalism led to the term "yellow journalism." Soon after the Yellow Kid's appearance, comic strips proliferated geometrically both in number and in popularity, their growth enabled by the creation of the comic strip syndicates. In a continuation of the Hearst-Pulitzer rivalry, the syndicates competed fiercely in their expansion, and continue to control the comic strip market in the United States to the present.

By the first decade of the twentieth century, comic strips, now commonplace in the daily papers and as special color Sunday supplements, had achieved enough popularity to warrant the publication of book-form reprint collections for both commercial and promotional purposes. Many of these collections—the first "comic books"—appeared through the 1920s. Published from 1929 to 1930, the thirty-six issues of *The Funnies*, a tabloid-format magazine printing original comic strips, represented the first four-color newsstand publication.

The format that came to be known as the comic book first appeared in 1933, thanks to the efforts of Harry Wildenberg and Max C. Gaines, members of the sales staff of New York's Eastern Color Printing Company. The Company produced a print run of 10,000 copies of *Funnies on Parade*, a 7½" x 10" magazine containing thirty-two pages of Sunday newspaper comic strip reprints, for the Proctor and Gamble Company to give away as premiums. Shortly thereafter Eastern Color, spurred on by the enthusiasm of Max Gaines, produced *Famous Funnies: A Carnival of Comics* and then *Century of Comics* in quantities of over 100,000. Gaines sold these comics to major advertisers such as Milk-O-Malt, Wheatena, Kinney Shoe Stores and others, for use as premiums and radio giveaways. The premium and give-away schemes were so successful that, early in 1934, Gaines persuaded Eastern to produce 35,000 copies of *Famous Funnies, Series 1.*

Distributed by the Dell Publishing Company to chain stores, the 64 page color comics, priced at ten cents, immediately sold out. Eastern promptly released *Famous Funnies* #1 in May (cover dated July) 1934, which became, upon release of #2 in July, the first regularly scheduled comic book magazine.

A new commodity form, the comic book experienced a period of rapid growth within the consumer market. Unlike the comic strip industry, which served the preexistent newspaper industry and was controlled by a handful of syndicates, the comic book industry was virgin territory, promising quick and easy profits. New publishers constantly entered and, in some cases, subsequently left, the field.

One of these entrants played a pivotal role in the creation of Batman. In 1935, the New York City-based National Periodical Productions entered the comic book market with the tabloid-sized *New Fun*. After a name change to *More Fun* and a format conversion to standard comic book magazine size, this publication became the first title regularly printing new material created specifically for the comic book market. Two years later, National Periodical Productions released *Detective Comics,* one of the earliest comic books devoted exclusively to a particular genre. Late in 1937, Harry Donenfeld bought National Periodical Publications and established *Detective Comics'* initials as the imprint for the company's entire output. Shortly thereafter, in the spring of 1938, DC moved onto the center stage of the industry with the publication of *Action Comics* #1.

A year after Superman's success, DC introduced Batman, created by artist Bob Kane and writer Bill Finger, in *Detective Comics* #27. At the time a young cartoonist in his early twenties, Bob Kane had begun his career in comics two years earlier in 1936 at the Eisner/Iger studio, the first company devoted to producing work for the comic book industry. Kane then worked briefly for the Fleischer Studio doing fill-ins, inking, and opaquing on Betty Boop cartoons. Upon leaving the Fleischer Studio, Kane returned to comics, getting a job at DC producing features such as "Rusty and His Pals," and "Clip Carson," both of which were scripted by a former high-school pal, Bill Finger. Finger had worked as a shoe salesman in the Bronx, but his passion for pulp magazines seduced him away from his job and into the allied field of scripting for the nascent comic book. Although Bob Kane received sole credit from DC for the creation of Batman, both the Batman character and the classic period, or Golden Age, Batman mythos were the co-creations of Bob Kane and Bill Finger.

The Batman mythos springs from the popular culture of the 1930s— movies, pulps, comic strips, and newspaper headlines—in which both Kane and Finger were fully immersed. According to Bob Kane, two movies contributed significantly to the formulation of the Batman character. *The Mark of Zorro* (1920) starred Douglas Fairbanks as Zorro, a wealthy landowner who maintained both an alter ego as a masked and caped crimefighter and a secret cave-hideout beneath his mansion. From this film came the Bruce Wayne-Wayne Manor/Batman-Batcave duality. *The Bat Whispers* (1930) featured a dual identity of a more schizophrenic nature: that of a detective and his alter ego, the murderer dubbed "The Bat," who dressed in a costume which inspired that of Batman. This film also featured a prototype of the Bat-Signal.

Finger's depiction of the Batman as a figure of awe and mystery as well as a master sleuth and scientist owed much to pulp magazine superstars Doc Savage and the Shadow, created by Kenneth Robeson and Walter Gibson, and to Sir Arthur Conan Doyle's master sleuth,

Sherlock Holmes. Chester Gould's comic strip creation, Dick Tracy, provided a prototype for Batman's square jaw as well as a model for Robin in Tracy's sidekick, Junior. The strip's cast of bizarre villains also provided major inspiration for the exaggerated visual representation of many of Batman's foes.

Newspaper accounts headlining the exploits of real-life criminals and gangsters such as John Dillinger, "Pretty Boy" Floyd, Bonnie and Clyde, Al Capone, and "Dutch" Schultz, often served as the catalyst for these crafted fictions. Operating outside the law, on their own terms, and at the expense of the status quo, criminals fascinated many a consumer of popular culture. Creating a figure who, like the criminals, operated outside the law and on his own terms, yet did so on behalf of the status quo, Kane and Finger originated a popular myth that has lasted for over half a century.

Despite his affiliations with the gangsters who have entered our popular mythology, Batman's opposition to crime and support of the status quo are clearly embedded in the character's narrative origin. First related in *Detective Comics* #33, six months after the character's initial appearance, the origin sequence centers around the criminal act that brought the Batman into existence: interrupted in the course of strolling home from a movie, in the company of their child Bruce, Thomas and Martha Wayne, wealthy, upstanding citizens, are brutally slain by a faceless, no-name thug attempting to rob them. The trauma that their murder inflicts upon young Bruce eventually leads him to adopt the alter ego of Batman. Swearing to avenge his parents' death by dedicating his life to combating crime, young Bruce devotes his youth and early adulthood to preparing his mind and body for the fight to come, his inherited wealth enabling his single-mindedness of purpose. Taking the appearance of a bat at his window as a long-awaited signal, the adult Bruce Wayne dons a costume to mimic this dark creature of the night and enters the world of crime that had spawned him.

Batman does not fight alone but is aided by a cast of supporting characters. The first of the supporting characters to appear, and the most consistently present, is Police Commissioner James Gordon. Introduced along with Bruce Wayne and Batman in the first Batman story, Gordon, at the outset a friend of Wayne's, soon allied with Batman, without ever becoming aware that the two were one and the same person. *Detective Comics* #38 (April 1940) introduced the character destined to play the most important supporting role in the Batman mythos. Robin, The Boy Wonder, represented a youthful duplicate of Batman. A member of The Flying Graysons trapeze act, young Dick Grayson witnessed the murder of his parents by gangsters. Bruce Wayne adopted the grief stricken lad and gained his confidence through disclosing that his parents were also murdered. Bruce revealed his secret identity and, after providing Dick with the necessary training, initiated him as his partner. Kane, Finger, and Kane's newly hired young assistant, Jerry Robinson, designed the Robin character to enable younger readers to identify more closely with the Caped Crusader's adventures. The character was an immediate success and so widely imitated that the junior sidekick emerged as one of the most important terms in the superhero lexicon. Three years later, *Batman* #16 introduced another permanent fixture in the Batman mythos, the only character privy to the secret identities of Batman and Robin. Alfred, the faithful butler of Wayne Manor and the Batcave, lent a homey touch to Batman's harsh environs and was ever ready to provide a steadying and reassuring hand.

Just as these supporting characters are integral to the Batman legend, so too are his foes and rivals. An immense and labyrinthian catalogue of criminals has crossed the path of the dark knight detective throughout his fifty-year history. Attempting to distinguish his adventures from the mundane cops and robbers genre, Batman's writers/artists have continually striven to create villains worthy of the attentions of a legend. Many of these villains mirrored aspects of Batman's character and development. The villains, like the Batman, frequently have their origin in a traumatic event or series of events that has forever altered their lives. In the case of the villains, however, the trauma invariably drives them to madness and a life of crime, if not a quest for world domination, the latter reflecting the anxieties about fascism that were particularly prevalent during Batman's early years. These villains often also share Bruce Wayne's status as a respected member of society.

Batman's earliest foes, Doctor Death (*Detective Comics* #29, July 1939) and Professor Hugo Strange (*Detective Comics* #36, February 1940) were both respected professionals who turned on society in a crazed quest for self-gain. Clayface (*Detective Comics* # 40, June 1949), an aging silent film star, transformed himself into one of his early roles to wreak vengeance on those he saw as robbing him of his immortality by remaking his early "classics." The Scarecrow first appeared in *World's Finest* #3 (Fall 1941), a title created to showcase Batman and Superman adventures. He was a professor of psychology who fell victim to his own obsession with fear. Adopting as his alter ego the derisive nickname "Scarecrow," jestingly applied to him by his students and colleagues at the university, he used his knowledge of fear as an extortionist's tool.

As a child, the Penguin (*Detective Comics* #58, December 1941) experienced the unending ridicule of his schoolmates, who constantly reminded him of his resemblance to the ungainly bird. Oswald Chesterfield Cobblepot dedicated his life to vengeance and, after attaining a degree in Ornithology and a knack for umbrella-engineering, used his knowledge and skills for evil-doing. Two-Face (*Detective Comics* #66, August 1942) had been the popular Gotham City District Attorney, Harvey Dent. Nicknamed "Apollo" by the press because of his out-standing good looks, he was permanently disfigured after a criminal he had convicted hurled acid in his face. Teetering on the brink of madness, Dent fixated on a defaced coin that had belonged to the man responsible for his fate. He decided that a toss of this coin would determine his actions: the unaltered side for good and the defaced side for evil.

Diverging somewhat from this pattern, the origins and identity of the archfiend of the Batman mythos remained a complete mystery for ten years. Introduced in the first story of *Batman* #1, the Joker proved to be the Batman's most implacable foe. The personification of the irrational, an agent of chaos, the Joker represented everything that Batman opposed. Inspired by a combination of a playing card joker and a still of German actor Conrad Veidt in the 1928 movie *The Man Who Laughs*, the Joker has elicited more popular response than any other character in the history of Batman.

While Bruce Wayne has courted many of Gotham's female socialites, Batman has tangled with those members of the opposite sex who oper-ate on the opposite side of the law. The third story of *Batman* #1 introduced the first and most important of these female offenders. Referred to in this initial appearance as The Cat, a jewel thief whom Batman, much to the consternation of Robin, allows to escape, The Catwoman, aka Selina Kyle, served to inject a hint of sexuality into the caped crusader's cavortings.

The first few stories introduced not only ongoing characters, but an array of bat-paraphenalia. The Bat-prefix made its appearance very early on with the Batgyro and Batarang both debuted in *Detective Comics* #31, though Batman's vehicle was not dubbed the Batmobile until *Detective Comics* #48 (February 1941). This issue is significant for another reason as well: it contained the first identification of Batman's locale as Gotham, the city having previously been referred to alternately as Manhattan and Metropolis, the latter the locale of Superman's adven-tures. The difference between Gotham and Metropolis succinctly sum-marizes the differences between the two superheroes. As current Bat-man editor Dennis O'Neil put it: "Gotham is Manhattan below Fourteenth Street at 3 a.m., November 28 in a cold year. Metropolis is Manhattan between Fourteenth and One Hundred and Tenth Streets on the brightest, sunniest July day of the year."

By 1942, writers and artists had established most of the basic ele-ments of the Batman mythos. Nineteen forty-two also found DC enjoy-ing the profits resulting from successfully marketing their premiere property, Superman, to Fleischer Studios, who were midway in their production of a popular series of Superman cartoons. Perceiving Batman as an established commodity in its own right, DC felt ready to market it as well. In 1943, Columbia Studios produced the first of its two fifteen episode Batman serials. The no-frills production, a blatant vehicle for World War II propaganda, presented a cast of no-name actors on a featureless low-rent soundstage.

The voice-over narration from the first episode, "The Electric Brain," speaks of a Batman and Robin who "represent American youth who love their country and are glad to fight for it" against "Axis criminals." These criminals hide in "a foreign land transplanted bodily to America: Little Tokyo" where, "since a wise government rounded up the shifty-eyed Japs," only one business, "The Cave of Horrors," still operates. This amusement ride camouflages the secret headquarters of a Japanese mad scientist, Dr. Daka, leader of "The League of the New Order," an Axis fifth-columnist organization. Hard at work against the American war effort, The League lures professionals away from their key posts.

The production abandoned many elements of the Batman mythos: a sunny, suburban "First and Maple" replaced the moonlit Gotham City; a bucolic Captain Arnold replaced Commissioner Gordon; a standard convertible sedan replaced the Batmobile. In fact, the production conveys no sense of Batman and Robin as characters, reducing them to the costumes Bruce Wayne and Dick Grayson don whenever they are about to enter a violent situation. The absurdity of the costumes is revealed when Batman says to Robin, "we don't want the police to find us in these outfits."

Since the 1943 serial achieved no great success, Columbia waited six years before producing another fifteen episode serial. Once again featuring a no-name cast, the 1949 production differed little from its predecessor. The one significant divergence was the restoration of elements of the Batman mythos: Commissioner Gordon, the Bat-Signal, a costumed villain, and, in a much more central role than she had played in the comic books, Bruce Wayne's girlfriend, newspaper-photographer, Vicki Vale. The second serial also conveyed blatant propaganda, this time focusing on cold-war paranoia. An opening montage of newspaper headlines progressing from "Crime" to "More Crime" to "Citizens Demand More Police" to "Batman and Robin Stop Criminals" and finally to "Batman and Robin Heros" set the tone. The plot revolves around the creation and subsequent theft of, search for, and struggle over a device capable of the "remote control of all machines." Commissioner Gordon, who has been put on the case by "Washington," calls upon Batman, who is "taken into upper echelon confidence" for "security reasons," to recover the device.

The combined total of thirty episodes of Batman serials served to establish the Dynamic Duo in the dominant medium of the day, while the Caped Crusader and the Boy Wonder continued their regular appearances in *Detective, Batman,* and *World's Finest* Comics. By the end of the 1940s, the superhero, the figure that had dominated comic books throughout World War II, was clearly on the wane. The overwhelming sense of victory at the war's conclusion stripped many superheroes, who had had their energies diverted from fighting crime to winning the war, of their raison *d'être.* Only those superheroes who kept abreast of the times, and even of those, only the most popular, survived. The creation of a more detailed backstory for the Batman character and the elaboration of key elements of the Batman mythos served to update the character. *Batman* #47 (July 1948) presented the first detailed origin of Batman, giving the murderer of Thomas and Martha Wayne a face, identity, and history. Batman is allowed the catharsis of revealing himself to small-time hood Joe Chill, his parents' killer: "I'm the son of the man you murdered! I'm Bruce Wayne." Chill retreats into the underworld and meets his demise at the hands of the hoods to whom he has disclosed his role in the creation of Batman. The very next issue of *Batman,* #48, continued to elaborate the Batman mythos with the cover feature of "1000 secrets of the Batcave."

Several years later, *Detective Comics* #168 (February 1951) set forth the origin of the Joker, heretofore a complete mystery. The Joker was a lab worker who decided to steal a million dollars from the Monarch Playing Card Company. He adopted the disguise of the "Red Hood," wearing a red helmet complete with oxygen mask. He escaped from the factory by swimming underneath a pool of chemical waste, but the noxious elements turned his hair green, his lips rouge-red and his skin chalk white. This rationalization of the most chaotic element in Batman's universe foreshadowed the sunny Caped Crusader of the 1950s who emerged as a response to pressures on the comic book industry.

As superhero titles continued to decrease, the comic book industry relied to a greater extent upon two other longstanding genres. Aimed primarily at children, the long established "Funny Animal" genre, led by the Walt Disney family of titles, including Mickey Mouse and Donald Duck, enjoyed its greatest success. The recently established "Teen" genre also experienced steady growth, much of which stemmed from the *Archie Comics* family of titles. During this same period, many comic book publishers experimented with the well-established genres of the mainstream print, radio and film media: crime, mystery, Westerns, horror, science fiction, and romance. While all of these genres had orginated before the War, the success of the superhero genre had relegated them to marginal status.

The comics industry in the post-war years faced problems more serious than the decreasing popularity of the superhero. Comic books did not escape the anti-communist hysteria and the valorization of domesticity and the nuclear family chararacteristic of the period, while the rise in juvenile delinquency during these years obviously contributed even more directly to pressures on the industry. Fredric Wertham, the most vocal opponent of the comic book, had devoted his career to the study of violence, focusing particularly upon sociopaths and psychopaths, and publishing *The Show of Violence* (Garden City, NY: Doubleday, 1949). Wertham next took on comic books, charging that they formed part of a conspiracy to destroy the American family by corrupting the morals and values of its youth. His book, *Seduction of the Innocent* (New York: Rinehart, 1954), depicted the undermining of American civilization from within by the comic book industry. Though Wertham concentrated his attack on crime comics' causal role in juvenile delinquency, he also launched a vehement critique of superheroes:

> The very children for whose unruly behavior I would want to prescribe psychotherapy in an anti-superman direction, have been nourished (or rather poisoned) by the endless repetition of Superman stories. How can they respect the hard-working mother, father or teacher who is so pedestrian, trying to teach common rules of conduct, wanting you to keep your feet on the ground and unable even figuratively speaking to fly through the air? Psychologically Superman undermines the authority and dignity of the ordinary man and woman in the minds of children. (pp. 97–98)

Wertham also cast aspersions on Batman's relationship with Robin.

> The Batman type of story helps to fixate homoerotic tendencies by suggesting the form of adolescent-with-adult or Ganymede-Zeus type of love relationship. . . . The feeling is conveyed that we men must stick together because there are so many villainous creatures who have to be exterminated. . . . It is like the wish dream of two homosexuals living together. (p. 190)

Wertham summed up his argument in his closing paragraphs. Said the psychiatrist: "Someday parents will realize that comic books are not a necessary evil." Wertham was "convinced that in some way or other the democratic process will assert itself and crime comics will go. . . " (p. 395).

While the comic book industry had successfully responded to the decreasing popularity of the superhero, Wertham and his ilk posed a more serious challenge. The release of *Seduction of the Innocent* signaled a shift in popular opinion and the industry began to feel pressure from all sides. In an effort to avoid external censorship or government regulation, a group of publishers, "The Comics Magazine Association of America," created the "Comics Code Authority" late in 1954. Designed to function as an independent regulator, the Code Authority screened all publishers' product prior to publication for violations of the Wertham-inspired Comics Code. Some of the Code's precepts follow.

> In every instance good shall triumph over evil and the criminal punished for his misdeeds.
> Crimes shall never be presented in such a way as to promote distrust in the forces of law and justice. . . .
> All lurid, unsavory, gruesome illustrations shall be eliminated.
> All situations dealing with the family unit should have as their ultimate goal the protection of the children and family life. In no way shall the breaking of the moral code be depicted as rewarding.

A comic book fulfilling these and other standards bore the "Approved by the Comics Code Authority" stamp, tacitly required of all titles beginning in 1955, in its upper-right-hand corner.

The adoption of the Comics Code marked a turning point in the history of the comic book industry. One by one titles, publishers, and even entire genres of comic books disappeared. With the exceptions of Superman, Batman, and Wonder Woman, the superhero vanished entirely for a period of several years.

The post-war tendency to a sunnier Batman evident before the Wertham crisis intensified after the Code's introduction. The first Batman titles carrying the Comics Code Authority stamp, *Batman* #90 and *Detective Comics* #217 (March 1955), signalled the inception of a makeover of the Batman mythos. *Detective Comics* #233 (July 1956) introduced the character of Batwoman, a mirror image of Batman, complete with a Batcave and Batcycle of her own. Perhaps intended to ward off further charges of homosexuality, Batwoman functioned as a female presence and potential love interest. Determined to establish both Batman and Robin's heterosexuality, the writers introduced Batwoman's niece as the Boy Wonder's possible girlfriend in *Batman* #139 (May 1961).

This introduction of females coupled with other textual alterations both reflected and contributed to the downward spiral in the sales of *Batman* and *Detective Comics* that had continued uninterrupted since the late 1940s. Throughout the late 1950s and early 1960s, Batman stories increasingly resembled science fiction scenarios that pervaded this anxious period in America's history, as the Caped Crusader faced alien menaces on the streets of Gotham and travelled through the universe to fight them on their home turf. During this same period, Batman began to behave more like a school prefect than a crime-fighter, confronting villains who had gradually evolved from criminals into pranksters. The character, severed from its roots as dark knight vigilante, was so ill-defined during this period that even Batman himself was subjected to periodic transformations, surreally assuming the forms of a variety of monstrosities as well as inanimate objects.

Nineteen sixty-four found Batman down and out, but over the next few years a variety of factors brought the Dynamic Duo back into the spotlight. At the start of 1964, Jack Schiff, editor of the Batman titles since 1940, was succeeded by fellow old-hand Julius Schwartz, who proceeded to overhaul DC's ailing property. Scwhwartz relieved Batman-creator Bob Kane of his charge of overseeing the ghost artists and providing the finished artwork. Bringing in artists he could work with more closely, he ordered a remodeling of everything from the Batcave to the Bat-costume. More importantly, he accelerated the return of the classic villains that Schiff had initiated before his departure.

This revamping coincided with the emergence into the public eye of the pop art and camp movements, which shared an aesthetic appreciation of the mass-produced commodity as a system of cultural signification. The soup-can paintings of Andy Warhol and the giant comic-book-panel canvases of Roy Lichtenstein epitomized pop art's physical representations of the camp sensibility's attitude towards mass culture. By 1965 the pop/camp movement, at the height of fashion, had repositioned and revalued comic books as central to its aesthetic. As a result, the previously unthinkable thought of a television series based on a comic book character emerged.

The recipient of a massive promotional campaign, *Batman*, the television series, produced by William Dozier and starring Adam West as Batman and Burt Ward as Robin, premiered on ABC on January 12, 1966. The show, structured around the movie-serial "cliffhanger" ending which enabled *two* prime-time episodes each week, shot to the top of the ratings. In no time "Batmania" sent comic book sales soaring and chased licensing profits out of the cellar and through the roof. Spawning a feature film released by 20th Century Fox and spanning three seasons of prime time, the *Batman* television series ran for 120 episodes. The show featured many Hollywood celebrities in regular appearances as Batman's foes and rivals, including Cesar Romero as the Joker, Frank Gorshin as the Riddler, Burgess Meredith as the Penguin, and Julie Newmar, Eartha Kitt, and Lee Merriwether in turns as the Catwoman. In addition, the series supplied impetus for the first Batman animated cartoons, which were aired Saturday mornings in 1968 and

1969 on rival network CBS's *Batman-Superman Hour*. Though the television series provided the DC property with the highest public profile in its 30-year history and temporarily increased sales of the Batman titles, it nonethless had no permanent impact, as the comic book adventures resumed their steady decline in sales even before the show's cancellation.

The widely-popular camp Batman of the television series did not appeal to the increasingly organized and vocal Bat-fans, who voiced their disapproval of the camp influences upon the comic book Batman. Perhaps expressing fan disaffection, the cover of *Batman* #183 (August 1966) portrays Batman reclining in front of a television set showing, "The Adventures of Batman," while Robin—functioning as a stand-in for the fan—entreats Batman to come out with him and fight crime. Editor Schwartz responded to fan discontent by bringing in present-editor Dennis O'Neil as writer and fan-favorite, Neal Adams as artist, who together returned the Dark Knight to his roots in a series of gritty and realistic adventures. Although this reconfiguration appealed to the fan community, it did little to help flagging sales, which continued to decline throughout the 1970s and into the 1980s, hitting an all-time low in 1985.

But even in the midst of this dismal period, one of the most significant developments in comic book history had occurred. During 1974, New York convention organizer Phil Seuling established the "direct distribution" system specifically designed to serve the needs of comic book fandom. This system resulted in the creation of the direct sales market, which has since grown to dominate American comic book sales. By 1981, the direct market had expanded to the point that it could support a company producing four-color comics exclusively for comic book specialty stores. This company, Pacific Comics, offered royalties and shared ownership rights to its creators, an event which produced the first loosening of the iron hold that the old established comic book publishers, especially DC and their chief competitor Marvel, had on their talent. Up to this point, creators had received only a flat rate per page produced, with all rights retained by the publisher. Soon, other companies formed and entered the direct distribution market, offering similar terms to creators.

As a result, by 1982 both DC and Marvel were forced to institute royalty payments that led to the creation of a comic book writer/artist star system. In 1983, in an unprecedented move to lure the super-hot Frank Miller away from Marvel, DC offered him ownership rights for his project *Ronin*, a six-issue series which was released in 1983–84. Upon completion of his *Ronin* series, DC offered Miller another contract, this time to work on an established DC property: Batman.

Miller's work on Batman related to DC's ongoing efforts to improve their market share. Nineteen eighty-five found the DC leadership so frustrated at the continually decreasing sales of practically all their properties that they decided to reconstruct the entire "DC Universe." Initiating this move was the twelve-issue series, *Crisis on Infinite Earths*, which rewrote the history of the DC Universe and killed off several major characters, including Supergirl and Flash. In addition, DC offered highly lucrative contracts to the most popular comic book creators to rework their three major properties: Superman, Batman, and Wonder Woman.

The four-issue, "prestige-format" series, *The Dark Knight Returns*, presented the last adventure of an aged and bitter Batman in Miller's vision of Gotham's future—a dark, corrupt and violent moral wasteland. A direct descendant of Kane and Finger's initial conception, the series provided DC with the big hit they so desperately craved, received unprecedented multiple printings and fed the Batman craze that subsequently became a raging inferno. In 1987 Miller, this time with visuals handled by artist David Mazzucchelli, followed *Dark Knight* with *Batman: Year One*, a hard-boiled representation of Batman's origin and first adventures centering on the formation of the relationship between Batman and police Lieutenant James Gordon.

Nineteen eighty-eight saw the release of the definitive treatment of the Batman-Joker relationship in the single-issue, prestige-format special, *The Killing Joke*, by the British writer-artist team of Alan Moore and Brian Bolland. *The Killing Joke* presents Batman and the Joker as distorted mirror images of each other on opposite sides of the law. The Caped Crusader was now more popular than at any time during the preceding twenty years, but the same could not be said for the Boy Wonder. In a call-in vote, the fans gave Jason Todd, who had replaced Dick Grayson as Robin in *Batman* #368 (February 1984), a big thumbs down. The new Robin died at the Joker's hand, clearing the way for Batman's solo flight up on the silver screen later that summer.

In October of 1979 major-league comic-collector and former attorney for United Artists, Michael Uslan, along with independent producer and MGM-veteran, Ben Melniker, obtained the rights for a Batman film. Several months later they made a deal with Peter Huber of Warner Bros., a division of Warner Communications Inc., which, incidentally, had purchased DC Comics in 1968. The project circled for years before finally touching down in 1988 on the ground prepared by *Dark Knight*, *Year One*, and *Killing Joke*. Warners committed to the project and put up $35 million to underwrite the film. Opening June 23 at 2,850 theaters and featuring a hit soundtrack by Warner Bros. recording artist, Prince, *Batman: The Movie*, starring Michael Keaton as Batman and Jack Nicholson as the Joker, broke every box-office record in the books. Breaking all precedents, the videotape was released a mere five months later and proceeded to set more records. "Batmania" returned with a vengeance and 1989 became the year of the bat.

DC took full advantage of such unprecedented success, producing new bat-texts in a variety of formats. Released simultaneously with the videotape of *Batman, Arkham Asylum* explores the pervasiveness of madness in Batman's world. Billed as a sequel to *The Killing Joke* and produced by another British writer-artist team, Grant Morrison and Dave McKean, the $24.95 hardback demolished existing records for dollar-volume sales on a comic book. *Arkham Asylum* presents Batman confronting his own "heart of darkness" as mirrored by his greatest foes, all of whom are kept locked up in the Arkham Asylum for the Criminally Insane.

DC also published bat-texts featuring alternative Batmen of the past and future. Released for Christmas 1989, *Gotham by Gaslight*, an "imaginary" tale set in Victorian Gotham, pits Batman against Jack the Ripper. The Spring, 1990 release of *Digital Justice*, a computer-generated graphic novel by Pepe Moreno, featuring a Bat-computer-entity analogous to those found in the cyberpunk novels of William Gibson, projects the Batman mythos well into the twenty-first century. Here Batman confronts his old nemesis, this time in the form of "the Joker virus." As Batman conquers time itself, it becomes increasingly difficult to keep in mind comic book-artist Robert Crumb's disclaimer: "Just remember kids, it's only lines on paper!"

2
Notes from the Batcave:
An Interview with Dennis O'Neil

Roberta E. Pearson and William Uricchio

Dennis O'Neil, one of the most prominent figures in the comics industry, has been an editor at both Marvel and DC, where, since 1986, he has edited *Batman* and *Detective Comics.* He started his professional life as a journalist but began writing comics in 1965 at Marvel. He worked on several long-standing titles at DC and Marvel, breathing new life into old characters, such as Superman, Green Lantern, and Captain Marvel. His Green Lantern and Green Arrow series in the early seventies were among the first comic books to deal with social problems. His collaborations with Neal Adams and Dick Giordano in ·the late sixties and early seventies transformed Batman from the campy comedian of the mid-sixties back to the Dark Knight Detective. Aside from his editorial duties, O'Neil continues to write: he scripted the first five issues of the third Batman title, *Legends of the Dark Knight*, and continues to do another DC book, *The Question.* He has also written teleplays, short stories, novels, film criticism and hundreds of book reviews.

Q. When you first started to write Batman, did you bring a new perspective to the character?
A. My brillant idea was simply to take it back to where it started. I went to the DC library and read some of the early stories. I tried to get a sense of what Kane and Finger were after. With the benefit of twenty years of sophistication in story telling techniques and twenty years of learning from our predecessors, Neal Adams and I did the story "The Secret of the Waiting Graves." Batman was kind of my assignment from then on. It was a different system in that writers or artists were not assigned to characters as they are today. I showed up once a week with a finished script and got another assignment and it just so hap-

pened for several years that that assignment was Batman—plus other things. You certainly couldn't survive writing one comic book a month then, but you would do okay if you could write four.

Q. What was your vision of the Batman?

A. The basic story is that he is an obsessed loner. Not crazy, not psychotic. There is a big difference between obsession and psychosis. Batman knows who he is and knows what drives him and he chooses not to fight it. He permits his obsession to be the meaning of his life because he cannot think of anything better. He is also rife with natural gifts. He is possibly the only person in the world who could do what he is doing. But he is not for one second ignorant of *why* he is doing it and even what is unhealthy about it, nor is he ever out of control. That is why I have to edit the writers who have Batman kill somebody. I think this is not something he does. The trauma that made him Batman had to do with a wanton waste of life. That same trauma that makes him go catch criminals will forbid his ever taking a life. He is not Dirty Harry. He is not Judge Dredd. He is, God knows, not Rambo, though some people want to make him that. I said this a couple of months ago to an audience in London and got the one spontaneous burst of applause I ever got in my life, which did my heart good. It shows there are some liberal humanists left out there.

Q. What kind of changes do you think the character has been through in the twenty years that you have been involved with him?

A. I started editing Batman about four years ago. I gather I got the job because I had written what people kindly considered to be something close to the definitive version of the character. Therefore, presumably, I would be able to edit the character. In the twenty years that I have been around Batman he has been pretty much the obsessed loner. However, there was a time right before I took over as Batman editor when he seemed to be much closer to a family man, much closer to a nice guy. He seemed to have a love life and he seemed to be very paternal towards Robin. My version is a lot nastier than that. He has a lot more edge to him. I think of Frank Miller's and my Batman as the same person. I think that Frank may have taken the concept further than I did but we were both working with the same material. Steve Englehart did a nicer version of the same guy who was no where near as obsessed as mine. I have to emphasize that none of these are wrong— they are just different.

Batman started off as a first cousin to the mystery men of the pulps in '39 and '40. He held that persona in varying degrees until the 50s when he became a sort of ebullient scout master for awhile. He was a bright, sunny fellow who would walk down the street in the middle of the day and people would say "Hey, Batman, hi, how's it going?" He could also be very science fictiony. Very light. The science fiction was really fantasy, only with a rocket ship instead of a magic carpet. He stayed like that until the '60s when he effectively became a comedian or a perpetrator of camp, which I think is a one line joke.

Q: How do you think Robin functions with Batman?

A: Robin as far as I can tell serves as a counterbalance. He has been a bright, cheerful, sunny presence in an otherwise grim world in the times when we have been playing Batman darkly. He is the equivalent of the comic relief scenes in Shakespeare's plays. This is not to say he is specifically there to introduce yucks, but he does bring a kind of light tone into all of this grimness and also effectively humanizes Batman. If Batman were a real person, Robin probably would be keeping him from crossing the line into nuttiness. It gets hard talking about these things because I don't have the critical vocabulary to differentiate between the character within the story and the character that is contrived for story purposes by a writer. But Robin functions in both areas. In the made-up universe of the stories, he is what keeps Batman and Bruce Wayne from going too far. In terms of the purpose he serves for writers, he allows the story to lighten up from time to time. When I was writing my *Legends of the Dark Knight*, which was without Robin, I found that I had to make Alfred a bit wittier than he usually is for exactly that purpose. I needed some lightness. I needed some humor in the story and it would have been out of character for Bruce Wayne and Batman to supply it so it fell to Alfred. Robin also serves the old hero sidekick role in allowing Batman to talk and explain things and therefore explain them to the reader. He allows for another dimension of human interest to come in. He has his functions both in Bruce Wayne's life and in the life of those of us who have to write about Bruce Wayne.

Q: Since Robin seems so necessary, why did Dick Grayson abandon his Robin role and become Night Wing?

A: I imagine the writers wanted to do *Teen Titans* and began to look around for popular teen characters. Robin was certainly the most popular of them and certainly the oldest teenage character in our little universe. Robin was simply a logical character to put in *Teen Titans* and he couldn't be Robin anymore, so they made him Night Wing. These decisions are seldom made with any long-range plans. It's usually more like, "Hey, it seems like a good idea now." Superman became God over the years because guys said "Wouldn't it be neat if he could freeze things with his breath? Okay, let's write that in." Not realizing that they were stuck with that forever. Many of the writers I know

now, having learned from our predecessors' experience, *do* worry about those things. We are not going to give a character a power that is going to make it impossible to plot future stories.

Q: When did the new Robin come in? Was that while you were editor?

A: No. It was 1983, I believe. He was invented by Gerry Conway in an origin that is a virtual duplication of Dick Grayson's Robin origin. I doubt that they were worried about creating a new character. I think they thought, "We've got to have a Robin in the series, so let's go with the tried and true. This Robin has worked for so many years so let's do him again."

Q: Why did everyone hate him so much? Why did he get killed?

A: Boy, that's a good question. They *did* hate him. I don't know if it was fan craziness—maybe they saw him as usurping Dick Grayson's position. Some of the mail response indicated that this was at least on some people's minds. I think this is taking the whole thing entirely too seriously. It may be that something was working in the writers' minds, probably on a subconscious level. They made the little brat a little bit more disagreeable than his predecessor had been. He did become unlikeable and that was not any doing of mine. But we became aware that he was not very popular. Once we became aware of that, of course, we began playing to it.

Q: And this decision was influenced by the fan letters you were getting?

A: Yeah. The general response. The fan letters and then being a comic book editor, artist and writer in the eighties means you go out and meet the fans a lot. What we get in the way of verbal response and mail is certainly not definitive, but it is probably as informative as the television ratings. It's sort of an informal sampling. I think that once writers became aware that fans didn't like Jason Todd, they began to make him bratty. I toned some of it down. If I had to do it again I would tone it down more. But you make these decisions from hour to hour and sometimes not under the best conditions. So we did a story, for example, in which it was left vague as to whether or not Jason pushed someone off a balcony. The writer, Jim Starlin thought he did—I thought he didn't, but we let the reader decide. There was certainly no doubt that throughout much of the story he wanted to push this guy off of the balcony. And then when we were building up to the death of Robin we made him rebellious—he ran away and in a way he got what he was asking for. He disobeyed Batman twice and that's what lead to his demise.

Q: How did you decide to come up with the device of the phone-in-poll as to whether he was going to live or not?

A: We were sitting around brainstorming at an editorial retreat. I mentioned the 900 number that had been used by Saturday Night Live and one or two other places and Jenette [Kahn] thought it was an interesting idea. We began to discuss how we could use it. I guess I came up with killing somebody and the logical candidate to be in peril was Jason because we had reason to believe that he wasn't that popular anyway. It was a big enough stunt that we couldn't do it with a minor character. If we were going to do it, it had to be a big, significant change. I don't think it would have had the impact we wanted if we had created a character and built him up and then put him in danger. It had to be something dramatic. This was the first time we were going to have real reader participation in comic books. Then I confess, it seemed like a great caper. It had that value to us. Like wow, what a neat thing to do.

Q: Well, it worked. You got a lot of publicity out of it.

A: Much, much more than we anticipated. I thought it would get us some ink here and there and maybe a couple of radio interviews. I had no idea, nor did anyone else, it would have the effect it did. I spent three days doing nothing but talking on the radio. Peggy [May], our publicity person, finally just said, "Stop, no more, we can't do anymore," or I would probably still be talking. She also nixed any television appearances. At the time I wondered about that, but now I am very glad she did because there was a nasty backlash and I came to be very greatful that people could not associate my face with the guy who killed Robin. I got phone calls that ranged from "You bastard," to tearful grandmothers saying, "My grandchild loved Robin and now I don't know what to tell him." That broke my heart.

I also forgot that there are John Hinkleys out there. A lot of us have gotten death threats. Miller got one when he killed Electra. I got kind of a death threat when I made Tony Stark an alcoholic character over at Marvel. Chris Clairmont got one when he killed Phoenix, a popular X-men character. Every once in awhile, I run into guys at signings that I think might be a potential danger. There are guys out there that don't seem to be able to grasp the difference between a story and reality. I call them the hoverers. They get a book signed and they stand back about six to ten feet from you and then they will dash up again when there is a break in the conversation. They often ask about violence. "Why doesn't Batman kill him? I just want him to kill him." I say, "Come on, it's just a story." And they just keep on saying, "I would kill all the criminals if I were Batman." Keep an eye on that guy!

Nothing has ever happened, but it's scary because I keep thinking it might.

The death of Robin caper also made me realize that all this goes a lot deeper in people's consciousnesses than I thought. All these years, I've considered myself to just be writing stories. I now know that that's wrong. That Batman and Robin are part of our folklore. Even though only a tiny fraction of the population reads the comics, everyone knows about them the way everybody knows about Paul Bunyan, Abe Lincoln, etc. Batman and Robin are the postindustrial equivalent of folk figures. They are much deeper in our collective psyches than I had thought. Because these characters have been around for 50 years, everybody in the country knows about them. They have some of the effect on people that mythology used to and if you get into that you can't avoid the question of religion.

Q: When you've got a character who has been around as many years as Batman and who, as you say, has a prominent place in the nation's psyche, how do you control character consistency across different titles?

A: Well, back in the old days you didn't. Julie Schwartz did a Batman in *Batman* and *Detective* and Murray Boltinoff did a Batman in the *Brave and Bold* and apart from the costume they bore very little resemblance to each other. Julie and Murray did not coordinate their efforts, did not pretend to, did not want to, were not asked to. Continuity was not important in those days. Now it has become very important, which is decidedly a mixed blessing. I sometimes want to say to these people who insist on continuity, "Hey, it is just a story. This is not real life. Don't get upset." Also, I think it's the idea of Batman that's important, the folklore/mythological roots of the character rather than the foolish consistency which, Emerson said, is the hobgoblin of little minds. Nonetheless, continuity is something our audience demands.

Q: Why more now than before?

A: I don't know. I think maybe the audience is more cohesive. Comic books are not read on a hit or miss basis anymore. They are read by fewer people than they were in the '40s but the current fans read a great deal more intently and with a great deal of care. Also, thanks to the direct market, it is now possible to get every issue of everything. Back in the old days, it was sort of newsstand roulette and fans couldn't worry about consistency because they didn't have all the stories. Also, letter columns did not exist back then so there was no arena to exchange opinions, nor were there conventions and all those other places where fans can get together and compare notes. Now, I keep coming back to the point that the Batman phenomenon has certain things in common with religion in that it is built around a mythology or psuedo-mythology and maybe that explains the concern with continuity. Anyway, for whatever reason, continuity and consistency have become important so DC has a guy like me to watch over things. Anything that has Bats in it I have to approve, therefore presumably I am the quality control. I am the guy who keeps the character consistent and says, "You may or may not do this with him."

Q: How do you go about making sure all your writers and artists are dealing with essentially the same character?

A: By giving people a bible which sets limits and by looking at the material. If Bats is doing something totally out of character then the writer will be asked to rewrite the story. It's as simple as that. It's more or less true of the other characters also. If were are going to do anything with Superman, Mike [Carlin] has to see it. If we are going to do anything with Wonder Woman, Karen Berger has to see it. We have lists of what characters are assigned to which editors. Obviously, Batman is a lot more important than the rest because of all of the brouhaha attending the character at the moment. But, two years from now Superman may be the big deal and Mike will have to do all this reading of other people's scripts.

Q: Is the obsessive return to the origin story for reasons of character continuity or is it just because of a turnover in readership?

A: The origin is the engine that drives Batman. The reason we didn't meddle with the origin when we were meddling with a lot of origins four years ago is that it's perfect. When the question of changing it came up, I said, "How are you going to improve on this?" It simply in one incident explains everything that anybody will ever need to know about the character. Why he does what he does and why he is who he is. The times I have written it, it just seemed organic to the story. In the old days, we would have repeated it every three years because the assumption was that the readership turned over every three years. This may have been true back then. The origin story has appeared a little too often recently. When I did it in *Legends of the Dark Knight*, I felt it needed to be there but I made it a dream and made the characters snowmen to at least make it a little different. I have put out one of my ban memos saying that nobody gets to do the origin for at least one year. I put one out about the Joker six months ago saying no Joker stories for at least one year because we have done him too much.

Q: Could we talk a little bit about the production process? Could you tell us on a very basic level what is the relationship among the editor, writer, penciller, inker, letterist, colorist and how does everybody work together?

A: Anything I tell you will be a broad generalization. One of the things that makes the job interesting is that there is no right way to do it. Every editor I have ever met, every editor I worked for, does it a different way and I do it a different way from day to day or hour to hour. Basically, in very broad general terms, a writer is given an assignment— it may be that he is assigned a series, it may be one issue or it may be that he comes in with an idea for a series. At any rate, he ends up with an assignment and meets with the editor, by phone, for lunch or in the office and talks about his story. The writer and editor agree on what the story is going to be about. That is pretty basic. From there on it can go a lot of different ways. My preferred way of working as a writer is to write a script, which looks very much like a television script. It's a format that I have developed over the years. There are panel and page numbers and descriptions of the visuals and dialogue and captions. The other method is that the writer does a plot. This has become known as the Marvel way of working since it was developed by Stan Lee. The plot can be anything from a paragraph, as it was in the early 60s with Stan, to something that is as long as a final script. Okay, the penciller pencils the story and at that point it comes back to the writer and the writer adds copy and if the writer is doing his job, he also does balloon placement.

Q: And how much dialogue do you usually put in a panel?

A: Depends on how big the panel is and what the needs of the story are. The rule I learned when I was starting out a quarter of a century ago was thirty-five words per panel. This is not a bad rule of thumb, though depending on the composition of the frame, it might accommodate fifty words and if it is a half page, it might accommodate 100 words. The idea is not to kill the art work. Don't have so much copy that you lose the picture.

Then the letterer does the panel borders, puts in the lettering and puts in the ballons working from the guideline he is given. Lettering is a great unacknowledged art form. It can make an immense amount of difference in how a job is perceived. The minimum requirement is that the lettering should be neat and very legible, but we are getting sophisticated to the point that we actually use it as part of the story. We'll use upper and lower case or italics or bold and also what I designate on scripts as spooky lettering. That can be anything the letterer wants to make it provided it is really different. It adds visual texture and I think in your mind you hear it differently. At least I do.

From the letterer it goes to the inker. At its crudest, his job is just going over the pencil with ink so it will photograph. But, like the letterer, an inker can make an immense amount of difference. He can do anything from redrawing and correcting the artist's mistakes, to adding textures, to giving depth to the picture by his placement of blacks, by his placement of sepiatone, by highlights. The best inkers are always intensely conscious of where the light source is in the panel. A good inker can take a mediocre pencil job and make it great and, conversely, a bad inker can take a pretty good pencil job and make it look awful. The guys who do this work tell me that it is a very different mind set to pencilling. A really good inker chooses to be an inker but probably could make his living as a penciller.

Q: But not many people do pencilling and inking do they?
A: No, they don't. The reason that pencilling and inking are separate jobs is just an accident of historical evolution. In the forties, comic books were mass produced and it was a lot faster if one guy did the pencilling and another guy did the inking. Now that is no longer true, but for most guys it's a matter of choice.

When all of the writing, pencilling and lettering is done, the editor has pages photographically reduced to a 6" x 9" comic book size. Those are given to the colorist. Until six months ago, I would have told you that colorists work with a palate of sixty-four colors. They are aniline dyes, which is a kind of water color. The colorist goes through, colors the job and, if he or she is conscientious, makes notations for instance, "R2 B2" which means 25 percent red, 25 percent blue. This is a notation to the separator for a specific dot pattern. Now, we are working with computer colors and the palate is a lot larger. On the upscale books, for example on *Digital Justice*, we have a sixteen million color palate. We aren't going to use that many. But we will probably use 500 of those. The letterpress books, which are half of our stuff, are not sophisticated enough to handle that many variations, but they will probably be able to handle well above sixty-four colors.

Coloring is another unacknowledged art form. The basic task in comic book coloring is to give depth to the picture. The easiest way to do that is dark colors come forward, pastels recede, so make the backgrounds pastel. When people are designing super hero costumes, they tend to do them in primary colors which simplifies the process. If a colorist wants to get a bit more sophisticated, he or she can emphasize story elements. The colorist can be part of the storytelling process. If the vase in the corner is going to be very important to the story, they will color the panel in such a way to subtly emphasize that vase without a little arrow pointing to it saying, "important clue." The very best colorists think in those terms. The worst of them just think in coloring book terms and they usually don't get much work. The colorist, like everybody else in the process, has to think of himself as one of the story tellers. The process of coloring is far harder than you would imagine because with super heroes, you have certain givens. Batman's costume is not going to change. That gives the artists real headaches in terms of what they can do in backgrounds. For example, how to handle the color of the clothing of the people around Batman, particularly since they move from place to place in the context of the story. It is really far more complicated than dabbing colors on the page.

Q: We want to talk about the business side of the industry and ask you if you see really significant changes in the relationship between creative types and the company over the past few years.

A: Oh Lord, yes. My timing stinks. When I started out the editor was God because it didn't make any difference who was doing the books, not a bit. Batman sold regardless of who the creative team was. So if a writer was giving you trouble, the hell with him. Get out your Rolodex, call the next warm body. Up till about ten years ago that is the way it worked. Then DC in particular began to emphasize the creators. The audience became sophisticated and began to demand a certain quality level. Now it is a very complicated relationship between the company, particularly as represented by the editor, and the creative people. Creative people have a lot more say in what goes down. We consult with them constantly about everything. In the old days, if there was going to be any kind of major change, the writer could find out about it the same time the readers did. I have been fired off books and didn't know it until I suddenly realized I hadn't done a Wonder Woman for four months and found out there had been six issues done in that time. We wouldn't dare do that now. If we are going to have any major change in policy, we call the creators.

Q: The artist and writers also started getting royalties a few years ago. Is that right?

A: Yes. That was seven or eight years ago. The probable reason was the rise of the direct market. I've heard that the business people here at DC were coming to believe that the direct market was the wave of the future and that this would create a body of knowledgeable readers. In the old days, when sales were all through the newsstands, quality didn't matter a lot, much less the names attached to that quality, because it was virtually impossible to be sure of reaching the readers who would care about good material and would notice bylines. With the direct sales shops, that isn't true. Those are precisely the readers you do reach through the comic shops and if that's the case, it's just good business to reward the creators who produce higher sales. You want to keep them working on your titles. A system of royalties was the obvious answer.

Finally, Paul Levitz came up with a royalty plan. When DC's plan was announced, Jim Shooter came up with a counterplan for Marvel which had also rejected the royalty idea up to this point. Jim claims he had proposed it two years earlier and had been rejected by his bosses. Anyway, DC's original royalty plan has been modified several times, always to the benefit of the creative people. One of the things we have done, for example, is reduce the break-even point from 100,000 to 75,000 copies, which means that on a newsstand book, after your first 75,000 copies are sold, you start making additional money. On our direct-only books, the break-even point is 40,000. But if you created the character, the break-even point is around 20,000, depending on the price of the book.

Q: Does this mean that people can write fewer titles?

A: Absolutely. Because of the sale of the five issues of *Legends of the Dark Knight,* if I were freelance, I would consider taking next year off. I wouldn't have to do a lick of work to live at my present standard because of the totally phenomenal and crazy sale of that one book. And Frank Miller coming off of *Dark Knight* probably didn't have to work for a couple of years at least. So if you were Miller or John Byrne, you could do a lot less work. Certainly, gone are the days when a top creator had to produce six stories per month. Of course, some of us would choose to do that. One of the realizations I came to a few years ago is that there are people who are prolific and there are people who are not prolific. Quality doesn't have very much to do with it. There are some people that just are not happy unless they are producing a large volume of work. Somebody like John Byrne, if he doesn't have quite enough comic book work, will look for something outside comics to do.

Q: How do the recent changes in distribution of the books affect the way you tell stories, particularly in terms of serial versus individual issues?

A: You used to have to tell one-issue stories because newstand distribution was irregular and your audience could not be certain if they bought *Batman* #28 of being able to buy *Batman* #29. You could have serial stories but you had to work in a flashback or exposition in each issue. I did that until about two years ago just as a matter of writing technique, even with the direct market. I gradually became aware writing *The Question,* that while its fans are not numerous, they are very loyal and they are going to buy everything. I have chosen to do a lot of one-issue stories because that is what I felt like doing. But if I wanted to do a three-issue story, any reference to the back story would be organic and help to propel some present tense piece of action in the same way that a novel will refer in chapter 20 to what happened in chapter 1 because it will be natural for the characters to make those references. You don't reach and twist and contrive to get back story exposition in. In *Legends of the Dark Knight*, I went full out and treated it as if I was writing a 125 page novel. The concession I made to the fact that it's episodic was to put a hook at the end of each episode, some reason why you will want to see where the story goes from there.

Q: Have you been reading Dickens lately?

A: I was going to say that novelists do that anyway. Particularly, people who write suspense fiction. Even if they are just writing a book, they will put those hooks in from time to time. Stephen King is great at it. It helps pull you through the story. But I am assuming that anybody who read issue 1 of *Legends of the Dark Knight* will read issues 2, 3, 4, and 5. On the other hand, this may not be true because I would guess that half of the people who bought issue 1 bought it because it was issue 1. It looks like issue 2 will sell considerably less.

Q: A lot of people are probably expecting issue 1 to appreciate in value.

A: Oh sure. And then we did that sort of sneaky stunt of bringing it with four different colored outer covers. I was in California signing copies last week and I signed a lot of sets. People felt that they had to buy all four versions of the first issue.

Q: We have been talking a lot about the readers and fans. We wanted to ask you a few questions about that. The letter columns seem to reflect an articulate readership and we were wondering if the letters you print are representative of what you receive.

A: Well, there is a bottom part of our mail where the letters are illiterate and we don't print them. Sometimes they are illiterate because they are from seven-year-olds, who are probably very intelligent seven-year-olds, but they are seven-year-olds. We may occasionally print one of those and clean up the grammar and spelling. But we try to make the letters representive. It's that sampling of fan opinion again. If 75 percent of our mail hated a story, we will reflect that in the letter column. Most of our readership is articulate. If you go out to schools, as I do, you will find that the kids who read comic books are the bright kids, the verbal kids. And then our marketing information shows that our average reader is twenty-four and male and very literate, so it is not surprising that we get a pretty high percentage of articulate, literary letters. That is one of the changes that has come about. I no longer feel very much need to write down to anybody when I am doing a comic book. I feel a very large persistent need to honor the tradition out of which I am working, but I don't have to worry about using big words anymore or even big concepts.

Q: So you think that your twenty-four-year-old males are pretty consistent readers then? The three- to four-year readership turnover has stopped?

A: The conventional wisdom about the turnover was that comic books were being read by children and when they got to the age of twelve they got into something else and they stopped reading comic books. We now know that they probably begin to seriously get interested in them at about that age.

Q: Do you think that the marketing of graphic novels like *The Killing Joke* and *The Dark Knight* in bookstores and even by the Quality Paperback Book Club have pulled in a new readership for you?

A: Sure, because people may have liked the form but felt the stories were too simplistic for them. Not interesting enough. Maybe the very crude version of super heroes, which is basically the male macho fantasy trip, *was* a little too crude for a lot of our potential readers. But, something like *Watchmen* or *The Killing Joke* is sophisticated and it gives the new readers the form they like with a content that is acceptable to them.

Q: Do you think a lot of women read Batman and, if not, how would you go about attracting a larger female readership?

A: I wish I knew. We have talked about this for at least fifteen years. We know that women are very much a minority of our readers though it is a minority that is growing. It may be because through one of those historical accidents, comic books have been about strong guys who vanquish evil. This is not a subject that a lot of little girls have a consuming interest in so there is nothing in them to attact this readership. When we did try and attract them, the stories were done by middle-aged men, who didn't have a handle on what a girl might really like. As I said, this is changing.

Q: Do you have plans to try to attract more female readers?

A: Yeah. I think the current version of Wonder Woman appeals to women—in fact, it may be too feminist for some peoples' taste. It's edited by a woman and written by a man who is certainly very sympathetic to feminist concerns.

Q: And what about Batman?

A: I don't know. I could guess that the movie will attract some women, but I think it's going to be a slow process because historically the character has not appealed to women. Women are going to have to discover comics on their own and then decide what they like and what they don't like.

Q: The industry seems to be unique in that a lot of creative people have started out as fans. What do you think the impact of this is? The pluses and minuses?

A: The pluses are that they are familiar with the material and with the vocabulary and the visual conventions of the medium. The downside is that they may become a little too concerned about repeating the stuff that they just absolutely loved when they first discovered comics. The good comic book writers who came up as fans at some point in their lives got interested in a lot of other stuff. Those that stay only interested in comics cripple their potential development as writers. Some of them are bright, talented guys but the medium has moved beyond what they loved when they were twelve years old.

Q: What do you think the difference is between somebody like yourself who comes out of a journalistic background and wasn't heavily into comics and the writers who were fans in terms of the different approaches to a character?

A: People with diverse backgrounds bring ideas and even fictional techniques from outside comics. In that way they push the envelope, they expand the possibilities, both in terms of subject matter and in terms of storytelling technique. They bring cinema to it. They bring novels to it. I think that Alan Moore, for example, has the instincts of a novelist—he has read a lot of novels and loved them. I think Frank Miller, is, in his soul, a visual writer, a very good one; he comes to it with the instincts of a movie maker. But the point is that they are both bringing to it something from outside comics. If you grew up only being interested in comics, you are probably only going to regurgitate, both in terms of content and in terms of technique, what has already been done. You can't get too radical and violate the medium, but you can expand it. It has to be a gradual thing. The Green Lantern stories I did in the '70s that got a lot of publicity at the time came about because I was a journalist and I brought a journalist's curiosity and social concerns to comic books. It wouldn't have happened if I had just been a comic book writer.

Q: When we talked to you the last time, you were using a lot of cinematic terms to describe art work. Is that something a lot of people tend to do?

A: No, that's something pretty much only I do. It's just because

I found it's the easiest way to do it. If I am in the middle of a story and I am really cooking and it's 3 a.m., hey watch out. It's a lot easier for me to write "ECU Myra" than "We see Myra's face close up." The nice thing about writing screenplays is that the language is such a nice economical shorthand. It's almost music notation. I have written two television shows in the last six months and I find it easy work because you don't have to work on transitions. You write "cut to . . ." and the camera man accomplishes the transition for you. It seems like a good thing to borrow from cinema insofar as we do a lot of the same things.

Q: But most writers don't use this cinematic shorthand?

A: No. Take Alan Moore, for example. His description for the first panel of *The Killing Joke*, one ninth of a page, is two and a half single space pages. It took me a day to read the script of *The Killing Joke*. It was a pretty good day though, I enjoyed it.

Q: How did Brian Bolland feel about the lengthy descriptions?

A: Alan will give you this incredibly detailed description of not only what is in the panel but why it's there, and what happened twenty years ago, and what the character had for breakfast this morning and what the kids were doing. Then at the end he'll say, "You could ignore all that and do whatever you want." So I think Brian basically followed what Alan indicated. At one point we thought about publishing Alan's script because it is so entertaining in itself and then ultimately decided that that would be a little bit like being invited back stage to a magic show.

Q: We saved one of the things we are most interested in for last, which is the relationship between comics and films. What similarities and differences do you see between the two?

A: Well, there is an awful lot that is similar but you can carry the analogy too far. Basically, if a comic book works, you will be able to get the broad story by looking at the pictures. But comic books are meant to be read. Reading requires more participation from the audience than cinema where if you are just passive you can still get it. You have to bring your brain cells to reading. I think that there is that interaction between the part of you that perceives images and the part of you that translates the very abstract stuff that is language. If you like comics, I think it's because of some kind of chemical process in your brain. Those two messages entering your consciousness at the same time through the same sense organ are very pleasing to you. If you are looking at a movie or television show, it's a different experience. You don't have to use your imagination as much, the language is coming in through the ear, the visual information is coming in through your eye. That's what you experience everyday in your life, it's not special in the way of perceiving a comic book.

3

Batman and the Twilight of the Idols:
An Interview with Frank Miller

Christopher Sharrett

If there is a single artist most identified with the resurgence in popularity of Batman it is without question Frank Miller. His 1986 graphic novel *Batman: The Dark Knight Returns* not only made Bob Kane's 1939 creation once again the most popular comic book hero, but played no small role in the incredible burgeoning in the '80s of the comics industry. Inked and colored by Klaus Janson and Lynn Varley, *Dark Knight* offered a troubled, suicidal, alcoholic Bruce Wayne in his mid-fifties who tries to repress the urge to again don his Batman persona after a ten year retirement. The worsening scene (Gotham City totally corrupt, the world on the brink of nuclear war, the Joker released from a mental institution) forces Batman into one last go-round that for Miller is the "Great American Superhero story," a four-part "opera" about the fall of the hero in a world that has rendered him obsolete. This book and a follow-up, *Batman: Year One* (a very grim retelling of Batman's origins), aside from recasting Batman and the other mainstay DC Comics superheroes, became part of a general reevaluation of hero worship in comic book narrative. Alan Moore and Dave Gibbons' mammoth graphic novel *Watchmen* (about a 1980s U.S. very similar to our own where superheroes are an accepted part of the landscape, with disastrous results), and Moore's *Miracleman* and *V for Vendetta*, use the superhero as a vehicle for challenging received notions of charismatic authority and leadership, among the driving strategies within the comic book renaissance.

Decidedly more romantic than Moore's superheroes, Miller's Batman is nonetheless offered as a radical opponent to the status quo, and an obsessed and brooding personality infinitely more three-dimensional than the type generally offered by the narrow moral universe of the comics industry. The renewed interest in Batman caused by *Dark Knight* and its successors far outstripped Batman's principal rival in pop fiction, Superman (described by a character in *Dark Knight* as "that big blue schoolboy") and spurred not only new Batmania but the impetus for bringing Batman to the screen after various scripts remained Hollywood back-burner projects for over a decade.

Aside from his Batman work, Miller has produced a number of other provocative works in the superhero genre, including the graphic novel *Elektra: Assassin*, and a celebrated run on Marvel Comics' popular *Daredevil* series, another character Miller virtually reinvented. As Miller's Batman books were enjoying great success and tremendous notoriety, Alan Moore made the field even richer with his own Batman novel (drawn by Brian Bolland) *The Killing Joke*, a melancholy meditation on the psychological relationship of Batman to his archrival the Joker. In 1987, at the height of one of the comic industry's most creative and productive periods, a new wave of censorship and a war over the industry's control of artists' work caused Miller, Moore, and a number of top creators to part company with DC and Marvel Comics. Miller has since written the screenplay for *Robocop II* and developed new characters for independent comics publishers.

In what follows Miller discusses his involvement with Batman, his earlier and future work, the state of the comics industry, and the meaning of the superhero as a symbol of our times.

CS: There is a perception that *Dark Knight* almost single-handedly started the new renaissance in comic books.

FM: *Dark Knight* got a lot of immediate attention because it was Batman and everyone recalls that character from the old TV show. But *Dark Knight* was only one of several things going on in the field that showed what comics could really do. Spiegelman's *Maus* got similar attention, perhaps from a slightly different audience.

CS: But *Maus* and *Raw* and such seem to be somewhere in the avant-garde. They still haven't gained the notoriety of a *Dark Knight*. Is it because Batman is simply such a strong popular icon?

FM: Well, I'd love to say that the success of *Dark Knight* was based solely on the talents of myself and my collaborators, but Batman after all is a major American folk hero who was due for a revival. About every ten or twenty years or so you see renovations of Superman or Batman, and in this case I was lucky enough to have almost complete autonomy and produce something that for me was ultimately very personal.

CS: You don't think that at least part of the interest was involved in the rather panicked search for heroes in 1980s culture? The incredible popularity of the work of Joseph Campbell also seems involved in a new phase of hero worship.

FM: Anytime a hero is done even reasonably well there's a *tremendous* popular response. Modern art and literature have so diminished the idea of the hero, at least up until a few years back, that there was a crying need.

CS: I want to come back to this idea of hero worship. Could you speak for a moment to the influence of *Dark Knight* on the image of Batman. We see constant references to the "dark knight" in the comics, but are the current Batman stories showing the type of complex character you created in the book? Some suggest that while Batman has become a "darker" character, more substantive ideas from *Dark Knight* have been dropped.

FM: The comics industry is dominated by two publishers, who don't believe in or even understand what comics can be. They shrink from censors whenever they appear. They have historically depended on a sweatshop atmosphere, even to survive. Since *Dark Knight*, very cynical editors have hired artists to trace off pages of *Dark Knight*, and they've hired writers to repeat what they think they understand about *Dark Knight*, which essentially is that it is very brutal, and that it includes little TV panels. Of course all this misses the point of the whole thing, so what we're seeing are a lot of third-rate imitations. I don't like saying this really. It's pretty embarrassing. The same publisher that bought Superman and Batman and totally corrupted them got a shot in the arm with *Dark Knight* and *Watchmen* and a few other things. And look what they've done with it.

CS: Are there any Batman books or mini-series which interest you and seem close to your sensibility? We've seen *Batman: The Cult*, *Batman: Year Two*, *Killing Joke*, *A Death in the Family* and quite a few other major Batman projects.

FM: *A Death in the Family* should be singled out as the most cynical thing that particular publisher has ever done. An actual toll-free number where fans can call in to put the axe to a little boy's head. On the other hand, *Killing Joke* was a very fine piece of work that came out at about the same time.

CS: Some of the Batman stories seem very opposite of *Dark Knight* with their one-dimensional moral simplicity. I'm thinking of *Ten Nights of the Beast* with the KGB supervillain.

FM: You're getting beyond me here. I haven't read that.

CS: It's not worth talking about. It's basically another example of turning back the clock on the whole genre.

FM: What offended me most was seeing the tracing off of David Mazzucchelli's drawings in the *Catwoman* series, and also seeing my own drawings traced off in *The Cult*. I really would have thought better of them. I would have thought the artists involved in those projects would do better than that.

CS: We've mentioned *The Killing Joke*. How close is Alan Moore's sensibility to your own in terms of the conception of Batman and his world, particularly to the image of the Joker?
FM: I disagreed completely with everything he did in that book but Alan did it all so beautifully I couldn't argue. And Brian Bolland's illustrations were gorgeous, some of his best work. You've got to understand that when I'm involved with these characters the involvement is total: I have to believe in them. Alan's view of the Joker was very humanistic. My Joker was more evil than troubled; Alan's was more troubled than evil.

CS: It does seem that *Dark Knight* contains a very metaphysical notion of evil, while in *Watchmen* and *Killing Joke* evil is produced by social forces.
FM: There is a wonderful line in *Killing Joke* about "one bad day."

CS: Yeah, that is a great line. Let's stay with Batman and the Joker. In the current conceptions of Batman, including the movie, we have this idea of Batman as rather insane, with the Joker as a kind of Doppelgänger.
FM: The Batman folklore is full of Doppelgängers for Batman. The Joker is one of them. The more accurate one, although a less interesting villain, is Two-Face. Two-Face is identical to Batman in that he's controlled by savage urges, which he keeps in check, in his case, with the flip of a coin. He's very much like Batman. The Joker is not so much a Doppelgänger as an antithesis, a force for chaos. Batman imposes his order on the world; he is an absolute control freak. The Joker is Batman's most maddening opponent. He represents the chaos Batman despises, the chaos that killed his parents.

CS: So it's control vs. the loss of control.
FM: Yeah. What really makes it so tantalizing is the sexual aspect of the whole thing.

CS: In terms of the Joker?
FM: In terms of the Joker and Batman. In a way, the Joker is a homophobic nightmare.

CS: Can you develop this a bit?

FM: In *Dark Knight* the Joker says he never keeps count of all the hundreds of people he's killed, but he knows Batman does and he loves him for it. To Batman, who's not asexual but really the essence of sublimation, this character represents every single thing he despises. It get's pretty weird.

CS: In *Dark Knight* the Joker seems more overtly gay than in other Batman narratives. In Chapter 3, his henchman Bruno seems to be a transsexual.

FM: Bruno is a woman. I have a hard time expressing the ways I initially conceived some of these rather bizarre characters without sounding like a psychopath. Anyway, Bruno was a woman, a cohort of the Joker. He never had sex with her because sex is death to him. Put more accurately, death is sex.

CS: There seem to be so many gay aspects to the Joker in *Dark Knight*. The makeup man at the TV studio taunts him about lipstick. The Joker actually wears lipstick. He calls Batman "Darling." A lot of gay signifiers there.

FM: I don't want to sound simplistic, but it seemed like a good idea at the time I was working on the character. I know we live in very rough times in terms of persecution of gays and gay stereotyping, but I wasn't trying to address this as much as portray this villain in a way I felt to be sensible and interesting.

CS: Of course an issue here is that the Joker is the only gay character in the book. There is no counterbalancing force in terms of a gay character who's more heroic. This is apparently one reason why *Dark Knight* was criticized.

FM: I've had flak from almost every group. I can only say that when I write my stories I honestly try to avoid targeting anyone. Working in Hollywood recently I've come to realize how many prohibitions there really are against even touching one group or another, to a point where the villain can't be female, can't be gay, can't be black. I understand this, but I still don't like the limitations placed on how you can go about creating characters. Anyway, yeah, the homophobic nightmare is very much part of the Batman/Joker mythos. It's always been there, I just spelled it out a little more plainly.

CS: If we can stay with the sexual theme for a minute, it seems that this has been developed increasingly after decades of repression, especially with Fredric Wertham's attack on the Batman/Robin relationship as gay. *Watchmen* insisted on superhero sexuality. Some readers have suggested that your Robin, Carrie Kelly, finally allows Batman

to express his sexual feelings for Robin since the character is suddenly
female. It's a subtle expression of his gayness.

FM: Come on. It's a father/child relationship. It's clearly defined
as such. This is where this stuff gets preposterous. When he says "Good
soldier" to her, he's holding this little girl. He's confronting his limitations as a human being. Batman isn't gay. His sexual urges are so
drastically sublimated into crime-fighting that there's no *room* for any
other emotional activity. Notice how insipid are the stories where
Batman has a girlfriend or some sort of romance. It's not because he's
gay, but because he's borderline pathological, he's obsessive. He'd be
much healthier if he were gay.

CS: I'd like to touch on *Dark Knight*'s politics. You're probably
familiar with the *Village Voice* review that called the book "Rambo in
a cape."

FM: It gets pretty silly. The book is what it is. In that *Village
Voice* attack they also said that the Mutant dialect was a disguised
black dialect, but it was taken almost word-for-word from a suburban
white dialect that Lynn [Varley] brought to it. Lynn co-wrote all the
dialogue with Robin and the Mutants, because it's all based on a dialect
in her home town, a predominantly white suburb, a real "Leave It To
Beaver" land. You check that place and you won't find it a center for
much urban black culture. The *Village Voice* reaction, along with a few
others, was a reaction based on the fact that *Dark Knight* did not offer
a didactic left-wing perspective. I was having great fun with parody,
and I've never been able to give up on the idea of superheroes. I couldn't
have done Batman and have been politically correct at the same time,
because the politically correct contingent won't allow for any character
with a larger-than-life status. Also, of course, violence is out, and Batman is an extremely violent character.

CS: Another criticism is that *Dark Knight, Watchmen, Batman:-
Year One, Miracleman,* and the works that reevaluate the superhero,
are essentially pessimistic. There is this apocalyptic vision throughout
these works.

FM: I don't know how I could write a superhero story and be
pessimistic. To go into history for a moment, what made the whole
superhero idea impotent was censorship. With fear on from pressure
groups, the industry adopted a self-censoring code. The code through
which most comics still pass insists on a benevolent world where
authority is always right, policemen never take bribes, our elected
officials always serve our best interests, and parents are always good
and sound people. They don't even make mistakes. The world we live
in does not resemble the world of the censors. I simply put Batman,

this unearthly force, into a world that's closer to the one I know. And the world I know is terrifying. I don't think *Dark Knight* is pessimistic because the good guy wins.

CS: But it seems that your hero finally loses at the end of *Dark Knight*. Moreover, it seems like these god-like characters are made irrelevant in the operatic atmosphere you create, with the nuclear backdrop and the contempt for superheroes expressed by the world at large. At the end Bruce Wayne immolates his Batman persona.

FM: For me that was a hopeful ending. He's looking forward to his next adventure after realizing that the methods of the past are no longer appropriate. The book starts with Bruce Wayne contemplating suicide; at the end he's found a reason to live. He's adjusted to the times.

CS: He's not going to be carrying on as a romantic superhero?

FM: The sequel I had in mind was as preposterous as the original. He would be much more direct in his actions, much more willing to mess with the order of things. He wouldn't be going after the poor bastards who are muggers. He'd be going after the people who make them muggers.

CS: So he would operate as Bruce Wayne, going after politicians and businessmen?

FM: Oh, I would have thrown all kinds of capes and cowls into it too, because that's the stuff of it. The key transition would be his recognition that he's no longer part of authority. That's really the transition at the end of *Dark Knight*, this knowledge that he's no longer on the side of the powers that be anymore, because the powers that be are wrong.

CS: So in that sense then the book is very radical, with Batman representing an antiestablishment image.

FM: Sure. And that's what I think these books can offer. Go back to the origins of Superman, before World War II. He was dragging generals to the front of battles. He was fighting corrupt landlords. He was *not* the symbol of the status quo he's since become.

CS: He was a real FDR/ New Deal character.

FM: Yeah, in a sense.

CS: So in the conservative '80s superheroes again represent very firmly the standing order, except for your work, *Watchmen* and a few others.

FM: There's tremendous pressure in the field, at the two major publishers, to do that. When Jerry Falwell and his ilk were riding high there was this edict down at Marvel Comics not to use words like "God," or "damn," or "Good Lord," or anything else that might by chance offend pseudo-Christians. You really have to keep in mind that Marvel and DC are scared chickens. If you can generate five letters they'll do what you say. And the characters reflect their publishers' fearfulness, so we have a Superman who's starting to spread around the middle and might have lunch with Nancy Reagan next week, and Batman has turned into a real jerk. Luckily there was a time when there was a little opening-up, and Alan Moore and Dave Gibbons and Lynn Varley and myself and a few others were allowed the opportunity to paint our own portraits of these heroes.

CS: What's your feeling about the Batman movie? It seems that it couldn't have come into being without *Dark Knight* paving the way.

FM: I didn't enjoy it. I disagreed with almost everything in it. I get locked into my visions of these characters and become resistant to other interpretations. I'm the last person who should attempt to review anything with Batman in it.

CS: OK. What about the constant use of the term "dark knight" in every Batman narrative?

FM: Well, I didn't make it up. It wasn't used very commonly in Batman folklore, it's true. Now DC is milking the idea for all it's worth. That's just the way they work. To me the whole killing of Robin thing was probably the ugliest thing I've seen in comics, and the most cynical.

CS: Has there been anything in the superhero genre lately that has really interested you?

FM: There's *Watchmen*. Back when we were doing *Dark Knight* and *Watchmen* there was a feeling among a few of us that we were reentering adolescence in working on this form. Now I feel that this has become true generally, with people going into this retrograde adolescence along several different directions. There's really no form of entertainment where the idea of the hero has been more fully explored than in comics, and now that public attention has grown there is a retreat to a more juvenile outlook. Marvel and DC are retreating to the styles of the '60s while keeping some of the trappings of the '80s. There's a little more violence, there's an occasional bare breast or whatever, but basically it's a retreat to the same material of the early '60s. Alan and I and a few others are trying to go our own way. I'm writing more stories about heroes. I'm not through with them yet.

CS: What's coming up?

FM: There are a few projects due later this year. One is called *Hard Boiled*, a kind of futuristic tough-guy series. The other is *Give*

Me Liberty, drawn by Dave Gibbons, which is a future history with a female lead. Geof Darrow is drawing *Hard Boiled*. I finished an *Elektra* book with Lynn Varley.

CS: You said *Watchmen* is the only book that interests you. That's now almost three years old and part of a time when you and Alan Moore were helping to change the industry. There's *nothing* else out there lately?

FM: Quality comes and goes, of course. I haven't been keeping up with the field. Someone may pop up with something amazing. You have to consider also what Alan and I were working on. I was working on a revivification of a folk hero, but I was also reaping all the benefits of fifty years of the hero's history. It's true also with Alan because you couldn't really approach *Watchmen* without growing up with the Justice League of America. Now I'm on much less steady ground because I'm creating characters out of whole cloth. I'm trying to build walls to push against. With Batman that's easy, because you know the rules of the game. If things are a bit fallow or bland right now it may be natural enough because there was an earthquake a few years back. I've seen things happening in the field, but not with superheroes. *Love and Rockets* is delightful; Spiegelman's work is of great value. Have you seen the new *Raw?* Excellent stuff. I'm especially interested in some imports—it's great to finally be able to read one of Milo Manara's books.

CS: Some fans suggest that after *Dark Knight* and *Watchmen* there isn't very much more to be said about superheroes.

FM: I heard that *before* those books came out. It's the old idea that there are only two or three stories that can be told about a character. It's just talk. There's plenty more work to be done.

CS: Does the sweatshop atmosphere of the publishers simply kill imagination?

FM: It's a combination of things. For one thing, you might notice that people's time at these publishers tend to be shorter and shorter. I spent a lot less time at DC than Neal Adams, for example, and certainly less than Gardner Fox did. You can't own your own work, or even a piece of it. You cannot control your work as you produce it. It's a condition intolerable enough to drive me and Alan and a number of other people away from those companies and therefore away from these essential folkheroes. So you have to figure what your options are if you want to work with the idea of the superhero. You can't just come up with an imitation Superman—that would be cheap and silly and not as good as the original. So for my part since I can't let go of these heroes I'm trying to come up with new ones without ripping off the old ones.

CS: I'd like to backtrack for a moment to some of the themes in *Dark Knight*. In that book and *Watchmen* there is a strong apocalyptic current. In *Dark Knight* there is a kind of near-miss nuclear attack that sets up a very bleak landscape for Batman to take a role in. In *Watchmen* a superhero causes a holocaust in order to usher in utopia. Most of the major superhero reevaluations seem intimately tied to an apocalyptic impulse in mass culture.

FM: Things don't look good right now. The environment is collapsing. That crisis may well be the next major theme in entertainment. I think it's finally sinking in that the planet is on its way to dying. Whether or not we decide to do something may be irrelevant. When we were doing those books nuclear terror was definitely in everyone's minds. It was obvious that everything could end very fast. *Dark Knight* and *Watchmen* were both an attempt to weave the superhero into that terror. That was sort of the basic backdrop. It was a bit of a stretch to weave Batman into it, but it seemed necessary, and it seemed to be good material.

CS: Some fans were let down that there weren't full-scale disasters at the end of *Dark Knight* and *Watchmen*, since you and Alan seemed to be building toward them and the end of the world seemed to be the culmination you were preparing us for.

FM: And these are the people who call us pessimists!

CS: Yeah, it's interesting. But obviously there's tremendous interest in these *Mad Max*-style narratives about a postnuclear wasteland out of which something new develops.

FM: Yes, well, science says that stuff is all wrong. I've never done a postapocalypse story. I just don't believe it. If that exchange ever happened there just wouldn't be any humans left alive. The planet might survive but there wouldn't be any people on it. Mad Max movies present the most reassuring fantasy of all, that we would somehow survive the catastrophe. As far as the interest in catastrophe in fiction, I suppose I tried to deal with this a bit with the Mutant gang. There is a suicidal, or rather genocidal, fantasy that all our problems will go away if we just get it over with and drop the bomb. It's also a sociopathic fantasy that we can just wipe everything clean instead of dealing with the much more difficult problem of how to maneuver our way out of it all. It's lessening a bit for the moment anyway with *perestroika*, but we still have a Republican in the White House so who knows where it will go. But the nuclear terror isn't quite so pronounced right now. I perceive the nuclear terror thing as a bit of a shill for some real problems in front of us, some of the deeper terrors going on in the planet. It's hideous. How we are going to write stories where superheroes deal with environmental issues is going to be a real bitch.

CS: That brings me back to the basic issue of superheroes. You seem to think that we need them, that strong, charismatic individuals are basic to history. *Watchmen* says the opposite. That book suggests that heroes can take you into hell and that each of us must take responsibility for history's direction.

FM: Like so many things Alan says, I would like to talk with him about this for about three hours, and I have. I just disagree completely with this particular idea *Watchmen* brings up. I don't believe that governments or committees or political movements accomplish much. I believe people do, individually. I'm in love with heroes, not because I think there are that many, or that there is any one individual who could do what Batman does or what Superman does, but because I think we're at our best when we're autonomous.

CS: I think one of Alan Moore's points is somewhat similar to Frank Herbert's argument in the *Dune* books, in that we tend to project too much onto individual charismatic father figures. No matter how well-meaning the hero might be, this abrogation of the will always poses disaster for society.

FM: When I create a story I take a very small thing and make it very big. It just happens to be the way I make my fiction. Someone mugs me and I make a Batman comic, to put it in the crudest possible terms. While there is room for political parody and while there is political meaning in all of this, presenting a hero is not presenting a case for political power. I don't want Batman as president, and I don't think the book says that at all. There's a tendency to see everything as a polemic, as a screed, when after all these are adventure stories. They can have a lot of ramifications, they can bring in an awful lot of other material, but anyone who really believes that a story about a guy who wears a cape and punches out criminals is a presentation of a political viewpoint, and a presentation of a program for how we should live our lives under a political system, is living in a dream world.

CS: But it's possible to see a character like Ozymandias in *Watchmen* as a powerful metaphor for specific political attitudes.

FM: Absolutely. That's part of Alan's brilliance. He did that wonderfully, but I'm just coming at this whole thing with a different attitude.

CS: But your Batman can also be seen as an image of a certain type of power.

FM: Everyone from Alexander to Hitler. But mostly Zorro. Batman doesn't work when he's a figure of authority. He'd would be a tyrant. Anyone who professes an absolute ideological point of view is a would-be tyrant. Batman doesn't do this. Heroes have to work in the society around them, and Batman works best in a society that's gone to hell. That's the only way he's ever worked. He was created when the world was going to hell, and *Dark Knight* came out when the world went to hell.

CS: Yeah. When Bob Kane created him the war was beginning.

FM: Sure. But he's also a dionysian figure, a force for anarchy that imposes an individual order. He's never been an authority figure except in some of the comics of the '60s that actually initiated the TV show, where Batman begins to wear a badge and whatever. But *Dark Knight* didn't end with Batman wanting to take over the U.S.

CS: That last panel of the book suggests he's become a kind of Jim Jones figure, creating a new cult out of the Mutants and whoever else he can pull together.

FM: That's what's fascinating about the character, the way he pulls together all these sinister urges. At the end Bruce Wayne is looking to the next stage, the next phase of his life.

CS: One of the problems with perceiving Batman as a dionysian, anarchical figure is that fact that he's a privileged person. Bruce Wayne is a rich man who seems self-satisfied despite his supposed trauma. We are asked to accept this man as a force for the common good.

FM: Anyone can be a victim. This is exactly what makes him a good character. It's how one uses the evil inside. It's how we use our rage, our venom. One of the things that makes Batman so strangely hip and unhip at the same time is that modern liberalism has totally divorced the forceful, violent aspect of the will from other aspects of personality. There is this view that this forceful aspect of individual will is just plain wrong and shouldn't exist in any form. You can see the kind of censorship in children's entertainment. There is no sense of individual will let alone violent individual will. We're not simple creatures. We all have God and the devil in us. Batman makes his devils work for the common good.

CS: There seems to be an attitude now that the Joker is at least as appealing as Batman in terms of the dark forces he represents. His kind of madness seems associated with the Ted Bundys of society, who seem to hold a powerful fascination for people in the '80s and '90s. An issue of *Film Threat* magazine calls mass murderers the "heroes of the '80s."

FM: It's fantasy. One of the big mistakes of modern times is to assume fantasy should be some kind of behavioral modification device. Fantasy is where we vent our spleens. Freddy Krueger—he's a child molester for Christ's sake! It all gets back to the term "role model" that castrates every hero or villain who falls under the sway of the censors. The Joker is popular right now because a charismatic actor played him, and because he represents doing whatever the hell you want to anybody at any time any way. It's the horror comics of the '50s. It's harmless. To think that our own fantasy lives must be censored is just crazy.

CS: Concerning your plans for the future, do you intend to stay with superheroes?

FM: Yes. I still have some things to say about superheroes, but I have some other projects I want to get into.

CS: For me what's more bothersome is the tendency of DC to cultivate this "adult market" with projects like Piranha Press. They drop terms like "expressionism." The whole thing is so mannered and forced.

FM: Oh god, isn't it awful? That stuff is about as painful as going to the dentist. I went to a comic store recently and spent about a hundred bucks just to see what's going on after a period of being a bit out of touch and feeling that things were rather barren right now. I'm very disturbed by the way that Marvel and DC looked at *Watchmen* and *Dark Knight*. All they got from them is that they were naughtier and a bit more brutal than other comics. They're interpreting stuff that was admittedly violent but they're making it all vicious and very small. When Alan and Dave were working on *Watchmen* and I was working on *Dark Knight* we were coming at the superhero from two different directions. I'm a real romantic. Alan's approach towards heroes, at least intellectually, is much more detached and skeptical. But when I saw that book I was absolutely knocked out. It was some of the most amazing stuff I've ever seen in the medium. It was so well thought out and so carefully crafted. But you have to take one position or the other.

CS: Alan commented in an interview with me that *Watchmen* was a political and moral fable that happened to contain superheroes and *Dark Knight* was a superhero adventure that contained political and moral ideas.

FM: Alan and I have had *many* conversations on the subject. My main comment was that I saw *Dark Knight* as profoundly American and *Watchmen* profoundly British. In *Watchmen* you can't help but see American icons reworked from a very European point of view. It's very hard to miss the whole British flavor.

CS: A couple of final things. Any thoughts on the current wave of Batmania?

FM: America is primed for a fad. It's been about twenty years since that thing happened. It just seems time for a good fad.

CS: I'm thinking how Superman's anniversary fell flat in comparison with what's going on right now with the tons of Batman paraphrenalia. Is there something more primal about Batman imagery?

FM: What better image for a time of despair?

CS: Since Batman indeed speaks to a very bleak attitude toward the future?

FM: Sad to say a very accurate one right now. We live in very dark times. It fits that this would be our hero.

4

"Holy Commodity Fetish, Batman!": The Political Economy of a Commercial Intertext

Eileen R. Meehan

Batman took the United States by storm in the spring and summer of 1989. Tee shirts, posters, keychains, jewelry, buttons, books, watches, magazines, trading cards, audiotaped books, videogames, records, cups, and numerous other items flooded malls across the United States with images of Batman, his new logo, and his old enemy the Joker.[1] Presaged by a much pirated trailer, *Batman* the film drew unprecedented crowds to theatre chains, of which the two largest (United Artist Theater Circuits and American Multi-Cinema) distributed four to five million brochures for mail order Bat-materials.[2] *Batman*'s premiere on the big screen was matched by appearances on the small screen. Film clips were packaged as advertisements and free promotional materials for the interview and movie review circuits on both broadcast and cable television; Prince's "Batdance" video played in heavy rotation on MTV. Over radio, "Batdance" and other cuts from Prince's Batman album got strong play on rock stations and "crossed over" for similarly strong play on black radio stations. Subsequently, retail outlets filled with Bat-costumes and Joker make-up kits for Halloween; Ertl Batmobiles and ToyBiz Batcaves and Batwings were being deployed for Christmas shoppers. In the specialty stores serving comics fandom, the *Advance Comics Special Batlist* offered 214 items ranging from $576 to $2 in price.[3] And in grocery stores, special Bat-displays offered children a choice between Batman coloring books, Batman trace-and-color books, and Batman magic plates. It would seem that Batman and his paraphernalia transcend age, gender, and race.

This deluge of material has generated a complex web of cross references as the major text, *Batman*, ricochets back in cultural memory to Bob Kane's original vision of a caped vigilante, then up to the more recent dystopian *Dark Knight Returns*, with ironic reference to the camp Crusader of television and all the intervening Bat-texts. This web of cross references creates an intertext into which we fit ourselves, positioning ourselves to construct different readings of the film and positioning the film and its intertext to suit our own particular purposes. When a text like *Batman* generates such a rich and complex intertext—in short, when Bat-mania takes the nation by storm—cultural critics are naturally drawn to analyze the text and intertext in order to discover why that text resonates with so many people, why it activates such widespread participation in the intertext.

If the prevalence of Bat-paraphernalia in the stores and the ubiquity of the Bat-logo on the streets are indicators, then indeed *Batman* has struck a chord deep in the American psyche. Certainly the temptation to speculate on the larger significance of *Batman* is strong given the irony of this dark, yet ultimately hopeful, film being released at a time when the mythic Gotham of the *Dark Knight's Return* and the mythos of the American Imperium both seem to crack under the strains of social injustice and personal irresponsibility.

This speculation, however tempting, is not quite fair to us or to the film. Such speculation requires an assumptive leap that reduces consciousness, culture, and media to reflections of each other. It assumes that the American psyche can be read off the film, which reflects American culture which determines how we see the world and how the film is constructed. This old and much criticized error retains its emotional force, despite the articulation of more careful theories about media texts and intertexts, about reception and reinterpretation of those materials by active viewers, as illustrated by the other essays in this volume. In this essay, however, I will argue that another dimension must be added to our analyses of media generally and of *Batman* specifically. Namely, economics must be considered if we are fully to understand the texts and intertexts of American mass culture. Most cultural production in the United States is done by private, for-profit corporations. These corporations comprise the entertainment/information sector of the American economy and encompass the industries of publishing, television, film, music, cable, and radio. Significantly, American capitalism organizes the creation of cultural artifacts as a process of mass production carried out by profit-oriented businesses operating in an industrial context. Profit, not culture, drives show business: no business means no show.

For much of American culture, corporate imperatives operate as the primary constraints shaping the narratives and iconography of the text as well as the manufacture and licensing of the intertextual materials necessary for a 'mania' to sweep the country. This is not a claim that evil moguls force us to buy Bat-chains: such reductionism is as vulgar and untenable as the assumptive leap from a film to the national psyche.

Rather, the claim here is that mass-produced culture is a business, governed by corporate drives for profit, market control, and transindustrial integration. While movies may (and do) flop, the decision to create a movie is a business decision about the potential profitability of a cinematic product. Further, as film studios have been either acquired by companies outside the industry or have themselves acquired companies in other entertainment/information industries, decisions about movies are increasingly focused on the potential profitability of a wide range of products. The film per se becomes only one component in a product line that extends beyond the theater, even beyond our contact with mass media, to penetrate the markets for toys, bedding, trinkets, cups and the other minutiae comprising one's everyday life inside a commoditized, consumerized culture.

To understand *Batman*, then, requires that our analyses of the text and intertext, and of fandom and other audiences, be supplemented by an economic analysis of corporate structure, market structures, and interpenetrating industries. These conditions of production select, frame, and shape both *Batman* as a commercial text and the product line that constitutes its commercial intertext. We begin, then, with *Batman*'s owner, Warner Communications Incorporated (WCI).

WCI: Structures and Industries

Warner Communications Inc. traces its history to the founding of Warner Brothers Studio in 1918. The four founding brothers have been the object of considerable scholarship as has their studio and its products, which include sound film, social realist films, TV Westerns, and cartoons.[4] Less well studied is the modern structure of Warner as Warner Communications Inc., a transindustrial media conglomerate. While much discussion has surrounded WCI's merger with Time Inc., that debate included little analysis on the impact of corporate structure on the content of cultural production. To see how that structure constrains content, we will trace the ways that WCI's external business pressures and internal markets shaped *Batman* as text and intertext. After sketching the emerging structure of Time-Warner, we will examine conditions at WCI from 1982 to 1989 and analyze the commercial intertext as a response to economic conditions.

WCI is now half of the newly merged, transindustrial Time-Warner. The combined holdings of Time and WCI in book publishing, cable channels, song publishing, cable systems, recorded music, television production, magazine/comics publishing, film production, television stations, and licensing make Time-Warner the predominant media conglomerate in the world. The Time-Warner merger signals a further concentration in the ownership of outlets, distribution systems, and content production across multiple media industries by a single company.[5]

Significantly, the major difference between the independent WCI and the new Time-Warner is a difference in size, not in kind. Prior to the 1989 merger, WCI had assumed the aggressive, expansionist pose typical of the 1970s and 1980s.[6] By the 1980s the company had joint ventures with American Express in cable operations, satellite distribution, pay cable channels, and basic cable channels (QUBE; Warner Amex Satellite; Showtime and The Movie Channel; MTV Networks comprised by MTV, NIK, and VH1). These rounded out WCI's wholly owned operations in film and television production, recorded music, cartoons and comic books, magazines, books, video cassettes, and licensing of characters. But WCI had pushed beyond these interests to purchase the Franklin Mint (collectibles by subscription), Atari (computers and home video games), Warner Cosmetics, Knickerbocker Toy, Gadgets restaurant chain, and other non-media firms. Throughout this expansion, revenues from WCI's core media companies remained strong.

However, the economic burdens of expansion almost capsized WCI when the home video game market collapsed in 1983[7] and when American Express moved to discontinue the joint ventures in 1985.[8] Only the willingness of the Chris-Craft Industries to expand its holdings of WCI stock saved WCI from a take-over attempt by Rupert Murdoch in 1983.[9] Having lost $420 million despite sales of $3.4 billion, WCI began selling assets both unprofitable (Atari) and profitable (MTV Networks to Viacom for cash and stock in Viacom) in an apparent attempt to both right itself and buy out American Express.[10] I say "apparent attempt" only because of WCI's willingness to accept stock in Viacom as partial payment along with much-needed cash. This suggests that WCI tried to solve its short-term crisis without sacrificing its long-term interest in retaining some influence over MTV Networks, the primary television outlet used to promote records. Despite its prodigious losses in 1983, WCI's film and television production units earned revenues of $109 million while the publishing division enjoyed $43.3 million in revenues. By reconcentrating operations in its profitable media operations, WCI began rebuilding profits, with earnings spiraling up to $693 million by October 1986.[11] With these revenues, WCI was poised for another round of acquisitions in December 1986.

This time, however, WCI focused its efforts more narrowly, absorbing and investing in companies that operated in the entertainment/information industries. Beginning with investment as a white knight in the Cannon Group (film production, home video, European theater chains),[12] WCI went on to acquire such firms as Lorimar Telepictures (film and television production, home video, television stations, television series including *Dallas* and *Alf,* licensing)[13] and Cinema Venture (theater chain co-owned by Gulf and Western),[14] and Chappell Music Publishing[15] before the culminating merger with Time Inc.

In economic terms, the initial diversification helped trigger a crisis that forced WCI to shed its non-media acquisitions and to sell off some of its profitable media operations. Because of continued profitability in film, television, publishing, and music, WCI soon found itself poised for reexpansion. However, this time WCI adopted a more restrained approach to expansion, emphasizing acquisition of media companies to achieve further integration in industries where it was already strong. The merger with Time marks an intensification in the extent to which operations in different media industries are subordinated under WCI (now Time-Warner)'s aegis. WCI's recovery and retrenchment transformed the Warner of 1982, a diversified conglomerate with strong media interests, into the prc-merger Warner of 1989, a highly concentrated and integrated media conglomerate.

Financing Recovery: Recycling

While WCI's retrenchment required that its media companies remained profitable, WCI's reemergence as a major media conglomerate and its subsequent expansion required increases in revenues and profits. This fostered greater cost efficiencies in film production as more profit was required from each project, whether directly from box office revenues or indirectly by repackaging sections of the film for recycling through WCI's non-film outlets. For instance, film soundtracks became much more important as a source of possible revenues since WCI could repackage soundtracks as records and music videos. For the film *Against All Odds,* this meant that two sequences were simply lifted out of the film, soundtrack intact, and intercut with shots of WCI artist Phil Collins lip syncing the words. Both videos were played in heavy rotation on MTV and on the daily show *NIK ROCKS* on Nickelodeon, thereby advertising both the film and the album. These videos for "One More Night" and "Against All Odds" were next recycled as part of the Phil Collins video album *No Jacket Required. Against All Odds* fed not only WCI's film operations but also its music publishing, MTV Networks, recorded music, and video cassette operations.

Similarly WCI's distribution of Prince's independently-made *Purple Rain* included an album, multiple music videos, and publishing materials. Perhaps WCI's reluctance to finance the film project may explain why *Purple Rain* looks like a half dozen videos stitched together by a loose narrative. In contrast, *Against All Odds* looks like a movie with two videos embedded in it. In any case, both projects not only earned revenues for WCI but also filled multiple WCI outlets with product to which WCI had first claim. Thus WCI created an internal market where product for one unit could be recycled to provide product for multiple units. This decreased costs of operations by decreasing the total cost of obtaining product for all media units. It also increased potential profitability per product since repackaging and recycling allow a product's component parts to earn multiple revenues. Thus the potential for repackaging and recycling become criteria for judging proposed projects.

The impact of these criteria on the finished product can literally be seen in *Against All Odds* and *Purple Rain*. Interestingly, such increasing cost efficiency in cultural production may ultimately decrease diversity of output. In any case, repackaging and recycling have the immediate effect of encouraging media conglomerates both to mine their stock of owned materials for new spin-offs and to view every project as a multimedia product line. WCI and Prince seem to have pioneered an intensified recycling of content.

Unlike *Against All Odds* and *Purple Rain*, the Bat-project began with a tried and true product that was already earning revenues for WCI: Batman, the only "normal" adult in DC Comics stable of superheroes. When DC was acquired by WCI in 1971, it was evidently viewed by the chair of WCI's publishing division (William Sarnoff) as a source of licensing revenues and movie materials.[16] However, both licensing and book sales were decreasing across the comics industry due to problems in distribution, an exodus of production personnel, and a perceptible drop in the quality of narratives, portrayals of characters, and artwork. Compounding this was the phenomena of underground comix (sic) with their explicit portrayals of drugs, sex, violence, political corruption, and the ills of capitalism. Although underground comix never achieved the mass circulation enjoyed by Superman or Batman, the undergrounds opened the way for a fully commercial line of comics aimed at adults. Often mixing neoconservative ideologies with vigilantes, victims of child abuse and explicit violence, these comics became the centerpiece of specialty comics stores, which served as the major retail outlet for all comics by 1984. Further, the clientele of these stores was mainly adults; buying by children continued to drop.[17]

To compete in its own industry, then, DC and its comics had to be reorganized. From 1976 to 1981, DC struggled to rebuild revenues, achieving profitability with one-third of its revenues from comics sales, one-third from licensing and one-third from other sources. Obviously movies helped, as *Superman* proved a box office smash in 1978 to be followed by three sequels (1979, 1983, and 1987) and one spinoff (*Supergirl* in 1984) all distributed by WCI. After six months of negotiating, DC granted rights for a Batman film to independent producers Peter Gruber and Jon Peters, whose films have all been released through WCI. With WCI's decision to bankroll as well as distribute the film, *Batman* achieved the status of an in-house blockbuster production on which vast sums would be lavished. Hence, it is notable that the film's director, Tim Burton, enjoyed a track record with WCI, having directed *PeeWee's Big Adventure* at a cost of $7 million with box office revenues of $40 million as well directing Michael Keaton in *Beetlejuice* at a cost of $13 million with box office revenues of $80 million. The latter film was credited by WCI as the keystone of the film division's second quarter earnings of $51.5 million in 1988.[18] With WCI risking $30 million with *Batman* in 1988, some assurances were necessary; hence the selection of producers, directors, and stars with solid track records at the box office. But WCI had other ways to build assurances given its internal markets, and the decision to release the film on Batman's fiftieth birthday.

Internal Markets and Batman

The mid-1980s marked the beginning of a process in which WCI both tested the waters and began building towards the release of *Batman*.[19] By issuing *The Dark Knight Returns* in comic form, WCI essentially test marketed a dark reinterpretation of Batman with an adult readership whose experience with the character would include the camp crusader of the 1960s. The four issues comprising the *The Dark Knight Returns* sold out, prompting DC to establish a recurring title and Warner Publishing to repackage the original series as a book. Priced at $12.95, the book sold 85,000 copies in bookstores to a general reading public. Besides WCI earning revenues twice from the *The Dark Knight Returns*, WCI tapped different systems of distribution, placing the *Dark Knight* in different kinds of retail outlets, tapping the markets of fandom and general readers to determine if the grim version of Batman could gain acceptance from both specialized and generalized consumers.

The *Dark Knight*'s success prompted DC's repackaging of classic superheroes in a 48-page anthology *Action Comics Weekly*, selling at $1.50 per issue and the Warner Books publication of *Batman: Year One*. Also, circulation figures for the Batman comic began rising as the Dark Knight's success rubbed off on the younger, less dystopian version of the character. The process of building an audience for the Batman film was thus started. It was intensified in 1988 when WCI let readers vote (via a 900-telephone number) on whether Robin should be killed off or retained. With 5,343 nays versus 5,271 ayes, Robin was duly killed in "A Death in the Family," which not surprisingly sold out. From comic sales of 89,747 copies in 1988, Batman sold 193,000 in 1988, as rumors abounded that Robin's cape would be taken up by a young woman. The entire incident was labelled a publicity stunt by both the *Comics Buyers Guide* and the *New York Times*.

Be that as it may, filming started in 1988 with the revenues from *Beetlejuice* safely in hand. Negative reactions from fans to casting decisions made the first page of the *Wall Street Journal*[20] with claims by the *Journal* that WCI would modify content in order to ensure fan attendance. From WCI's use of its publishing division, WCI already had market measures that fans and the general public were willing to buy a darker interpretation of a lone vigilante. Just as important, WCI had information on the identity of fans from an industry survey funded by DC's main rival Marvel, which described the average reader as a 20-year-old male spending $10 a week on comics. As a male-oriented action film, *Batman* would rely on the public personae of Jack Nicholson and Michael Keaton to widen the audience. Similarly, WCI would rely on the film to feed its internal markets in both the short and long run.

The $30 million sunk into *Batman* is not entirely the cost of a single film. Rather, it includes the root costs of a film series. The construction of sets, development of props, total investment, and plot presume that sequels will be shot. In the long run, WCI's investment in plant for *Batman* can be spread out across two or four other films. While revenues per sequel can be expected to decrease as the number of Bat-movies increase, the major cost of sets for each sequel was largely included in WCI's original $30 million budget. The costs of recurring cast members would seem fairly manageable, although the initial expense of Nicholson's Joker probably precludes that character's resurrection. Keaton is the only necessarily recurring cost in the cast; should contract negotiations take an unacceptable turn off-screen tragedies can easily explain the absence of either Vicki Vale or Alfred. WCI will probably use casting to build talk about the sequels just as it used the original casting of Nicholson and Keaton to create news stories about *Batman* and thereby gain free advertising for the film. Similarly, with the principle themes established in the orchestral soundtrack, new scoring can be limited largely to themes for villains and sidekicks leaving WCI another chance to showcase one of its recording artists in the sequels (à la Prince on the first soundtrack). Similarly, the sequels should provide the raw materials for novelizations and comic books. Over the long run, then, WCI's $30 million investment in *Batman* has built the basic infrastructure necessary for manufacturing a line of films, albums, sheet music, comics, and novelizations.

In the short-run, this investment served as the seed money for a line of Bat-media to be distributed through WCI's non-film media outlets. The script for the film was adapted to both novel and comic book forms. The novel retells the film with only minor differences; the comic's visuals reproduce the shots of the film with slight variation in plot and pictorials. Thus both the plot and the movie's visuals were broken out to earn income. Similarly, the soundtrack was broken out as two products: an album by Prince[21] with songs from the soundtrack and songs inspired by the film (with the album going double platinum) plus an orchestral album by Danny Elfman which surpassed the usual sales for orchestral scores with sales around 150,000. Both album jackets featured the Bat-logo, differentiated only by decals stuck to the wrappers, thereby realizing a slight cost efficiency in album production although perhaps at the risk of some confusion among purchasers. In a departure from previous practice, Prince's video of his album's lead song, "Batdance", featured no footage from the film. Instead, "Batdance" broke out dialogue from the film, using the actors' lines as the basis for rap elements in Prince's funk sound.[22] The video played with Prince's usual themes of sexuality, androgyny, and punishment. "Batdance" was frequently featured on MTV, the music channel targeted primarily to middle class whites from youth to middle age.[23] The use of a rap-funk style secured airplay on radio stations targeted to black audiences. This was a rather significant extension of Prince's audience, which WCI had pegged as white females in their late 20s to middle 30s. The crossover had the effect of cultivating black audiences and Bat-logos began to crop up on black male performers featured on MTV's rap segments. But if rap elements generalized "Batdance"'s appeal, Prince's performance in the video replayed the themes that endeared him to his longtime fans and made *Purple Rain* a hit at the box office and in the record store. In this way, the decision to showcase Prince as a musical guest on the film's soundtrack promoted the film to an audience atypical of comic fans (white women); the style of Prince's musical performance promoted *Batman* in terms of black culture to black youth despite the minimal role of black actors (including Billy Dee Williams) in the film. All this had the effect of widening the pool of potential ticket-buyers for *Batman*.

This also earned revenues for WCI. Both albums represented extra income from an integral part of *Batman:* musical score and dialogue. Similarly, the sheet music from the film score and from Prince's songs inspired by the film provided fodder for WCI's song publishing operation. This had recently expanded to become the largest song publisher in the world with WCI's acquisition of Chappell, thereby also enlarging WCI's need for music to publish. And with sequels in the planning,

Batman promises to feed WCI's interests in comics, books, albums, sheet music, film production, music videos, MTV Networks, film distribution, theaters, and home video cassettes for quite sometime.

The relative swiftness of those sequels is suggested by WCI's video cassette release of *Batman* on November 15, 1989, less than six months after the film's premiere. Taking the trade press by surprise, this decision should serve to hasten *Batman* into the tertiary distribution circuits of pay cable and home video, cutting short the film's booking in second-run theaters. This promises to feed product to WCI's home video operations as well as Time-Warner's HBO/Cinemax pay channels and WCI's pay-per-view channels on QUBE. Eventual distribution to basic cable raises suspicions that Time-Warner's 17% interest in TBS may shape Time-Warner's selection of a basic cable channel. However, regardless of which major cable channel carries *Batman*, one can expect wide distribution of the film over Time-Warner's ATC cable systems. The final distribution of the film on network television may even earn revenues for Time-Warner's television stations. Each redistribution means more income from the basic product; repackaging means more distribution through more outlets to earn more revenues. Further, each step promotes the entire product line by getting the logo and characters before the potential consumer in yet another setting.

WCI's use of the Batman product line to feed its internal markets for media products indicates how media conglomerates bring together media industries that were once distinct and separate. The interpenetration of the music, film, print, and video industries does not arise in response to demand from movie goers, record buyers, or comics subscribers. Rather, this interpenetration is orchestrated by the conglomerate in its search for more profitable and cost-efficient ways to manufacture culture.

But internal markets, corporate structure, and interpenetrating industries are not the total sum of economic structures that constrain cultural production. External markets are also important in show business. Earning profits from shows means working in two very different external markets. The first is the market for licensing, a closed market in which a limited number of corporations secure exclusive rights over copyrighted materials. The second is an open market where real people go to movies, listen to favorite songs, read murder mysteries, change channels, and rent videos. After feeding internal markets, media conglomerates sometimes turn to external markets and negotiate licensing agreements with firms whose concerns lie outside the pale of the licensor's operations. By granting exclusive use of copyrighted materials for use in the manufacture of particular product categories (e.g., toys figures, keychains, etc.), the licensor guarantees a secondary source of income from images, logos, and characters from the original media product. Since licensing is both a form of promotion and a source of income, we turn next to a discussion of WCI's expenditures for advertising and arrangements for income from promotion. Since internal markets shape deals in the closed market, we'll begin by analyzing that market and *Batman.*

External Markets and Bat-mania

The extent to which WCI could make *Batman* a "must see" film depended on promotion, comprised by advertising and licensing. While the former is a cost, the latter is a source of revenues. However, the $10 million WCI spent on advertising would not be a complete loss even if the film did poorly at the box office. Under US tax law, advertising is an ordinary cost of doing business and deductible as such. When advertising is accompanied by licensing in a promotional campaign, the producing company has the opportunity of earning revenues from licenses to toy companies, clothes manufacturers, fast food chains, etc., even if the film flops. Licensing is increasingly used, then, to augment revenues and licensed products are used to augment advertising for the film.

Because of WCI's cartoon properties, licensing has always played a role in the company's revenues. For *Batman,* WCI licenses two different properties: *Batman* the movie or Batman of comics and television fame. Potential licensees could opt for the film's logo or the traditional logo; for the Dark Knight or the Dynamic Duo; for Keaton's body armor or Adam West's costume; for Nicholson's Joker or DC's Joker, Riddler, Penguin, and Catwoman. This mix-or-match approach gave WCI's 100 licensed manufacturers considerable latitude in devising merchandising campaigns to cash in both on WCI's ad campaign for the film and on Batman's anniversary. Manufacturers could license images appropriate to their targeted consumers: children as traditional consumers of Batman; young adult males and bookstore patrons as consumers of the Dark Knight; the forty million people estimated as the viewership for reruns of the syndicated Batman television show;[24] ticket buyers for films rated PG13/Parents Strongly Cautioned (as Batman was). Depending on its targets, plus available information on consumption habits and Batman, manufacturers could license the line of images that seemed more likely to trigger purchases in tandem with the film's much-advertised opening.

Having seen *Batman*'s extraordinary box office (a record-breaking $40.49 million in its first three days),[25] it may be hard to believe that manufacturers could question the film's ability to sell merchandise.

However, as late as 28 February 1989, surveys showed low response from consumers to Batman as a character in general.[26] Consultants "in the know" counseled potential licensees to stick with the old images. While hindsight may set heads wagging, WCI's own merchandising suggests an attempt to hedge its bets. WCI's product mix included merchandise using the film images as well as the old comics images. Importantly, WCI's entire line of Bat-products was energetically promoted in theaters where a positive reaction to the film could be conveniently translated into purchases. Besides offering a limited line of Bat-products for sale in theaters, WCI provided two major theatre chains with special forms to mail order Bat-products. Offering each theater in the chain a 2% rebate on orders received, WCI reported receiving 1000 forms per day for the first eleven days of *Batman's* run with an average order of $75 per form. This practice fostered the interests of all licensees by cultivating demand for Bat-products, thus promoting WCI's direct and indirect revenues earned by Bat-products.[27]

Licensing can also expand markets for Bat-products beyond the film's targeted audiences to reach consumers who may be blocked by parents attending to the "PG13 / Parents Strongly Cautioned" rating. Interestingly, movie-related products targeted for preteens do not necessarily require parental permission. The prices of ToyBiz's Batwing ($16.99) or Batcave set (figures not included, $19.99) may block unsupervised purchases; not so Ertl's Batmobile ($1.99) nor Topps' *Batman: Official Souvenir Magazine* ($2.95) nor Topp's packages of trading cards with sticker and bubble gum, the 132 cards in the series featuring visuals from the film with a running plot summary on the back. Similarly, Topps' magazine mixes visuals from the film with a sketch of the plot and information on special effects. These materials are sandwiched between an article on Batman's history and a closing article on the joys of collecting Bat-products. The centerfold is Keaton's Batman standing in front of the Batmobile. Five pages are given to advertising: ToyBiz Batman action figures and toys; Data East Batman video games (using comic images); movie tee shirts, jewelry, and posters from DC/WCI and Great Southern Company; DC/WCI Bat-books; DC authorized Batman role playing game (an abridged version of the DC heroes game) with Mayfair Games. This intermixture sets the new *Batman* in the context of the old, collectible Batman products and new Bat-products with images from comics, television, and film versions of Batman. Not only does the souvenir magazine operate as an advertisement and a revenue earner, but it also operates as a particular system of cross references, as an intertext. And that particular intertext meshes with the web of cross references created by WCI's entire promotional campaign.

The commercial intertext that results from this combination of advertising and licensing intermixes old themes with new, camp motifs with grim visages, cartooning with live action, thus generating a rich and often contradictory set of understandings and visions, about justice and corruption in America. And it does this because of manufacturers' perceptions about acceptable risk, potential profit, and targeted consumers. Simultaneously, the plethora of Bat-products intersects with $10 million of paid advertising and a flood of free advertising ("Bat-dance", reviews, news stories, interviews) to hype the movie —making *Batman* the "must see" film of the summer. This brings us to the third market, in which WCI transacted its Bat-business with the moviegoing public.

The Last Market: Show

In this last market, the "show" in show business finally becomes important as the show itself finally earns revenues directly from people through ticket sales. However, this market has some distinctive features, which differentiate it from other media markets; but it is similar to most consumer markets in advanced capitalist economies since the market for movies depends on advertising to stimulate consumption of products selected by an oligopoly of producers.[28] Like most consumer markets, the market for films is not driven by demand; WCI was not picketed by millions of moviegoers demanding a Bat-film. Quite the opposite: once WCI decided to go ahead with the Bat-project, the company needed to test market the new Bat-image and to convince people that we wanted to see this particular film of *Batman*. So, while we count in this market, we count as consumers who must be enticed to buy a ticket, thus renting a seat for one viewing of a particular film selected from all movies currently playing. Obvious though this process is, it has some rather subtle consequences: in the market where people consume shows, all shows compete against each other regardless of the manufacturer's identity. So if WCI releases five films, each movie competes with the other four films by WCI as well as with all the other films released into the marketplace.

As a result, it is in the interest of film producers to control the number of releases per year, artificially decreasing the number of films available in order to decrease competition between films.[29] By limiting our choices to a handful of films and by consolidating release dates into two 'seasons'—summer and Christmas—the major film studios create a business cycle that alternates forced choices between a limited number of "hot films" with stretches of doldrums. This industry-generated business cycle sets up conditions of production that favor the funding and distribution of relatively few films by each major studio. By limiting releases, a studio decreases the amount of competition between its releases. Since every studio follows this policy, the effect is a decrease in competition over all films in each season. To augment each season's line-up, a studio will selectively contract with semi-independent producers for a limited number of additional films. Willingness to accept such product varies inversely with the amount of a studio's own product that it has slated for release. Further, releases within a season are staggered so that most studio product (and the more favored semi-independent product) shares its opening date with no other major release. Such favored films are proceeded by massive advertising campaigns in an attempt to pack the house for the film's premiere. Taken together, these components create a market in which even "failures" earn a minimum box office, like the $8 million earned by the WCI flop *Supergirl*. This potential for failure regardless of advertising, business cycle, etc., is rooted in the market itself, as we will discuss later.

This decreased competition among films regardless of studio has decreased competition among studios for screens and ticket- buyers. It also has the effect of channeling money from multiple projects into one or two projects, so that major theatrical releases become increasingly expensive with production costs running into millions of dollars, before millions more are spent for advertising. In fact, the enormous cost of a film can be an impetus for news coverage, hence gaining free advertising providing one reason to see the film. For *Batman*, the press reported figures ranging from $30—40 million plus another $10 million for promotion.[30] The sheer size of production costs may well be the source of studios' willingness to pay similarly high costs for promotion. The $10 million figure for *Batman* represents an attempt to hype the film as a "must see," to fill theaters across the nation for the film's premiere performances. By releasing *Batman* after most major films had opened, including the sequels (*Indiana Jones and the Last Crusade, Star Trek VI*), and by hyping that release through the radio, television, cable, print, and film industries, WCI tried to ensure that its early revenues would be as high as possible. Even if word-of-mouth damned the movie, the early revenues could carry the film into a respectable slot on *Variety*'s chart of moneymakers.

All this joins together to create a market for theatrical release films that stresses high production costs, limited seasons, limited number of releases, slightly staggered releases within a season, and extensive pre-release advertising, as film companies try to cope with the vagaries of this last market.

Where people are the prime purchasers, revenues can not be completely shielded from the direct responses of consumers. Word-of-mouth can break a film designed as a blockbuster, or elevate an obscure movie to the status of a cult film or even a sleeper. Thus, expensive films may be box office bonanzas or big-time disasters. Where some media revenues are protected by the habits of subscription, film remains in direct relationship with an open, unstructured market of potential ticket-buyers. This encourages film producers to cultivate 'brand loyalties' in an attempt to establish purchasing habits so that consumers routinely select a particular genre, personnel (actor or director), recurring characters, and continuing stories. For consumers, the decision turns on projected satisfaction: we can not know if the film is worth the price until after viewing it. Thus word-of-mouth and published reviews may shape our willingness to pay. Similarly, genre, personnel, recurring characters, or continuing stories can be used to make quick decisions based on past experience when selecting from a season's releases. Sequels and stars can be used to manage demand just as pre-release advertising can be used to inflate revenues from premieres before word-of-mouth makes its rounds. For WCI, building a Bat-series required both extensive pre-release advertising to produce a "hit" premiere as well as a sufficiently solid foundation to earn a steady income after the hype subsided. By holding the film until June 23–24, WCI could count on post-premiere drops in attendance for the early releases. After that, the summer-long success of *Batman* at the box office would depend on the film itself, its ability to resonate with our experiences and visions, and to tap into the conflicting ideologies through which we make sense of social life.

From Cultural Economics to Economic Culture

That leads us back to the audience for *Batman* and to *Batman* as text and intertext. However, as we again approach *Batman*, Bat-mania, and Bat-audiences, our discussion of economics reminds us that text, intertext, and audiences are simultaneously commodity, product line, and consumer. Separating reader from text/intertext is the complex structure of interpenetrating cultural industries and the corporate interests of media conglomerates. This complex structure is generally invisible to us. Our personal and shared experience of media—including *Batman*—is emotional, imagistic, interpretive, and pleasurable. Thus the commodification of text, the commodity fetishism of intertext, and the management of consumption are obscured behind the "soft and fuzzies" feeling of experience. The economic logics of profit and cost efficiency suggest that *Batman* is best understood as multimedia, multimarket sales campaign. Yet, although that campaign's primary purpose is to earn revenues and decrease production costs, it also "sells" ideologies—visions of the good, the true, the beautiful. Herein lies the contradiction of capitalist media: to understand our mass media, we must be able to understand them as always and simultaneously text and commodity, intertext and product line. This contradiction is well captured in the phrase "show business." In our fascination with the highly visible show, let us not overlook the less visible business that ultimately shapes, constructs, recycles, breaks out, and distributes the show for a profit. No business means no show and doing business means constructing shows according to business needs. These are the ground rules, recoverable through critical analysis, from which we can safely approach the analysis of a commodified culture and the products of show business. One might well exclaim: "Holy commodity fetish, Batman!"

Notes

1. The author would like to thank Tim Emmerson for research assistance and Alfred Babbit for word processing this text.

2. Jim Robbins, "Orders for Batstuff Bring 2% to Exhibs (sic); Brochure System Cheered," *Variety*, 5 July 1989, p. 8.

3. *Advance Comics* is a catalogue listing comic books and fan materials that are scheduled to be distributed to specialty stores in two months time. Resembling a black-and-white comic book, issues include an order form.

4. Charles Higham, *Warner Brothers* (New York: Scribners, 1975); William R. Meyer, *Warner Brothers Directors* (New Rochelle, NY: Arlington House, 1975); Ted Sennett, *Warner Brothers Presents* (New Rochelle, NY: Arlington House, 1971); Nick Roddick, *A New Deal in Entertainment: Warner Brothers in the 1930's* (London: BFI, 1983), with the analysis of finance capital and C1 in Janet Wasko, *Movies and Money* (Norwood, NJ: Ablex, 1982) or the structural analysis of WCI, QUBE, and MTV, see Eileen R. Meehan, "Technical Capability Versus Corporate Imperatives" in Vincent Mosco and Janet Wasko (eds.), *The Political Economy of Information* (Norwood, NJ: Ablex, 1988), pp. 167–187.

5. For a complete listing of Time's and Warner's holdings, consult *Standard and Poor's Corporation Descriptions*, New York; 1989 and *Who Owns Whom: 1989 North America*, Dun Bradstreet International: England.

6. *Standard and Poor's Corporation Descriptions*, Standard and Poor Corporation, New York, 1980–1989.

7. This collapse elicited considerable commentary in the *Wall Street Journal* as suggested by representative titles: "Atari to Idle 1,700 at California Site, Move Jobs to Asia," 13 Feb. 1983, p. 6; Laura Landro, "Warner's Atari Staff Facing Shake-Up; Merger of Video and Computer Divisions Set," 31 May 1983, p. 5; "Warner's Atari Unit Reorganizes Its Lines in Bid to Stem Losses," 2 June 1983, p. 20; "S and P Adds 4 Makers of Home Computers, Games to Credit Watch," 27 June 1983, p. 41; "Warners Ratings Cut by Standard and Poor's; Atari Troubles Cited," 28 Oct. 1983, p. 48. The effect on Warner was duly chronicled in the *Wall Street Journal* with such headlines as "Warner Communications Stock Continues to Slide as Analysts' 2nd (sic) Period Loss Estimates Growth" (20 July 1983, p. 55) and "Warner Lays Off

30% of its Staff at Headquarters" (14 Oct. 1983, p. 3). Headlines in the *New York Times* were equally grim "Warner's Profit Falls by 56.5%," 17 Feb. 1983, p. D14, "Warner Amex Cable Cuts 57 More Positions" (17 May 1983 p. 2) "Warner Posts a $283.4 Million Loss," 22 July 1983, pp. D1 and D5 and $122.4 Million Loss at Warner," 15 Oct. 1983, p.37, "Layoffs Predicted at Warner Amex" (28 December 1983, p.4). "Warner Loses over $400 Million—More Workers Are Dismissed," 3 Aug. 1984.

8. American Express attempted to end the joint ventures by forcing Warner to either buy it out or to let American Express buy out Warner with the understanding that American Express would sell the ventures to either Time or TCI or to a Time-TCI joint venture. Warner was reluctant to exit the cable industry, particularly if its cable, satellite, and programming operations would be absorbed by the two largest operators of multiple cable systems, Time and TCI. The maneuverings of all parties were thoroughly reported in the financial pages of the *New York Times* (representative titles: "Warner Amex Bid Confirmed," 30 May 1985, pp. D2 and D19; "American Express Bids for All of Warner Amex," 18 July 1985, p. 2; "Warner to Buy Out Amex Unit," 10 August 1985, pp. 31 and 33) as well as in the *Wall Street Journal* (representative titles: "American Express Offers to Purchase Rest of Warner Amex for $450 Million," 18 July 1985; "Meeting Is Delayed Again by Warner Communications," 12 July 1985, p. 15; "Warner to Buy Partner's Stake in Cable Firm," 12 August 1985, p. 31.

9. The *Wall Street Journal's* "Heard on the Street" featured items on Murdoch's attempt to take over Warner (30 Sept. 1983, p. 59 and 20 Dec. 1983, p. 55) and covered the story in some detail from the start (representative titles include: "Murdoch Can Tap Healthy Empire If He Moves to Take Over Warner," 9 Dec. 1983; "Warner Communications Stake Is Boosted to 7% by Murdoch—Control Isn't Sought," 16 Dec 1983, p. 10) to finish ("Murdoch Loses Round in Fight for Warner as FCC Approves Christ-Craft Stock Swap," 9 March 1984, p. 6; "Warner's Plan to Buy Back Shares from Murdoch Boosts Chris-Craft," 19 March 84, pp. 35–38).

10. Laura Landro, "Warner to Post $5 Million Net for Quarter But $420 Million Deficit for the Full Year," *Wall Street Journal,* 16 Feb. 1984 p. 4; "Viacom Gets Its MTV," *Broadcasting,* 2 Sept. 1985, pp. 50–52; Bill Abrams, "Viacom Will Pay Warner $500 Million for Stakes in MTV Networks, Showtime," *Wall Street Journal* 27 Aug. 1985, p. 4.

11. Geraldine Fabrikant, "How Warner Got Back Its Glitter," *New York Times,* 14 Dec. 1983, section 3, p. 1

12. "Warner Pact Helps Rescue Cannon," *New York Times,* 24 Dec. 1986, p. 2.

13. Geraldine Fabrikant, "Warner and Lorimar in 'Early' Talks, "*New York Times,* 8 Mar. 1988, Section 4, p. 1; Richard Gold, "WCI to Appeal N.Y. Court Ruling Against Its Merger with Lorimar," *Variety,* 5 Oct. 1988, p. 3; "Warner Merges with Lorimar," *New York Times,* 12 Jan. 1989, p. D19.

14. Laura Landro, "Warner Is Cleared to Buy 50% Stake in Cinema Venture," *Wall Street Journal,* 14 Dec. 1988, p. B6.

15. "Purchase of Chappell Music From Investors Is Completed," *Wall Street Journal,* 8 Oct. 1987, p. 16.

16. Philip S. Gritis, "Turning Superheroes into Super Sales," *New York Times,* 6 Jan 1985, p. 6.

17. Kurt Eichenwald, "Grown-Ups Gather at the Comic Book Stand," *New York Times,*

64 *Meehan*

30 Sept. 1987, pp. 1 and D5; Richard W. Anderson, "Biff! Pow! Comic Books Make a Comeback", *Business Week*, 2 Sept. 1985, pp. 59–60.

18. Joe Morgenstern, "Tim Burton, Batman, and the Joker", *New York Times Magazine*, 9 April 1989, pp. 45, 46, 50, 53, 60.

19. Information on the *Dark Knights Returns*, on circulation, demographics and Robin is taken from: Georgia Dullea, "Holy Bomb Blast! The Real Robin Fights On;" New York Times, 10 Nov. 1988, p.23; Alexandra Peers, "Given His Costume, It's a Wonder He Didn't Die of Embarrassment," *Wall Street Journal*, 26 Oct. 1988, p. B1; Lisa H. Towle, "What's New in the Comic Book Business, " New York Times, 31 Jan. 1988, p. 21; "Growing Up into Graphic Novels" and "America Is Taking Comic Books Seriously," *New York Times*, 31 July 1988, p. 7.

20. Kathleen A. Hughes, "Batman Fans Fear the Jokes on Them In Hollywood Epic," *Wall Street Journal*, 29 Nov. 1988, pp. 1 and 8.

21. Kevin Zimmerman, "Soundtracks: Not Too Much Noise in '89," *Variety*, Jan. 3, 1990, pp. 49–57.

22. Nelson George, "Prince Is Back on Wings of 'Batdance'," *Billboard*, 24 June 1989.

23. From the start, MTV was targeted for white audiences, 14–34, with an average income of $30,000: Jack Loftus, "Warner Amex Preps All-Music Cable Channel," *Variety*, 4 March 1981, p. 1; (Young adults 14–34, stress on 14–24 year olds) Sally Bedell, "All Rock Cable-TV Service Is A Hit," *New York Times*, 2 August 1982 p. 15; Ed Levine, "TV Rocks with Music," *New York Times*, 8 May 1983, pp. 42, 55–56, and 61.

24. "Cape, Mask, Platform Heels, "*The Economist*, 14 Jan 1989, p. 84.

25. Joseph McBride, "'Batman' Swoops to Conquer: WB Pic Sees Hottest B.O. Action in History," *Variety*, 28 June–4 July 1989, p. 1.

26. Bruce Horovitz, "Holy Tie-In! Batman Bores Consumers Just as Retailers Prepared for Film," *Los Angeles Times*, 28 Feb. 1989, p. 6.

27. Robbins.

28. Thomas Guback, "Capital, Labor Power, and the Identity of Film," paper presented at the Conference on Culture and Communication, Philadelphia, March 1983. Also, Wasko.

29. This market structure arises from two conditions. The first condition was the divorcement of film production and film exhibition required by the decision rendered in U.S. v. Paramount Pictures (334 U.S. 131, 142, 161). This decision resulted in the studios' divesting themselves of their theater chains, which freed the studios from the necessity of producing "B" movies simply to fill screens. Such production became less attractive partly due to the availability of "free" entertainment from broadcasters, which eroded the guaranteed audience that had once existed for any film (cf., Thomas Guback, "Theatrical Film," in Benjamin M. Compaine, *Who Owns the Media?* (New York: Harmony Books, 1979, pp. 179–250 and Wasko, pp. 103–147). Currrently, WCI and other conglomerates with interests in film studios are reintegrating film production and exhibition, while also pursuing further intergration of film as an industry with the once distinct industries of television, cable, recorded music, book publishing, etc. Reintegration may encourage the production of more film product for the screen, since that product can also be recycled across the entire array of distribution channels, including pay cable and videocassette rental. Reintegration may also encourage the current practice of playing a single title on multiple screens at cineplexes, followed by shortened runs at independent

theatres and a quick turn-around to cable and rental. The precise dynamics have yet to be worked out by the relevant companies.

30. The $30 million figure is the most widely reported, generally with $10 million given for advertising costs. The $40 million figure tends to be cited without a separate figure for advertising.

5

Batman and his Audience: The Dialectic of Culture

Patrick Parsons

Introduction

The grim story of personal psychosis, cultural deterioration, political neo-fascism and social angst that is Frank Miller's *Dark Knight* speaks many tales to its audience, but one of the simplest and clearest is: this isn't just kids' stuff. And if the work itself insufficiently communicates that message, the people at DC Comics will only too gladly point it out. They have, in the past five years or more, moved vigorously to reposition their products to appeal to an older, more sophisticated audience; they have repeatedly told reporters, readers and retailers that they're after a new buyer, a college-age, college-educated Batfan.[1]

Yet, the hordes of movie goers waiting in line two hours and spending five dollars a ticket just to see the trailer for the Batman movie months before the film's release were not thirty-five-year-old stock brokers, but the army of twelve to seventeen-year-old boys that has traditionally constituted the bulk of the superhero fans.[2] Similarly, the Batman lunch boxes, pajamas, toys and Halloween costumes remain the domain of the pre-college set.

What then, is the nature of the audience for Batman specifically and superheroes generally? What do we know about the influence of such comics on their audience, and what does that audience have to do with the nature of the superhero character? This paper seeks to address the occasional neglect of the audience in studies of cultural commodities. In analyses of the cultural influence of comics, researchers working out of behavioral and laboratory-bound settings may assume too much about the generalizability of their data.[3] Critical and literary analyses of the production of such material often ignore the role of audience.[4] Both types of research and criticism can benefit from a broader understanding of the complex interaction between producers and consumers.

In the production of cultural commodities, audiences play a variety of roles. They are active consumers, interpreters and critics[5] as well as an integral part of the production process itself, especially in the more specialized media. The forms of influence are reactive and proactive in nature, and often substantial, creating an ongoing dialectic relationship between consumers and creators. There are few areas more dynamic and intricate than the evolutionary links between Batman and his audience.

This paper, then, seeks to outline the history and nature of the audience for superhero comics, considering the relationship between this material and its readers. Contrary to the assumptions of some in both the popular and scholarly community, the impact of readers on content may be greater than the impact of content on readers.

The Rise and Fall of the
Comic-Book Audience

Accurate, detailed historical data on circulation and readership in the comic book industry are difficult to locate and verify. Circulation figures for individual comic books are not generally reported in any uniform, national manner. The two major comic companies, DC and Marvel, are reluctant to report most information pertaining to readership. A handful of distribution companies around the country do have such information but it's scattered by region and goes back only a few years. *Ayers Directory of Periodicals* and *Standard Rate And Data Service* have reported total monthly circulation for the major comic producers since the beginning of comics. The varying mix of monthly, bi-monthly and quarterly issues and the failure of the majority of the hundreds of smaller presses to report to these services, however, render this information imprecise.

In addition, circulation in comics is not a one-to-one indication of readership, because regular comic readers do not read just one comic book a month or even just one comic title, such as Batman, Superman or Spiderman, a month. While there is at least one Batman fanzine,[6] the vast majority of Batman readers, like comic readers generally, buy and read many different comic titles every week. Tastes and reading habits do vary and collect across certain types of material, but readers normally do not specialize to the point of reading only one comic title exclusively. Readers become involved in a number of characters or the titles of a specific company (such as DC, Marvel or First). They may even follow the work of a specific artist. The audience for Batman, then, must be understood as an audience for comics generally and superhero comics specifically.

Table 1.   Estimated Monthly Circulation of
Comic Books

1940	3.7
1944	28.7
1950	45.6
1952	59.8
1956	34.6
1961	33.7
1965	33.5
1971	30.4
1974	23.3
1979	18.5
1984	20.5
1989	20.0

*Sources: Ayers Director of Periodicals, Standard
Rate and Data Service,* "Capt. Marvel Returns to
Lead Comic Revival," *Advertising Age,* Feb. 5, 1973,
p. 39; "Comic Book Heroes Expand Marvel Business," *Advertising Age,* Dec. 17, 1979, p. 12; "Direct
Sales Rescues Comics," *Advertising Age,* June 25,
1984, p. 110.

Despite these difficulties, available circulation reports and sporadic
readership studies can generate a sense of overall readership. Table 1
provides a crude index of comic book popularity from their inception
in 1938 to today.

Table 1 shows the slide comics have taken in the past 30 years.
Monthly circulation grew through the 1940s reaching a peak of somewhere around sixty million in 1952, but then began an uneven downhill
ride. The steepest drop came in the mid 1950s, and although the figures
suggest another drop from the 1960s to the 1970s, these numbers may
be misleading. For reasons to be discussed later, actual sales may have
been smaller in the 1960s than reported above.

These figures, of course, reveal neither the actual size of the audience
nor the reason behind the changes in circulation. The history of the
changing audience is complex and fascinating.

The 1940s and 1950s

Superman appeared in the first *Action* comic in 1938. He was an
immediate success and a wave of imitators followed. In 1939 there were

sixty comic titles, by 1941 there were 168.[7] Within the wave was Batman, who first appeared in *Detective Comics* # 27 in May of 1939. Robin was introduced in *Detective* # 38 in April of 1940.

Comic books surged in popularity during the war years. Muhlin reported in 1949 that forty-four percent of the soldiers in Army training camps read comics regularly.[8] Comics were reported to have outsold popular magazines such as *Life* and *Reader's Digest* ten to one on army bases at the time.[9] The Armed Services, in fact, used the comic format in training material distributed to the troops. Muhlen additionally reported that forty-one percent of the civilian male population and twenty-eight percent of the civilian female population regularly read comics.[10]

National Periodical Publications, the predecessor of DC, created many of its most famous superheroes during the war, including Green Lantern, the Flash and Hawkman. On the shoulders of these Batman associates, the company built wartime monthly sales of more than twelve million copies. The DC superheroes reflected the nationalism and war-fervor of those times. But with the end of the conflict, their popularity dwindled. The comics industry generally, however, kept expanding through the late 1940s and early 1950s, adding new characters, titles and companies. Mysteries, romances, westerns, comedies, and children's animal stories (including Disney characters) took comic book form.

Despite the adult interest in comics, the medium was assumed to be primarily a pastime for children and teenagers. Moreover, most popular and scholarly writers considered comic book reading to be ubiquitous among American youth.[11] Some studies attempted to quantify the assumed habituation; Table 2, from a 1950s article on the psychological aspects of comic reading, is illustrative:

Table 2. Comic Book Reading Habits, 1944

Age	Percent reading comics regularly		Average N Per Month
	males	females	
6–11	95	91	12–13
12–17	87	81	7–8
18 +	41	28	6 +

Source: Bakwin, Ruth Morris "Psychological Aspects of Pediatrics: The Comics," *The Journal of Pediatrics*, (1953): p. 633.

In 1944, the younger audience, those six to eleven years old, reportedly read an average of about fifteen comic books a month, teenagers

Table 3.   Comic Book Reading Habits by Grade, 1950

comics per wk	3		5		7		9		11	
	m	f	m	f	m	f	m	f	m	f
10+	25	23	26	26	29	26	17	14	7	9
1—9	48	43	34	49	46	49	59	59	59	42
None	26	24	30	25	25	25	24	27	33	49

Source: Lyness, *Journalism Quarterly*, Vol. 29:1, p. 49.

about twelve comics a month.[12] (It is interesting to note that girls read nearly as many comics as boys, a situation no longer true today.)

A study of more than 1,400 Des Moines, Iowa, school children examined comic reading patterns in 1950, near the height of comic popularity.

Anywhere from fifty to seventy-five percent of all school-age children in the study read comics regularly and read them vociferously, up to sixty comics and more a month.[13]

Much of what we know about the audience during this period developed out of scholarly and public debate about the impact of this burgeoning media on children. With the success of the comic book came a concomitant parental fear that such material sowed the seeds of youthful corruption.

In retrospect, this reaction is unsurprising. Virtually every new form of mediated culture has, in the twentieth century, been greeted by the same type of frantic parental concern, which in turn has spurred the funding of social science research and led to various public policy debates. In cinema, the Payne Fund Studies of the late 1920s and early 1930s are the classic example. In television, the list of research projects numbers in the tens of thousands and Congressional and administrative oversight have been ongoing since the mid-1950s. The most recent example involved the lyrics of popular music, and lesser examples include the "invention" of rock 'n' roll itself in the early 1950s, and the introduction of video game parlors in the 1970s. In every case, younger audiences typically have been the first to approach and adopt a media innovation, and often the material has involved violent or antiestablishment messages. The political climate of the 1950s additionally renders the hostile adult reaction to comics understandable.

After fifteen years of fear and deprivation, the American public sought nothing so much as security and cultural stability. Any perceived threat to the long-denied promise of domestic tranquility was bound to elicit a strong response. The debate over the potentially corrupting influence of comic books, then, was caught up in the broader social paranoia that served as the underpinning of the McCarthy era.

While concern about comics began with the sale of the first Superman comic book, serious debate over the psycho-social implications of the books arose in the late 1940s. Initially perceived as a dialogue among psychologists, the issue quickly emerged on the national agenda, due largely to the efforts of one crusader.

The genre of horror and crime comics that comic industry pioneer William Gaines established in 1950 brought matters to a head. After his company, Educational Comics (EC), failed in a line of literary and classic titles,[14] the company changed its name to Entertaining Comics and began publishing titles such as *Crypt of Terror, The Vault of Horror* and *Weird Science.*

Those who saw the demons of juvenile delinquency and the death of western culture issuing forth from newsstands across the country rallied against EC's product. Dr. Fredric Wertham, Senior Psychiatrist for the Department of Hospitals in New York City, author of numerous scholarly articles and texts, and an established and influential figure in the psychiatric community, led the anticomic campaign. Wertham contended that comic books were the opiate of the nursery, that all comic books were bad and crime and horror comics were the worst. Instruction booklets for criminal behavior, they led, almost inevitably, to the moral destruction of their readers and the addition of increasing numbers of sociopaths to the already overcrowded prisons.

Wertham's views were supported by some psychiatrists,[15] attacked by others,[16] and ignored by most.[17] The theoretical analysis was based primarily on Freudian psychology and the methodology limited almost exclusively to case studies Wertham had done with emotionally-troubled children. Within scholarly circles, Wertham made little progress, but he tapped into the general cultural paranoia of the period through the continual and effective use of the popular press. In 1948 he published no fewer than five articles attacking comic books.[18] From the late 1940s through the early 1950s, he circulated his arguments in the *Saturday Review, Colliers, The Ladies Home Journal,* and *Reader's Digest.* His 1954 book, *Seduction of the Innocent,*[19] was a featured Book-of-the-Month Club selection.

With Wertham's help, the National Parent Teachers Association took up the case against comic books. PTA chapters across America lobbied at home, in the grocery market and in public fora for a crackdown on comics. Retailers felt the pressure, publishers scrambled to enact guidelines on content, and at the highest level, the U.S. Senate subcommittee on Juvenile Delinquency called hearings to investigate the role of comics in crime.[20] Wertham, as well as teachers, preachers and comic book publishers, testified during the hearings. In many ways it was the "Red Scare" in microcosm, although in this case the McCarthy of the comic books scored something of a victory. To prevent potential government intervention and repair the public relations damage, the industry adopted its own code of self-regulation.

With adoption of the Comics Code in 1954, the crime and horror titles, which by Wertham's count had reached more than fifty percent of the total titles published by 1953, began to disappear.[21] At the same time, the bad publicity and pressure by conservative women's groups forced retailers to drop or radically reduce their carriage of comic books. *Ayers* listed more than twenty major publishers in 1948, but only about ten by 1956.

The "comic scare" of the mid-50s undoubtedly damaged the trade by stigmatizing the comics and reducing availability. Nevertheless, the industry probably could have recovered if underlying consumer demand had remained steady. It did not. Data suggest that a more powerful source of the long-term decline in comic book sales was the result not of the ideological battle, but of television and its role in siphoning off the comic book audience.

In 1946 there were about 8,000 television sets in the United States (Table 4). By 1960, the figure had grown to nearly fifty seven million. Nearly eighty percent of all U.S. homes had a TV set by 1955. A general movement from comic books to TV should not, then, be surprising.

A team of Stanford researchers conducted one of the more prominent studies of children's media habits in the late 1950s.[22] As part of their work, they examined television's impact on the use of other media, including comic books. Table 5 shows some of their findings.

Although reading varied between rural (Rocky Mountain) and metropolitan (San Francisco) areas—with the researchers attributing the difference to availability of television and general levels of education—Schramm and his colleagues found that forty-one percent of eighth grade boys in 1960 (San Francisco group) read nine or more comics per

Table 4.   Adoption of Television in the United States

	Sets in Use	Sets per HH
1946	8,000	.0002
1949	4 mill	.0949
1950	10.6 mill	.2438
1955	37.4 mill	.7826
1960	56.9 mill	1.0600

Source: DeFleur & Ball-Rokeach, p. 96.

Table 5. Mean Number of Comics Read Monthly

	2nd		4th		6th		8th		10th		12th	
	m	f	m	f	m	f	m	f	m	f	m	f
San Fran	1.1	0.2	2.6	1	3.3	1.4	4.5	3.3	3	1.3	.9	.7
Rocky Mtn					8.5	4.7			2.1	.5		
Teletown					5.0	4.0			.1	.1		
Radiotown					10.5	10.2			10.0	6.5		

Source: Schramm, Lyle, Parker, Table VII-22, p. 261.

month. In comparison, the 1950 Des Moines study reported that up to sixty-five percent of seventh graders read similar amounts. The fact that in 1950, researchers measured reading in number of comics *per week*, often more than fifteen (sec Table 3), but by 1960 measured reading in number of comics *per month* underscores the decline over the decade.

More tellingly, the 1960 study used a matched pair of Canadian towns, one with television and the other without.[23] Table 6 shows comic reading patterns in the two groups, dubbed Radiotown and Teletown.

A first-grader in Radiotown read an average of about four comics per month as opposed to about one and one-half per month in Teletown. Across all study groups, the median number of comics consumed by sixth-graders in the non-television town was significantly greater than the other communities and for tcnth-graders, three to ten times greater.

The contraction of the industry in the 1950s stemmed, therefore, from a variety of causes, including the political attack, the loss of cultural sanction, the decline of outlets and, importantly, the advent of television.

The 1960s

The early 1960s are generally considered a resurgent period in comics, especially superhero comics.[24] While the plethora of Superman and Batman clones that flourished during the war did not survive the mid-1950s, in 1959 National reintroduced the Flash, opening the so-called Silver Age of comics. The fan movement formed part of the resurgence.

Table 6. Percent Who Read 10 or More Comics A Month

	6th	10th
Teletown	34%	6%
Radiotown	87%	49%

Fans, who are usually somewhat older than the general comic readership, originated as an ongoing industry component in the 1960s.

(There was an aborted attempt to create a fan following in the 1950s, based on EC comics. According to Robert Overstreet, a number of older readers published the first comic fan magazines or fanzines, around 1953, focusing on EC enthusiasts. Response to the effort was disappointing, however, with one fanzine editor estimating the average EC reader to be between nine and thirteen years old. According to Overstreet, "This fact was taken as discouraging to many of the fan-eds who had hoped to reach an older audience." They consequently gave up their efforts and turned to science fiction fandom, which historically has had an older following.[25])

The first modern comic fan magazines appeared in the early 1960s. The editors of National, and later Marvel, encouraged the organization of superhero followers through the letters columns. While comics never again reached the circulation levels of the early 1950s, then, the Silver Age characters did attract a steady audience and, more importantly, gained the interest of slightly older readers, with the fan organizations in particular reaching people in their twenties and above.[26] Underground "adult" comix also began to appear in the late 1960s.

For Batman, the popularity of the top ten television show in 1966–1968 seasons aided sales, but the Marvel heroes created by Stan Lee began to capture an increasing share of the market.

In relation to the available school age audience, circulation continued to slip, however. Table 7 is from a study of more than 1,500 children in Southern California in 1970.[27]

The percentage of sixth graders reading nine or more comics per month was down to nineteen percent. In comparison, magazine reading was relatively more popular, as Table 8 illustrates.

While comic books remained a part of adolescent life through the 1960s, they were increasingly a smaller part of it. A following of hard core fans and collectors did develop during the decade, but they numbered, at best, in the low thousands.[28]

Table 7.   Comic Book Reading Habits, 1970

N of comics read in last month	6th Grade	10th Grade
None	35%	64%
1—4	32	24
5—8	13	6
9+	19	4

Source: Lyle, Hoffman, p. 156.

Table 8. Magazine Reading Habits, 1970

N of mags read in last month	6th Grade	10th Grade
None	29%	32%
1—4	48	54
5—8	12	9
9+	10	5

While television continued to play a role in the decline of the industry, other important factors also contributed. (Television, in fact, often helped spur sales through the promotion of comic characters on Saturday morning children's programs and, of course, through the Batman series. The cancellation of the Batman program meant a loss of the readership driven by that short-lived fad, however.) More importantly, the distribution system that had served the comic industry since the 1940s was rapidly deteriorating and the producers were having increasing difficulty getting their product to the remaining audience.

Comic book distribution, for decades, had piggybacked on the magazine distribution system in which comic titles went from the publisher to a dozen or more national distributors, then to hundreds of regional wholesalers and from there to the retailers, which for comics consisted mainly of newsstands, drug stores and small groceries. Comics were discounted at each stage, leaving profit margins on the dime-priced commodities low. Those copies that went unsold were returned to the publisher (accounting, in part, for the uncertainty of reported circulation figures). The system also resulted in slim profit margins and erratic, unpredictable sales.

In addition, the staple outlet for comic books through the 1950s and 1960s, the Mom' n' Pop corner store, was dying out. In its place arose the large supermarket chain which avoided comics because of the industry's tarnished image and the crowds of loitering children comics supposedly attracted. The newsstands ceased to carry comics because of the low profit margin, clearing their shelves for more lucrative periodicals. Going into the 1970s, mounting problems both in distribution and consumer demand faced the industry.

The 1970s

Riding the popularity of Spiderman, Marvel did well through the early 1970s. And supported by Saturday morning television programs, DC Comics, Archie Comics, and even such books as *Richie Rich*, published by Harvey Comics, continued to attract buyers. The Superman movies gave DC sales a boost in the latter 70s and Marvel produced a *Star Wars* series that proved very successful.

Nonetheless, the bulk of the school-age audience was eroding. Total reported monthly circulation, which had been running as high as thirty-six million copies during the run of the Batman TV show, dropped into the twenties in the early 1970s. Beginning in the mid-1970s total circulation started a slow but steady decline. Marvel reported losing up to thirty percent of its readership per year through the late 1970s and early 1980s, and in 1979 cut the number of its titles from forty-five to thirty-two.[29] Artists at Marvel publicly expressed unhappiness with the direction of the publications, complaining that licensing of the comic characters, now becoming more lucrative than actual comic sales, was the primary focus of management.[30] In the face of decreasing sales, DC in 1978 also cut back, paring its titles down to fifteen. Two publishers that produced comics almost exclusively for children under twelve, Gold Key (distributor of the Warner Brothers and Disney character comics) and Harvey Comics (with such titles as *Huey*, *Little Audrey*, *Sad Sack* and *Richie Rich*), ceased publication completely.

Competition from television and the loss of convenient sales outlets had, by the turn of the decade, reduced the industry to dependence on the hard core fans and collectors. But the industry began its restructuring through this audience segment in the 1970s.

Using the letter columns of DC and Marvel, and subsequently the emerging fanzines, fans by the late 1960s had developed a small network of clubs and correspondence.[31] While not a dominant segment in absolute numbers (the first edition Overstreet's *Comic Book Price Guide* sold about 3,000 copies in 1970), fans represented a powerful one due to the intensity of their interest and their large per-person purchases. These older readers, more serious about comics and privileged with greater disposable income, had prodigious buying habits. Collectors were known to purchase hundreds of a given title for investment purposes alone, and, in fact, still do.

In addition, through the 1970s, a small market for the non-code adult comics that were the progeny of the 1960s underground publishers remained. A small number of specialty comic shops provided service for this group and the collector-fans—groups which often overlapped. These comic shops dealt in adult titles that regular stores and newsstands would not carry due to the nature of the content and the irregular publishing schedules of the independent companies. The specialty shops additionally carried back copies of comics, servicing the collector.

The first specialty shops opened in the San Francisco Bay area in the early 1970s. It is estimated that by the mid-1970s there were about 100 of these shops around the country.[32] The owners discovered, however, that stocking new comic book titles posed difficulties. For reasons already noted, the normal newsstand distributors did not give comics high priority, making service poor, and the comic shops didn't always know from week to week what titles or how many copies they were going to receive. Further, the multiple tier distribution system had not changed, so discounts and profit margins remained low.

Responding to this, a comic dealer named Phil Seuling proposed a new system in 1974. He devised with DC a plan to purchase comics from the company, through his newly-established Seagate Distribution Co., and supply the specialty shops directly; there would be no returns and discounts would be higher. This "direct distribution" system was tremendously successful. The major companies began sending fliers to comic shops promoting their upcoming issues. The shops would place orders for certain numbers of comics, thereby stabilizing press runs, reducing waste and increasing efficiency for everyone.[33]

While the traditional comic market and older distribution system was withering, then, the direct-sales market began to blossom. From 1980 to 1986, at least 4,000 specialty shops began operation. Toward the end of the 1980s, some 5,000 to 6,000 shops were in business.[34] Market share followed. In the early 1970s, at least ninety-five percent of all comic sales went through newsstands, drug stores, etc. By the end of the 1980s, the specialty shops accounted for probably at least seventy percent of all unit sales and, because comics sold in such stores at higher prices, probably at least eighty percent of dollar volume.[35]

In light of the shrinking audience, many credited the specialty shop and the direct distribution system with saving the industry from collapse. At the same time, the growth of the new distribution network served to reinforce the existing demographic trends in the comic book audience. As the lack of interest in comics and operating inefficiencies in the old distribution system worked to dry up the popular market for comic books, a smaller, more specialized audience gathered at and was limited to the specialty store.

The Audience for Comics Today

Size

According to those in the industry, a regular comic shop customer in the early 1990s will purchase from four to fifteen comics per week. Collector/investors often buy several times that. If one assumes conservative figures of twenty million comics sold monthly at sixteen copies per customer, the size of the domestic comic audience can be estimated at about 1.25 million. Single issue sales of the most popular recent titles, which tend to be Batman titles, have reached as high as 500,000. Based on that figure, some in the business have estimated the size of the regular comic reader audience at less than one million. Obviously, however, there remains a substantial number of occasional readers, children who purchase a comic once every month and parents who buy them for birthdays and Christmas. Accounting for this fringe market, the number of people regularly buying comics at any given time might go as high as four or five million. There are currently about twenty million children between six and twelve in the United States[36] and another twenty-five million teenagers.[37] As a small percent of the market is substantially older than this, it suggests that something less than ten percent of U.S. school children are regular comic readers.

Age

The comic audience, since its inception, has been heavily skewed by age. Historically, children seven to eleven have constituted a large portion of the audience, with peak reading experienced between sixth and eighth grade. As the previous tables indicate, comic consumption falls off considerably by high school. In the 1970s, the changes in media habits coupled with changes in the distribution system acted to reduce radically the number of younger (seven to eleven) comic readers. Loss of this market segment probably accounted for the bulk of the circulation decline. It also meant that the remaining readers, the specialty shop customers, were on average older. Marketing studies by Marvel in the late 1970s showed that the average *newsstand* buyers of comics ranged in age from six to seventeen with a mean age of about twelve.[38] Subsequent studies of *comic shop* patrons show them ranging in age from sixteen to twenty-four with a mean age of around eighteen.[39] Comic shop owners interviewed for this paper reported very little activity from children under ten or eleven.

Gender

The comic book audience in the 1990s is overwhelmingly male. The limited research available on comic shop customers indicates that only six to ten percent are female.[40]

Education

The comic reader today is probably more educated than in past decades. Early readership studies showed that income and education were inversely related to readership.[41] For example, children considered to be brighter "discovered" or came to comic books at an earlier age, but then were quicker to stop reading them as well (a pattern duplicated in studies of television viewing among adolescents).[42] And comic reading, especially among older adolescents, was associated with low cultural status. In the 1980s, DC has reported its average reader to have had at least some college education.[43]

Demographics and Content

The demographic breakdown of the comic audience into its major component parts begins to reveal the interaction between the audience and content. Historically, different age and gender categories have followed different comic types. Early readers have been attracted to the animal character comics and "funny" comics, but as readers age they move into adventure, action-adventure and superhero comics. Female readers traditionally have been drawn to romance and 'teen' comics, such as *Archie.*

When interest in superhero comics flagged after World War II and new topics and titles developed, childrens' interests diversified. In the 1950 study of media habits, the comic most often mentioned as a favorite across all age groups was *Donald Duck*, followed by *Roy Rogers*, and for girls, *Archie*. Westerns, including *Gene Autry* and the *Lone Ranger* were more popular than Superman, who was the only superhero character reported.[44]

As late as 1970, those who read comics were interested in a broad spectrum of types. Data from the Lyle-Hoffman study are revealing:

Table 8

Types of Comic books preferred	6th m	6th f	10th m	10th f
None	21%	25%	41%	36%
Mystery/Detective	8	6	4	1
Western	4	1	1	1
Romance	3	9	2	10
War	8	0	5	4
Horror/Sci Fi	15	3	4	2
Teenage	10	26	7	19
Animal Characters	12	12	8	3
Adult Humor	20	15	28	26
More than one type	2	3	1	1

Source: Lyle-Hoffman, 1970.

The largest category, adult humor, is described by the researchers as comics "such as Peanuts." Interest in this category increases over time, as interest in all other categories diminishes. The strong relationship between comic type and the gender and age of the reader also is apparent. Boys, especially in the sixth grade, are more likely to read mystery, science fiction, or war stories. Girls, again, are more interested in romance and teen comics.

Most importantly for present purposes, readership of the category likely to capture Batman and superhero readers, horror/science fiction, suggests that this group was a relatively small percentage of the overall comic audience.

At the same time, even in the late 1960s the greatest number of comic titles in circulation were superheroes. According to Nye, the January 1969 *Magazine and Paperback Sales Guide* listed 231 comic book titles, and "by far the greater number fall into the Superman-Fantasy-Space Adventure category, including *Batman*, *Aquaman*, *Hawkman*, *Ironman*. . ."[45] In short, a small segment of the comic buying audience in the 1960s probably made the majority of purchases.

This situation became more pronounced in the mid and late 1970s, with the decline and near death of both the animal character comics, geared for younger readers, and the romance and teen comics, aimed at women. As noted, those publishers responsible for comics such as *Casper*, *Harvey*, *Sad Sack*, *Bugs Bunny* and *Daffy Duck* ceased operation near the turn of the decade. In its reorganization in the 1970s, DC eliminated its romance line, which had traditionally trailed the superhero comics in circulation. At the beginning of the 1980s, the hard-core comic fan and a small but growing number of collectors, both interested primarily in science fiction and fantasy comics (not the least of which was Batman) constituted the majority of readership.

The science fiction bent of current readership reveals itself in two other demographic characteristics associated with comic shop patrons. According to the reported industry research, a significant portion of the comic shop audience has an academic or professional interest in math, engineering or science. While percentages are unavailable, the connection is intuitive and strong enough for DC and Marvel to note in comments to the press.[46] Secondly, there's a significant overlap with non-comic science fiction and fantasy literature, especially among older readers. First Comics, for example, reported that eighty percent of its audience reads science fiction books regularly.[47] And comic fans often progress naturally into science fiction novels and magazines.

An Overview

The comic book market today has some small degree of diversity due to the influx of independent publishers in the mid-1980s. Those independents that survived through a period of economic shakeout and into the late 1980s brought with them a number of "adult" titles. Nonetheless, Marvel and DC, with their preponderance of science fiction and fantasy titles, still control at least seventy percent of the market. The audience for this material roughly breaks down into three groups.

At the top end, in age, income and education, are the fan-collectors. Sales of Overstreet's *Price Guide*, a crude indicator of the size of this group, reached about 100,000 in 1989.

Closely following this group are those older non-collectors attracted to the adult comic titles, which feature more realistic themes and characters than do the superhero genres. These titles are largely the domain of the independents. First Comics ("Shatter") estimates its average reader to be twenty-five years old.[48] Judging from circulation figures of the independents, this group attracts fifteen to twenty percent of the audience, at best.

The bulk of the comic book market is probably comprised of fifteen-to twenty-year-old males, largely involved with superhero-fantasy comics. They provide the heart of the readership for *Batman* and the other DC and Marvel titles.

These audience segments are not, of course, either precisely defined or mutually exclusive. Any given seventeen-year-old may consume a wide variety of superhero titles, adult titles and may even be a young collector. But it does begin to sketch the nature of the available audience for *Batman* comics.

Consumers outside these profiles still exist although they probably do not constitute a habituated audience. *Archie* comics, for example, still sell up to 1.5 million issues a month, primarily through newsstands and more recently in book store chains. According to the publisher, Archie's average reader is about eleven years old and sixty percent of the audience is female.[49]

In summary, the industry in the late 1980s appeared to be contracting and specializing. It had devolved from a mass medium in the early 1950s to a specialized medium in the 1990s. Like the magazine industry, its mass audience has been usurped by television and it has reoriented toward target market niches. While it seeks to expand in several directions, its existing base is limited demographically and psychographically. In this, comics have been subject to the same socio-political centrifugal forces that are creating specialized audiences across media, magazines and cable television being only the most prominent examples. Unlike many of these other forms, of course, the comic book is only the hub of a far-flung merchandising empire that propagates its cultural products in endless manifestations. And analyses of the industry must consider both the limited nature of the cultural source as well as the global reproduction of the licensed characters.

Audience and Content: The Interaction

The issue of the dynamic interaction between audiences and content opens along two fronts. First is the question of the impact or influence of the material on readers and second is the influence of readers on the production of content. This dichotomy is drawn for discursive purposes, understanding that in fact the process is one of continuing interaction and change.

Consumption and Interpretation

In the 1940s and 1950s, the issue of the impact of comics on young readers generated the serious debate that led to the Senate Hearings discussed previously. The concern, of course, focused on the potential for crime and horror comics to cultivate violent or otherwise criminal behavior in the readers.

Critics alleged that comic reading served as a primer for pathological behavior among the young and impressionable. A rather crude social learning theory model which either implicitly or explicitly assumed unmediated modeling effects, often accompanied by an equally simple Freudian interpretation of comic content, formed the theoretical core of these fears. The Werthamesque critique, however, rested only on anecdotal evidence and clinical case studies. Controlled research and more sophisticated models of media socialization suggested the fears to be largely unfounded.

The simple theoretical point that, for those who read them, comics are but one source of information about social roles and social expectations must be underscored. It is easy to overestimate the influence of that source by forgetting that readers come to a text with a developed and complex configuration of social and cultural norms; that the meaning of a given comic is subject to the varying interpretation of each reader. Further, comics serve as but one set of role cues in an intricate web of often competing socializing forces, each with varying degrees of salience and levels of positive and negative reinforcement.

Moreover, cultural values attached to an unlimited variety of social topics are distributed in various normal and non-normal ways throughout the social structure. Any given subgroup will have its own particular and complex ideological configuration. There are few hard or thick boundaries compartmentalizing sections of society, of course. As Blau points out, the larger cultural fabric is woven of continually cross-cutting intersections of human behavior, what he calls structural heterogeneity.[50] Still, clusters of interests, values and backgrounds are real. And it is out of its own socio-historical grounding that any given subgroup seeks certain media forms and it is through its given ideological lens that it approaches and interprets, often critically, that given content.

The gay audience may find a meaning in the Batman and Robin relationship special to their particular group, but that reading is not, obviously, going to be shared by born-again Christian conservatives or most twelve-year-old boys. The influence of comic reading on a given individual or closely defined group of individuals must be considered in its unique normative setting.

Given the common heritage and shared identity that to some extent must bind the broader culture, this range of acceptability may be conceived of as some normal curve of distributed meanings, with a central tendency and with extremes of interpretation arising from outlying values. The gay community and Dr. Wertham may, at the two extremes, share a given interpretation of the Batman-Robin relationship, albeit with widely contrasting reactions, while the tendency among the bulk of population may be to translate the relationship in nonsexual terms.

To carry the argument further, a similar phenomena of distributed meaning can be found in the content of media itself. Newcomb has long made the argument that television, for example, is a kaleidoscope of diverse images, values and ideologies.[51] There are obvious boundaries and limits to this and a synthesis of Newcomb's heterogenous prime-time universe with, say, Hall's cultural hegemony, suggests again a distributed curve of meanings with a tendency toward some cultural mean.

While the "spread," if you will, of the curve will be much narrower for a specific program or cultural commodity, a character like Batman offers a wider array of potential meanings than a new television sitcom due to the iteration of the character across licensed media forms. That is, Batman has been mediated through a panoply of merchandising channels. In the process, much of the comic book bound lifestyles, norms, and values of the characters are modified. While the Batman movie may carry with it some of the grit of Miller's *Dark Knight*, the lunch boxes, earrings, tee shirts and Saturday morning cartoons, do not. For the audience at large—that is, the non-comic book consumer—this sanitized version may be the only one to which they have access. A recent personal experience of the author brought home this point vividly. "Sasha," age four, told the author of his keen interest in Teenage Mutant Ninja Turtles. "Sasha" discovered the Turtles through television, and despite the author's repeated insistence, steadfastly refused to believe there existed a Mutant Ninja comic book, which in fact was the origin of the characters.[52] Moreover, while the black and white comic book version of the Turtles is graphic in its violence, the TV Turtles do little more than hurl pizzas at their enemies.

For Batman, the result may be that the thick web of history, personality, drives and fears that constitute the character in his comic book form are lost, and he becomes an icon, a social marker that taps into any number of more generic western values.

The complete process, then, is one of interaction between two curves of cultural meaning, one embedded in the audience and one embedded in the narrative, each arising jointly out of a particular socio-cultural environment, which premises the norms, or central tendencies, of both. Given the common cultural heritage of the two curves, and the precepts of individual cognitive homeostasis, the most typical interaction will be one of ideological reinforcement. But to understand the meaning a given reader ascribes to Batman, one must be able to locate both the position of the individual along the curve of cultural meaning and the location of the specific content consumed along its companion curve. (In fact, due to the complex interaction of clustered values, the curves are best conceived of in at least three dimensions.)

It is beyond the scope of this paper to treat, in detail, the perspectives and interpretations of the hard core comic book reader—that job is best left to the ethnographers. The above model suggests, however, that this group will not necessarily share the perspectives of the culture at large in its evaluation of Batman. Its strongly antagonistic reception of the *Batman* television program in the late 1960s is but one example.

For the general audience, Batman and the other superheroes may be thought of, then, as cultural and perhaps even sub-cultural icons. They are symbol sets serving to designate a certain rather special and limited constellation of fears, aspirations and fantasies. For the reader more deeply involved in the comic universe, Batman is a complex, changing, but familiar figure rich in history and meaning. And in the production of Batman, this reader plays an important reactive and proactive part.

Audience and Production

More interesting in many ways than the influence of the content on the special or at-large audience, is the influence of the audience—the specialized comic audience—on the content itself, and more to the point, the manner in which the audience has been responsible for the changing nature of the content.

The impact of the audience can be articulated in at least three major forms: the changing demographics of interested readers, the direct communication between fans and comic artists and writers; and the rise of writers and artists out of the fan audience.

The general lines of the first form of influence already have been traced. Comics in the 1980s have matured. Frank Miller's *Dark Knight* is only the most prominent example of a shift in the superhero form from the classic, innocent clash of good and evil to the raw, doubting, often cynical vision of postmodern capitalism. This vision is often repeated in the non-superhero adult comics. And both the tarnished, or at least flawed, superhero and the 'adult' comic forms emerge in large part from the changing core of comic consumers. As interest on the part of younger and female readers waned in the 1960s and 1970s, the industry reorganized around the remaining audience, leading to a growing reliance on superhero titles. At the same time, one can argue that the culture itself was maturing, that the teenage comic buyer of the 1980s was in many ways more worldly and mature than his 1950s cohort. One of earliest signs of and greatest testaments to this change was the success in the 1960s and 1970s of Spiderman and the other Marvel characters. Their popularity over DC's superheroes stemmed primarily from the perceived greater reality and human turmoil of the characters. Unlike the 1960s Batman, Spiderman grappled, often unsuccessfully, with the problems of real life in an often hostile world. The Marvel characters provided the early models for the even harder edge that Batman took in his 1980s incarnation.

The audience was changing, therefore, not only in terms of average age, but also in terms of general cultural sophistication. While the older collectors and fans helped drive the development of comic shops and the burgeoning independent comic publishing industry, the overall maturation of the audience influenced the general stylistic character of all comics.

Both DC and Marvel were, of course, sensitive to this, marketing more aggressively to the existing audience, especially the more lucrative comic shop buyer. Marvel in the mid-1980s divided its line into three, tiered segments, the "Star" line for toddlers, the "Marvel" line for sixth- to ninth-graders and the "Epic" line for high school age students.[53] The editorial nature, reading level, and price varied accordingly. DC more aggressively courted the older audience, forsaking comics aimed at the younger reader and establishing a general line of superheroes, including Batman and Superman; a mature line (which included an emotionally-troubled Green Arrow with a drinking problem), and a non-superhero adult line called "Piranha" ("comics with teeth").[54]

One sees in the industry's marketing an interesting blend of characteristics typical to specialized magazines on the one hand and mass media on the other. To the extent that the rather well-defined and

limited set of audience interests have provided the changing parameters
for content and character, one is reminded of hobby-related media, such
as magazines for model-train collectors or astronomy buffs. On the
other hand, Warner Communications is a multibillion dollar corporation with an array of sophisticated marketing tools at its disposal. The
comics industry thereby rides the cusp of the specialty and the mass
media forms in some of its activities.

With respect to two other types of audience interaction, however,
the industry demonstrates a much stronger similarity to the small,
homogenous world of the subculture. Serious comic fans are not passive
consumers of cultural product; they are in many ways active participants in its creation. The producers receive constant, enthusiastic and
serious feedback from comic readers. The letters, pouring in to Marvel
and DC daily from fans who continually monitor, critique, judge, suggest, and complain, provide the most direct line of communication.
If a superhero performs out of character, if a change in plot line is
unsatisfactory, if there is a small mistake in art work, the fans do not
hesitate to express their feelings. Furthermore, the comic community
knows and follows the work of the principle artists and writers. In the
columns of the comics themselves, fans and artists exchange views,
accept compliments, justify story lines.

Fans also organize themselves into clubs and groups, socialize at
regular comic conventions, and communicate through the various fanzines, which serve as additional fora for the examination and critique
of developments in the industry.

The extent to which this fan oversight has a direct impact on content
is impossible to say, of course, but role theory would suggest that any
individual creator is subject to a variety of role cues and influences. In
most mass-media situations, the voice of the audience is far removed
from the daily grind of production.[55] But given the relatively close
nature of the comic community, it is quite likely that the audience
constitutes one of several direct and significant influences on the creative process. Illustrations of this impact can be seen in the strenuous
and expensive efforts of Warner to reassure the fans of Michael Keaton's
ability to do justice to the Batman role, after a wave of hostility rolled
through the comic community when casting for the movie was announced. The telephone polls deciding the fate of a somewhat unpopu-
lar Robin is also but one of the more prominent examples of fan power.

Finally, the role of the audience is realized through the fact that many
of the individuals who write, draw and sometimes even manage the
comics, themselves come from the fandom community. Unsurpris-
ingly, those who are attracted to comics at an early age, stay with
them and are most serious about them, often turn into the creators

themselves, carrying with them the norms, values and life vision of the fan. DC Comics executive vice president Paul Levitz began writing a fanzine called the *Comic Reader* when he was in school, and started work for DC as a freelancer.[56] Jim Shooter got hooked on comics at age twelve, went to work as a teenager for DC writing Superman and Superboy and at twenty-five succeeded Stan Lee as editor-in-chief of Marvel Comics.[57]

A Closing Remark

The point, then, is that the nature of the current Batman is the product of a variety of cultural and industrial factors. Some of them have to do with the process of creating cultural commodities. But the characters—their ambitions, psychoses, strengths and weaknesses— are also the product of individual creators and those creators have ties of numerous types to a relatively small and well-defined audience. To the extent that the audience is part of the larger culture, Batman and other modern superheroes reflect, iconically, the attributes of that larger culture. But the comic audience is also a specialized subculture, a modern media-bound specialized community, and so the various demographic, psychographic and ideological peculiarities of that community must be taken into consideration when critically analyzing the social significance of the many lives of the Batman.

Notes

1. "Bang, Pow, Zap Heros are Back," *Time*, October 6, 1986, p. 62; Benjamin DeMott, "Darkness at the Mall," *Psychology Today*, February 1984, pp. 48-51; "Comic-Book Heroes to the Rescue," *Newsweek*, December 12, 1983, p. 27.

2. Bill Barol, "Batmania," *Newsweek*, June 26, 1989, pp. 70–74.

3. See, for example, Alexis Tan and Kermit Scuggs, "Does Exposure to Comic Book Violence Lead to Aggression in Children?" *Journalism Quarterly* 57(1980)4: pp. 579–583.

4. See, e.g., commentary by Anthony Giddens in *Central Problems in Social Theory* (Berkeley: University of California Press, 1986), pp. 9–49.

5. See, for example, John Fiske, *Television Culture* (New York: Methuen, 1987); Janice Radway, *Reading the Romance* (Chapel Hill: University of North Carolina Press, 1984).

6. Martin Noreau, ed., *Batman Fans: The Midnight Conference* [newsletter] (St-Hubert, Quebec, Canada: np).

7. Judith Duke, *Children's Books and Magazines: A Market Study* (White Plains, N.Y.: Knowledge Industry Publications, 1979), p. 116.

8. Norbet Muhlin, "Comic Books and Other Horrors," *Commentary*, Vol. 7 (1949): pp. 80–88.

9. Bernard Rosenberg and David Manning White, eds. *Mass Culture: The Popular Arts in America* (Glencoe, IL: The Free Press, 1957), p. 187.

10. Muhlin, p. 81.

11. See, for example, Lauretta Bender and Reginald Lourie, "The Effect of Comic Books on the Ideology of Children, American *Journal of Orthopsychiatry*, Vol. 11 (1941): 540—550; William Marston, "Why 100,000,000 Americans Read Comics," *The American Scholar*, Vol. 13 (1943–44): 35–44; Robert Thorndike, "Words and the Comics," *Journal of Experimental Education*, 10 (1941): 110–113.

12. Muhlin, pp. 881–882.

13. Paul Lyness, "The Place of the Mass Media In the Lives of Boys and Girls," *Journalism Quarterly*, Vol. 29:1(1952):43–54.

14. Les Daniels, *Comix: A History of Comic Books In America*, (New York: Outerbridge and Dienstfrey, 1971), p. 62.

15. Sharon Lowery and Melvin DeFleur, "Seduction of the Innocent," in *Milestones in Mass Communication Research*, 2nd. ed. (Boston: Longman, 1988), p. 215.

16. Frederic Thrasher, "The Comics and Delinquency: Cause or Scapegoat" *The Journal of Educational Sociology*, 23(1949)1: 195–205.

17. Lowery, p. 215.

18. Lowery, p. 215.

19. Fredric Wertham, *Seduction of the Innocent*, (New York: Rinehart, 1954).

20. U.S. Senate, Judiciary Committee. Hearings before the sub-committee to Investigate Juvenile Delinquency, 83rd Cong. 1st & 2nd Sess., 84th Cong., 1st Sess. (1954–56).

21. Lowery and DeFleur, p. 220.

22. Wilbur Schramm, Jack Lyle, Edwin Parker. *Television in the lives of our Children* (Stanford, Ca.: Stanford University Press, 1961).

23. The extent of television's penetration is underscored here in that the researchers could not find a matched pair of communities in the United States that included a town without TV (pp. 15–16).

24. Robert Overstreet, *Comic Book Price Guide*, 19th ed. (New York: House of Collectibles, 1989), p. 55.

25. Overstreet, p. A-55.

26. Overstreet, p. A-55.

27. Jack Lyle and Heidi Hoffman, "Children's Use of Television and Other Media," *Television and Social Behavior*, Vol. 4, *Television in Day-to-Day Life: Patterns of Use*, ed. E.A. Rubenstein, G.A. Comstock, and J.P. Murray (Washington, D.C.: National Institute of Mental Health, 1971), pp. 129– 256.

28. Telephone interview with Robert Overstreet, October, 19, 1989.

29. N. R. Kleinfield, N.R. "Superheroes' Creators Wrangle," *New York Times*, Oct. 13, 1979, Section D, pp. 25–6.

30. Kleinfield, p. 25.

31. Telephone interview with Robert Overstreet.

32. Eddy Christman, "Direct Sales Rescues Comics," *Advertising Age*, June 25, 1984, p. 110.

33. "Specialty Stores Increasing Share of Comic Market, Boosting Sales," *Variety*, July 8, 1987, p. 28.

34. Kurt Eichenwald, "Grown-Ups Gather at the Comic Book Stand," *New York Times*, Sept. 30, 1987, p. 1.

35. "Specialty Stores Increasing Share of Comic Market,"

36. Horst Stipp, "Children As Consumers," *American Demographics*, February, 1988, p. 28.

37. Doris Walsh, "Targeting Teens," *American Demographics*, February 1985, p. 21.

38. Christman.

39. Tom Bierbaum, "As Typical Comics Reader Skews Older, More Adult Themes Raise Questions and Eyebrows of Kiddies," *Variety*, July 8, 1987, pp. 27, 42.

40. Bierbaum, p. 42.

41. Lyle and Hoffman, p. 206.

42. Schramm, Lyle, Parker, p.

43. Bierbaum, p. 42.

44. Lyness, p. 43.

45. Russel Nye, *The Unembarrassed Muse: The Popular Arts in America* (New York: The Dial Press, 1970).

46. Christman, p. 110; Beirbaum, p. 42.

47. Steve Roth, "First Comics Is Still Third, but Has Firsts of Its Own," *Publishers Weekly*, December 6, 1985, p. 43.

48. Roth, p. 48.

49. "Archie Comics: Three Generations In the Business," *Publishers Weekly*, Dec. 6, 1985, p. 42.

50. Peter Blau, "Parameters of Social Structure," in *Approaches to the Study of Social Structure*, Peter Blau, ed. (New York: The Free Press, 1975) pp. 232–235.

51. Horace Newcomb and Paul Hirsch, "Television as a Cultural Forum," in Horace Newcomb, ed., *Television: The Critical View*, 4th ed (New York: Oxford University Press, 1987) pp. 455–470.

52. Personal Interview with Sasha Rush, Lemont, Pa., Nov. 11, 1989.

53. "Marvel Expands Its Lion's Share with Early Reader Line," *Publishers Weekly*, December 6, 1985, pp. 38, 42.

54. Bierbaum, p. 42

55. See, for example, Muriel Cantor, *Prime-Time Television: Content and Control* (Beverly Hills: Sage, 1980), 81–96.

56. "From Fan to Superexec, Levitz Stresses DC Comics' Creativity," *Variety*, July 8, 1987, p. 27.

57. "Biff! Pow! Comic Books Make a Comeback," *Business Week*, September 2, 1985, p. 59.

6

Batman: The Ethnography

Camille Bacon-Smith with Tyrone Yarbrough

Introduction

In June of 1989, *Batman* swept the movie theaters of the nation, carried on a wave of publicity that rivaled *Gone With the Wind* in its fanfare. In the University City area of West Philadelphia, located between the ivy league University of Pennsylvania and low income inner city housing, scalpers sold tickets outside the theater for the preview showing of *Batman* at the AMC Walnut III on Walnut Street. During the preview, determined fans filled the aisles and the back of the theater, at first sitting or reclining, then standing as the crowd grew. By 4:00 on the 23rd of June, some of the more avid fans waiting in line at Olde City Cinema for the third showing of opening day had already seen the movie and were returning for a second look.

For popular culture scholars, the phenomenon of the blockbuster movie presents a number of interesting questions about audiences and their behavior:

1. Who are the fans who stand in line on opening day, who return for repeated viewings of the movie, and who encourage their friends to do the same?

2. How does a particular group, defined as an audience, respond to a given example of a highly publicized "big movie" such as the recent Warner movie, *Batman*?

3. What significant meaning does the audience construct out of its experience of the movie, to produce a secondary, "memory" response?

4. What social mechanisms drive these responses?

With the Batman movie, all of these questions are inflected by the history of the character in comic books, graphic novels, novelization of the script, and the television series. Accordingly, we must refine our definition of audience to recognize that in one "mass" viewing group that filled the theatre for any showing of the film, various "audiences" were present:

1. Long term fans of the comic books, who added the graphic novels, novelizations, and other forms of presentation to their repertoire as they appeared, and who judged not only the movie but also the mass media hype and promotional clips based on prior knowledge of the characters.

2. Short term fans with less direct experience with the primary sources—the comic books, graphic novels, etc.—who relied on word-of-mouth and references in the meta-literature such as *Comics Journal* and *Comic Buyers' Guide* and some promotional material to fill out the understanding of the *Batman* characters they bring to viewing the movie.

3. Fans of the television series, who filled out their understanding of the *Batman* characters with promotional pieces on screen and in the press.

4. Audiences who were not fans of Batman in any sense, but who attended because the movie was touted as an event, and who drew all of their information about the characters from word-of-mouth and promotional materials.

How researchers find answers to these questions depends on their training. Many scholars begin with a theory of how social mechanisms produce responses, and then examine actual consumers to see if the theory works.[1] As folklorists, we begin with a method for examining the responses of a given audience and then apply the particular theory out of a repertoire of possibilities that seems to fit what we find.

Part I: A Method to the Madness

Qualitative Ethnography

Ethnography is a data-intensive method in which the researcher studies the culture of informants where they gather in their own native habitats—difficult to do with a heterogeneous mass audience. Comic book fans, however, have established gathering places where the researcher can interact with the informants on their own ground. This study, therefore, focuses on the first two "audiences" described above: fans of comic books who have a history of commitment to the form and the characters created within it, but whose understanding of the specific characters of the Batman corpus may vary.

The ethnographic method used in this paper relies heavily upon the work of Dell and Virginia Hymes, and on the work of Clifford Geertz. From ethnolinguist Hymes[2] comes the deceptively simple dictate: If you want to know what something means in a culture, ask. But, to understand the answer, you have to speak the language—the special symbolic dialect—of the community, the audience you wish to study. Critical theorists have their own dialect, as do folklorists. So, too, do Star Trek fans, Ralph[3] members, and the fans of Batman, Wolverine, "Spidey"[4] and "Supes."[5] Meaning becomes transformed for the scholar who explores it in the language of the community as it unfolds in the interplay between observed use and expressed gloss. Again, however, we must understand the language of the explication, as well as the limitations the researcher's outsider position places on his access to specialized knowledge.[6] Ethnography takes time, but in this case, specific researcher experience made a short-term study feasible. Camille Bacon-Smith had eight years' experience studying media and science fiction fan groups that interconnect with the comic book fan interest. Bacon-Smith brought to the study a prior knowledge of some of the fan language, activities, and organizing principles. Tyrone Yarbrough had both folkloristic and literary training, and a lifelong interest in comic books. Yarbrough brought to the project extensive prior knowledge of the comic books characters as well as the fan debates that play out in the semi-professional publications: he "knew the language."

Quantitative Method: the Baseline

For this study, the authors chose to combine particularistic qualitative research—observing fans, conducting extended interviews with individuals and groups in their "natural habitats"—with a more quantitative approach. The quantitative method provides an additional range of general information on the fan community while it acts as a "baseline" or norm against which the qualitative can be tested. We chose to quantify three areas of the study:

1. Who are the comic book fans?
2. How important is Batman to comic book fans? and
3. How do audiences in the theatre respond to the *Batman* movie?

Each question carries with it the problem of selection bias. The choice of venue may effect the range of the survey group, so we chose to examine as many venues as possible. These included:

- All three major comic book shops in downtown Philadelphia, Pennsylvania, with particular attention to "Fat Jack's Comicrypt." "Fat Jack's" is the best known of the shops in the Philadelphia area, and draws a cross section of customers from all the comic-book reading publics. Time constraints limited our research to the major comic outlets, and we did miss at least one smaller shop and several locations where comic book resales represent a significant portion of the business.

- Five movie theaters. These included all the major first run venues in the city that we could find: one in the University of Pennsylvania area, one in the Society Hill tourist area (both with audiences mixed as to race, class, gender, age, profession), one in the down-town area that usually attracts a high percentage of Black teenage males, one in northeast Philadelphia, generally described as a "working class neighborhood" in local media, that attracts primarily White families. Serendipity provided an opportunity to compare city audiences to one in the Princeton, New Jersey suburbs that primarily draws an upper-middle-class[7] White family audience.

- One animation fan club in Center City Philadelphia, the members of which share a strong interest in comic books. (The researchers could only find the one such organization in the city.)

- One comic book convention in New York City, chosen because it was the biggest and most heavily advertised convention in the Middle-Atlantic region.

Once the research team had decided upon the venues for study, the next question became one of limiting the demographic analysis. At this point, the team had a choice: we could count every body in a certain venue during a sampling period, in which case we had to limit our survey to those factors we could see immediately, whether they were important to the study or not; or we could select less visible variables, and work with a smaller sampling of people who would willingly answer questions or hand in questionnaires.

We decided to measure visible factors, and selected three categories that we could distinguish quickly: race, sex, and slightly more problematically, age. We broke the group into teen and adult for the comic book shops, and occasionally had to ask the age of a late-teen/young-adult for proper registering. This one quick question did not inhibit our basic goal of counting everyone who entered the store. At each venue, we took a demographic sampling of the customers, audiences, or participants. We gathered information from June 9, two weeks prior to the release of the film, until July 28, roughly five weeks after the film opened.

The team conducted the greatest amount of demographic research at the three comic book shops, with special concentration on Fat Jack's Comicrypt, located on Sansom Street in Philadelphia's downtown area known as Center City. Owner Mike Ferrero and the staff at Fat Jack's were consistently supportive of the work and this attitude carried over to the patrons who accepted our counting and the occasional "how old are you?" with aplomb. The store itself is big enough that our presence did not seriously hinder patron browsing, and we found that many fans consider Fat Jack's to be the center of comic book activity in the city, which made it ideal for our purposes.

We applied the same method at the Greenberg's comics convention in New York City, collecting data from our checkpoint at a juncture between two display rooms: the team counted everyone who passed this point during the one-hour collecting period. For the convention, we added an age category for children, and a race category for Hispanic. No other venue had a measurable number of either group.

At the theater, patrons with tickets waiting on line at 3:45 for the 4:00 showing of the *Batman* movie were counted. We did not have the opportunity to do a formal count at the Anime Society meetings, but a quick scan found the group to be primarily White males of college age or older, with only three or four women and about as many men of other races in attendance:

Location	Comic Shops Philadelphia	Convention New York	Movie house Philadelphia
Black Male Adult	24%	9%	20%
Black Male Teenager	20%	3%	13%
White Male Adult	27%	34%	14%
White Male Teenager	17%	18%	10%
Asian Male Adult	1%	1%	00%
Asian Male Teenager	3%	5%	00%
Other Male Adult	1%	4%	3%
Other Male Teenager	00%	4%	3%
Black Female Adult	1%	00%	14%
Black Female Teenager	2%	00%	7%
White Female Adult	2%	7%	12%
White Female Teenager	2%	00%	4%
Asian Female Adult & Teen	00%	00%	00%
Other Female Adult & Teen	00%	2%	00%

Demographically, the numbers are significant in and of themselves. In Philadelphia, the percentages of Black males buying comic books in the specialized shops equals that of White males, and exceeds the percentage of White males for the audience waiting to see the film at the Olde City Cinema. While this particular movie house caters to mixed audiences, it generally attracts more White ticket buyers, both because of its proximity to an expensive and fashionable urban residential area and because it generally runs "upscale" mainstream films. Batman clearly attracted Black viewers as strongly as it did White viewers, and in subsequent exit interviews no audience member mentioned any racial issue as motivating his or her response to or opinion about the film.

In addition to the basic information the demographics provided us about who bought the comics or the tickets, we used these figures to ensure proportionate representation of all the demographic groups in our more intensive qualitative investigation. We also compared the responses we received in interviews by demographic group, to see if certain attitudes did in fact seem influenced according to the categories we established. When a correlation between our categories and attitudes did not occur, we tried to determine how the responses to the movie *did* organize. (For the purpose of testing the qualitative results, a consistent negative result is as significant as a consistent positive one. The keyword is consistent.)

The second question, "How important is Batman to the comic book fans?" gave us a kind of context into which our study fit. We knew that, when asked about Batman, all of our informants could offer an opinion and a bit of history about the character, and could name some of the recent graphic novels. But was Batman as important to the fans as it was to our study? Did the importance of the character to the fans change after the movie opened? A smaller objective study, carried out at Fat Jack's Comicrypt from two weeks before the *Batman* movie opened to two weeks after the movie opened, posed the question more obliquely: "What are your favorite comics?" We made it clear that the patron could suggest more than one series or character, and that he did not necessarily have to be purchasing the favorite at the moment. Surprisingly, we found that Batman places as the favorite in the lists of very few fans, and continues to fall below such perennial favorites as X-Men and Spiderman even when sales figures for Batman products surpass those of the more frequently mentioned books and characters. Of sixty-three responses, only two chose Batman as a favorite, tying with such disparate choices as *Captain America, Ralph Snart Adventures, Lum,* and *Superman.*[8] By contrast, *X-Men* scored the highest with eleven mentions, closely followed by *The Amazing Spiderman* with ten.

This response is consistent with qualitative findings that many fans are making high-volume purchases of Batman ephemera as an investment strategy while holding the movie and the surrounding hype at arms length from the "real" business of comic book fandom. According to Mike Ferrero, comics distributer and owner of the Fat Jacks Comicrypt chain, *X-Men* has been the leading seller in his sales area for the last ten years, nudged out of first place only by the flood of Batman ephemera that accompanied the movie.

That is not to say that Batman has no place in the consciousness of the fan community. In qualitative reporting, we found that few fans answered general questions about comics or fan involvement with examples from Batman (*X-Men*, and *Watchmen* came up with much greater frequency), but when asked directly about the character, all fans had an opinion or an experience with the character to relate. It seems that, like Superman, Batman is a character that many fans meet early in life, and that they may return to from time to time when a particularly interesting interpretation is introduced by the publishers. In general, Batman represents part of the background of common history that fans share rather than the immediate source of fan interaction on a day-to-day basis.

Batman: the Immediate Response

To establish a context in which later responses to the movie could be examined, we conducted a rigorous preliminary survey of the preview showing of *Batman* in the University City area. The survey included brief interviews with audience members before the movie began, and a detailed record of kinesic and paralinguistic responses during the actual viewing of the film. It is important to keep in mind here that the researchers were "reading" the audience, not the film. Bacon-Smith rarely looked at the screen at all, while Yarbrough did make a conscious effort to register the screen action for specific responses. Responses were "read" based on stress, volume, tone (ascending or descending), duration of response, uniformity of response, movement (both in the theater and leaving and returning to the theater). Audible comments from the audience were used as corroborative evidence.

Short interviews with audience members waiting for *Batman* to begin indicated that most people did not have preconceived expectations for the movie. Some were aware of the controversy over Michael Keaton, best known for his comedic turns in *Mr. Mom* and *Beetlejuice* before taking the role of Bruce Wayne, the Batman. Most had seen trailers, or features from the flood of speculative "industry news" about the film that swamped spring television. On *20/20* and *West 57th Street*, endlessly on *Entertainment Tonight* and on a number of syndicated "preview specials," viewers were warned that this would be no camp return to the sixties, but a darkly moody eighties Batman.

Although more women were present than usually frequent the comic shops, the audience at the AMC Walnut III preview reflected the same demographic mix that we found the next day at Olde City Cinema. Few of those waiting to see the movie said they were there because of the comic books or any special affinity with Batman. Groups seemed to be made up not of fans, but of friends among whom one or two enthusiasts persuaded the others to attend. Between dating and married couples, the man generally made the decision to see *Batman*, the woman going along for a night out. However, the women did show some familiarity with the character from a variety of sources.

For the most part, however, preview moviegoers seemed conscious more of being present at a major *event* than at a narrative film. Before the 10:00 p.m. preview showing at the AMC Walnut III in University City, one audience member stated that he had never read the comics. He knew the character from the television show, but it had been the television entertainment pieces and preview specials that drew him to the first public showing of the film. When the interviewers asked a woman in the audience what brought her to see a movie at 10:00 on a Thursday night, she replied, "The publicity behind it, there's been so much publicity, the hype, the hype and the promotional things."

There was an undercurrent of aggression in the preview audience in University City. The theater had problems with the sound, and the crowd shouted for the projectionist's attention sporadically for some time even after the movie had begun. The Batman opening music drew the crowd's attention, however, and explosive applause greeted Jack Nicholson's name on the screen. (Entrance interviews here and at Olde City Cinema on opening day confirmed that the star's name carried the allusive guarantee of quality.) On a scale of 1–10,[9] with Jack Nicholson a 10 and Kim Basinger a 1, the Batman Logo received a 5, Keaton a 3, Billy Dee Williams a 7, and Prince an 8. No other name received notice at all in the credits. Subsequent responses to the film are charted in the appendix at the end of this article, but to quickly summarize, the "raw" response of the audience with mixed expectations and no guidance as to appropriate response was very different from the response of later audiences.

At no point did the film seem to catch and hold these viewers' attention for more than a scene or two. Audience responses were primarily of two types: shock and intertextual recognition, with the latter being most common. The audience responded with pleased laughter at remarks that played incongruously with the well known, like "American Express, don't leave home without it!" (spoken by muggers early in the film), or Knox's question, "What's he (Batman) pulling down after taxes?" Some lines that had figured prominently in the advertising

campaign, such as "I'm Batman," not only drew a strong positive response, but had audience members reciting along with the screen even
for the preview.

Shocking scenes brought a mixed reaction. Early in the film, when
muggers shot Batman, some audience members laughed when he fell,
but the response to Joker's fall into the vat of acid drew a uniformly
horrified response. (Surprisingly, the emergence of his now-whitened
hand from the river drew no response at all). The destruction of the
fine-art museum brought a mixed reaction: many men seemed to find
the scene funny, while women responded with dismay or horror. Large
portions of the movie drew little audience attention and no reaction.
Even at the preview, scenes with Vicki Vale seem to have picked up
the dubious status accorded the special effects scenes in *Star Trek: The
Motion Picture:* a good time to nip out for popcorn or a bathroom break.
The batmobile drew a favorable response, but the batwing did not. Most
fight and chase scenes met with bored inattention; the audience seemed
most "up" for Joker's oneliners. For preview audiences, the film developed little internal textual tension. Some viewers fell asleep, others
began to leave the theater before the denouement had run its course,
and the closing credits met with mixed response—some applause, and
some boos.

David Bordwell has said that "Every film trains its spectator."[10] Based
on in-theater response and later interviews, however, *Batman* seems
not to have done so. The preview audience remained unsure how to
respond at almost every point: was the film a comedy or a drama? Was
the Joker frightening or humorous? Why was Vicki Vale interested in
Bruce Wayne, and why was he interested in her? Did it matter? When
did the film end? (Preview audiences began to leave after Commissioner
Gordon lit the Bat Signal. They waited in the aisles when the film
continued with Vicki Vale entering Bruce Wayne's Rolls Royce. Only
the die-hards waiting for the final credits actually saw Batman standing
in silhouette on the rooftop.) The immediate response was conflicted
and ambivalent, and the audience seemed to abandon its generic expectations about the time that Bruce Wayne entertains Vicki Vale for
dinner at "stately Wayne manor." At no point did response[11] anticipate
action, but from the aforementioned scene, the response also lost the
brief lag that accompanied the effort to fit the pieces of an unsolved
narrative puzzle together. Response turned on the line, the image—
MTV as standup comedy.

Though the film did not train its spectator, the newspaper reviewers
took up the slack. By the first regular showing (11:00 a.m., June 23,
1989) at the Olde City Cinema, many viewers had read the reviews of
the movie in the *Philadelphia Inquirer* and the *Philadelphia Daily*

News, both morning papers. The *Inquirer* targets a more sophisticated audience, and reviewer Carrie Rickey emphasized the film's visual "postliterate" quality, comparing *Batman* to *Blade Runner, Brazil,* and *Metropolis* in postmodern terms, and putting it in the category of visual cult classic. *The Daily News,* a more working class paper,[12] gave credit to the popular-culture origins of the Batman and Joker characters, but reviewer Gary Thompson drew on a Shakespearean model to describe Batman: "And Batman is not comfortably Good—he has a terrible lust for vengeance that would put hair on Hamlet's chest."[13] Like Rickey, Thompson compared the film to Terry Gilliam's *Brazil.*

Armed with the information that *Batman* is a dark film about vengeance and the Joker is a psychotic with a twisted but droll sense of humor, opening-day audiences responded more "appropriately" to the film. The early, uncomfortable laughter dropped away dramatically, as did much of the confusion about where the movie was going. Reviews did not change the response to the romance portion of the film, however: scenes including Vicki Vale and other secondary characters continued to lose audience interest. Audiences at The Orleans, patronized almost exclusively by White working and lower middle class families responded with silent attentiveness characteristic of that group. The standing room only audience laughed rarely, but gave the movie a standing ovation at the end credits, an extravagant demonstration of approval for that group. At exit interviews, however, even long-time media fans, who discuss the details of movies and television series at length at social gatherings, could offer few comments about why they enjoyed the movie. The most telling was the comment by one woman that she expected the movie to be terrible, and so was pleasantly surprised that it exceeded her expectations.

The mixed audience at the Midtown three weeks into the movie's run had clearly seen the movie before: viewers interacted with each other and the screen, and had few of the shock or surprise responses we had seen in earlier audiences. At times the crowd seemed overwhelmed by the response to the movie *Lethal Weapon II* playing next door. In the Princeton area suburb late in the run, the matinee audience filled only about one quarter of the theater, and its responses were subdued, although a number of the audience members said that they had seen the movie a number of times and liked it very much.

It is difficult to draw conclusions about the popularity of a movie in different areas based on the raw responses in the theaters. First, one must consider culturally appropriate behavior. The standing ovation of the respectfully attentive audience at the Orleans expressed an enthusiastic approval of the film equal to the laughter and applause that interspersed the showing at the Olde City, and in fact some comic book fans mentioned that they deliberately sought out theaters in neighborhoods where silent viewing was the norm so that they could listen more attentively to the film. Other fans deliberately attended showings in more exuberant movie houses to enjoy the audience participation.

One thing does remain clear, however; the preview audience response remains an anomalous reading of the film. In spite of the intertextual information provided by previews on television and trailers before other films, in spite of the articles in magazines and explication in magazine-format programming, the preview audience did not know how to react to the movie, and left the film with mixed feelings that ranged from loving the film through finding it boring and inexplicable, to hating it.

Part II: The Comic Book Fan Response

Fat Jack's

In the sixties, the area around 2006 Sansom Street represented Philadelphia's version of Haight Ashbury. Today the street is quieter, but it has never lost its counterculture aura. A few doors down from Fat Jack's Comicrypt, past the bicycle messenger service, is the Wilma Theatre Group's headquarters. Across the street the Roxy Screening Room shows art films, with *The Rocky Horror Picture Show* at midnight on the weekends. The neighbors all rub elbows at Fat Jack's back issue bins: this is the place to be for comic book fandom.

From the outside, Fat Jack's looks like a tiny box of a store—just wide enough for a door and a bay window at the front. Several yards into the store, however, it opens to twice the width, and extends back thirty or forty feet to a storeroom with still more comic books. In the shop itself, new arrivals for the week appear to the right of the window, while current issues are displayed on the left, from the front of the store to the rear. Back issues are grouped in clean white bins by publisher, alphabetized by title and stored in plastic sleeves. The bins fill the center of the shop, with aisles wide enough for customers to browse and chat with friends. Some fans come in, buy their books and leave alone, while others come in groups and still others come to the shop to meet other fans, forming interlocking knots of enthusiasts that meet and pass on. Mom, the cat, presides over the activity from a basket on top of the back issue independents. Thursday the new books are put on the shelf, and the store is packed with the regulars through Saturday. Members of the Anime Society show up most Friday afternoons.

The Fans

On the afternoon of the ninth of June, Bacon-Smith talked to the director of promotions for the Roxy. He's twenty-two years old and in to buy the week's new books (*X-Men, Spiderman, Avengers West Coast,* but his favorites are *Animal Man* and *Doom Patrol*). He'd seen the *Batman* film at a special exhibitor's showing, and readily talked about the experience, which seemed to reflect some of the response we saw in the preview audience:[14]

Informant: I thought it was really disappointing. Umm, I think our worst fears of casting have come true. Michael Keaton was, was very wrong. I mean uh, Batman's supposed to be swaggering and handsome and tall and virile and Michael Keaton's a munchkin and uh, wasn't convincing. It also had a lot of attention to design and detail in the film, kinda similar to like *Metropolis,* or *Blade Runner* or *Brazil.* Have you seen the film?

Bacon-Smith: I have not, I have not seen *Batman,* but I've seen *Metropolis, Blade Runner* and *Brazil.*

Informant: It's overwhelming, the design. And it's not done as well as uh, the other three films. It just doesn't have like the wit that, like *Brazil* had. I didn't think Tim Burton, the director—he does mayhem well, but he doesn't do action well. The action scenes, like the hand to hand combat, didn't work. And they also had too much emphasis on this relationship he [Batman] had with Vicki Vale—Kim Basinger's character. And it was just too much time. I don't know, I wanted to see it much grittier, Batman stalking in the night and that sort of thing. . . . I mean Vicki Vale has more screen time than Batman does in the film. And it's like, what new outfit, and how's her hair going to be this scene. You know, look at the Art Deco design in this room. It was just disappointing. I mean, Jack Nicholson, however, was fantastic. I mean he's worth the film alone. (pauses, then laughs) Yeah, Jack Nicholson's great, I mean, he's a total scene stealer. I mean, you actually get to a point where you're rooting for him instead of Batman. Which can work against them. . . .

Bacon-Smith: Now, did you see it with a group of people at a screening?

Informant: Ahh, yeah, they were all exhibitors.

Bacon-Smith: Yeah. What was their response?

Informant: It was reserved applause, I mean there were some people that clapped. I mean, the group that I went

> with, there were six of us from the theater and two
> really liked it and two really disliked it. . . . I really
> wanted to love the film.

Like the above informant, Martin King, one of the new middle class
Black artists and writers for DC Comics, saw the film at a special
screening—not, however, the one Warner Bros. held for DC in New
York:

> King: I saw the film on a special sneak preview on Tuesday.
>   . . . I wasn't expecting to be going, I thought—I had
>   work to do, and also, there was a DC sneak preview
>   in New York that I thought I was going to —
> Bacon-Smith: DC's preview was on Wednesday, wasn't it?
> King: They didn't have one for the staff. It was actually just
>   for the editorial people.
> Bacon-Smith: Oh.
> King: So we were, like, really, how could you do this to us,
>   you know? But, uh, my friend, he had a ticket, and
>   another person that was supposed to go with [us], he
>   couldn't make it, so I had his ticket. So I went and
>   saw it then.

Seeing the film at a special showing in Philadelphia went a long way
to repair King's original disillusionment with the producers of the film
for excluding creative staff from the DC preview in New York. When
we talked at Fat Jack's on the eighth of July, King had already returned
to see the movie four more times. His description of his initial response
and his efforts to reconstruct that response parallels the experience of
many fans coming to terms with their own ambivalence about the film:

> Bacon-Smith: What kind of folks were in the [first] audience?
> King: Well, let's see. There were a lot of people who had
>   won tickets, so it wasn't a massive comic book crowd.
>   It was very strange, because uh, you know, the tension
>   that was there, there was people who didn't know
>   what to expect. I was one of them, you know, because
>   like I was saying, when I first was hearing stuff about
>   the movie. . . . I was reluctant to see it. I said I have
>   to go see it. This is my life, this is my employer, so
>   just out of respect I am going to go see it. The first
>   trailers and clips I was seeing I was still kind of
>   shaky—iffy about it. I finally saw the long, extended,
>   long trailer, and it was like, 'wait a minute, now I'm

> impressed. Now I am really impressed, so I had to go
> see it.

Like the informant from the Roxy, King had important personal reasons for wanting to like this movie: "This is my life, this is my employer." For King, *Batman* is a public expression of his identity as a comic book professional. As the event approaches, his doubts resurface:

> By the time, getting up in the theatre to see it, I was—started—feeling uneasy again, like, I don't know what to expect anymore. It was bizarre. The first time I saw it I was mixed on it. . . . I was also gauging audience reaction. I was sitting right next to the reviewer from the *Inquirer*, and so, like, you know, he's (sic) kind of like, leaning over to hear us because like, everybody [in King's party] was comic book people. So, my first reaction to it was, you know, what a wonderful Joker film. He was, you know, spectacular.

As a comic book artist, King describes Nicholson's performance in terms of artists' renditions of the Joker. At the same time he rationalizes the audience's lukewarm reception as ignorance of the vital context of comic book lore:

> You know Jack Nicholson made—you know, it was so bizarre, be-cause I was watching him on the screen I kept getting images tem-plated over him of comic book images. I was like looking at him, and "oh my God, that's a Jim Aparo Joker drawing" I shake my head, and there's a Brian Bolland. He's amazing, he's all Jokers in one, you know? I mean, he captured the thirties, forties, sixties, seventies, eighties, all of them all in one, without doing massive research. He just became part of it, and I was going , 'wow, the Joker film,' because the Batman, he's a smaller role, you know. And like I said, unfortu-nately the audience reaction wasn't the best because the audience didn't seem to be people who were Bat-people. They were people who were going 'I won a ticket to this big **event** that everybody wants to see, and it had better be good' so they were I guess mentally biased, you know.

The description of mood here seems to parallel the aggression noted at the preview audience. The Warner hype had led consumers to expect not just a movie but an event. It had not, however, defined what makes their movie stand apart from the summer adventure films, what that **event** was to be. The movie itself gave them few clues that the uniti-ated could interpret:

King: So, we're sitting there watching the film, and like,
             certain scenes which were rallying points, you know,
             which, you know, we're going, 'this is the part where
             you are supposed to be cheering, stomping and
             screaming' the audience was like looking around.

Bacon-Smith: What were some of those parts to you?

King: . . . [A] big rallying point was the last scene of the
             movie where he's standing there with, you know, the
             Bat signal. And most people were saying, well, that
             didn't work because it was more Superman than Bat-
             man. In the original script and in the book, they were
             saying he was crouching down like one of the gar-
             goyles. And they pulled back and you see it is not a
             gargoyle, it's Batman. But then to have him standing
             there, you know, heroically, you know. It didn't fit in
             what you were portraying by the entire film . . . that
             was another point they [the audience] didn't go for.

The interpretive process going on throughout King's description becomes clearer, and we begin to see how clues missed by a general
audience can be discarded by comic book initiates. King references the
original script, transtextual analysis, and resituates the clue—Batman's
heroic stance at the close of the movie—into a more appropriate (to
him) context: the Superman universe of heroic righteousness, rather
than the murkily neurotic world of Batman. *Batman* is ambiguous
because it sends mixed messages to the comic books fans that are
outside the contextual experience of the general audience.

King next sees the movie after the reviews have come out, with an
audience that has been trained to read the movie by the reviews:

King: The second time I saw it the audience did go crazy
             for it, but it was, like, more of a general audience, of
             people who wanted to see this film.

Bacon-Smith: So, when did you see it the second time?

King: The second time I saw it on the weekend. We saw it
             in New Jersey. . . . Things that didn't work the first
             time did work the second time, you know, like be-
             cause uh, the underplayed Batman, at first it didn't
             work for me. I'm going, 'well, it's his movie. It's not
             the Joker's film. But, a friend of mine pointed out
             something that I'd said, and reversed the thought on
             me, and I said, you know, 'now it does make sense.'
             That I was saying like the audience in a sense is kind
             of like Gotham City. The audience is—we are all

> Gothamites, because we don't know anything about
> Batman, and we are finding out about Batman the
> same time as Gotham City and Vicki Vale does.

Here we find the most interesting aspect of 'rehabilitation.' Fans, because they are fans, want to like the products that feature their interest. When the product falls short of fulfilling the fans' need, viewers make use of an extreme form of traditional fill-in-the-blanks interpretation. Rather than fill in the action with what the movie has led them to assume should be there, fans substitute plot twists that change the meaning of the on-screen evidence. As an important part of this process, fans impute to the creators of the film conscious motivations for the unsatisfying direction of the film (which may or may not have actually guided the film) that allow the viewer to see the film "in a different light":

> King: And, of course the Joker comes across as more flam-
>   boyant, because, as he says in the film, you know,
>   'Where's Batman? He's home somewhere. I'm here
>   giving out money.' You know, the Joker is this kind
>   of flamboyant image, and the contrast is, to most
>   people, so like, here's this guy dressed as a clown,
>   who you're seeing on television. . .
>   And Batman is this shadowy thing that you didn't
>   know who or what he was. And then, it worked, you
>   know. At first it's more like, well, you didn't make
>   him, you know, "Batman" as efficient as he is in the
>   comic books, and he came across slightly inept. But
>   the understanding again is, against the Joker, who in
>   a sense has been mentally the Joker since day one,
>   You know, the chemical just gave him a new motif,
>   you know. Batman was basically a new person.

Sometimes, however, even these efforts to rehabilitate the film break down. We can hear the distress in the repetition of the key phrase, "hero line," and in his anticipation of criticism of Batman in the same scene:

> I mean like, in a scene where you know, Batman's strafing the ground,
> and the Joker gets—he gets a *hero* line, you know. He looks at the
> batwing, and the Joker says, "come and get me you grotesque son of
> a bitch." And that's a hero-line. In any other film, that's what the
> hero says when the villain, the monster, the creature comes rushing
> at him. . . .

Still, the unequal positions of Batman and the Joker seemed to bother
him:

> And you know, I say Nicholson and the character are so flamboyant
> that they kept stealing scenes right out of the hands of Batman, you
> know. The fight scene at the end of the movie, when Batman is
> beating him up is like, really exciting. And then there's the one hit
> where, you know, the Joker falls back, and like is a bloody mess and
> drops something out of his mouth and we all jump back, and it's
> chattering teeth. He's just stolen the scene away. . . . It's bizarre,
> because you are feeling, you know, "what a great guy!" for a madman.

The Anime Society

The society meets the second Friday of every month in three rooms
on the ground floor of the Friends' Service Committee building at
Thirteenth and Spruce Streets in downtown Philadelphia. Members
gather to watch Japanese animated films in the back room, to buy
Manga—Japanese comic books—in the center room, and to talk comics
of every kind in the outer lobby. Martin King is a member, as are many
of the Friday afternoon regulars at Fat Jack's. These days the most
discussed books other than the Japanese are *The Sandman* and *Watch-
man* series. Few members continue to follow the traditional superheroes regularly, but everyone we interviewed had read them, and continued to keep a casual eye on the developments in that form.

Like other comic book fans, many Anime Society members already
had seen the film *Batman* when we talked to them at the July 8th
meeting. Again like other fans, their opinions varied, from those such
as fan artist Sue Humphries who hated the film, to others including a
group of friends who loved it in spite of its flaws:

> Humphries: I saw the movie. . . . I thought the movie stank.
>
> Bacon-Smith: Did you have any reason for thinking it stank?
>
> Humphries: Yes, I have lots of reasons, you want my list? Keaton
>   should not have played Batman. He's supposed to
>   be a 'millionaire playboy', right? Well, he got the
>   eccentric and millionaire part right, but that was a
>   recluse, not a playboy (laughs). Problem number one.
>   Problem number two . . . Where did it [the Batman-
>   Vicki Vale relationship] come from? . . .
>   But they spent more time developing the Joker's
>   character—and they let you know that he was a little
>   bit crazy to begin with. Getting shot through the face,
>   and, and falling into the chemicals, and seeing what

his face looks like drove him really crazy. And so you know what the hell is going on in his brain. But they just whisked by the history of Bruce Wayne. You don't know. I mean, really, he went through a helluva a lotta training, y'know, he worked himself, (pounds table), he was a maniac (pounds table loudly). In order to do what he was doing. And they—skipped it. They just left it all out. So you don't have any of his real motivations.

It just didn't work. I mean, I can't find one thing that I really liked about the movie . . . especially not with all that hype, it sure as hell wasn't worth all that hype. I'm glad I saw it as a matinee.

Judging the movie against its publicity much as a voter judges a politician's actions against his campaign promises, Sue Humphries finds the movie lacking—a disappointment because it does not keep its promises. Other fans at the Anime Society disagreed with her assessment, judging the movie on different terms:

Fan One: I loved it. . . . I think they kept it fairly faithful to what was expected of it as far as the actual story content, such as what some of the better writers have done.

Um, like you said, the city was the big thing. There was a complete aspect. You felt as if you were within Gotham City, you weren't just watching it as much. . . . I especially liked, for example, the way they amalgamated everything from the thirties to the eighties in one sort of non-time universe if you will, because if you take a look, you'll notice, although the women dress fairly fashionably in the film, all the men are dressed in forties pinstripe suits and things of that nature. . . . Uh, also if you noticed, there was other scenes where, for example, the reporter is using a little microcassette recorder, but during the press conference, the microphones they are using to talk into are those big 1940s radio microphones. And, Uh, I liked a lot of that throughout.

Perhaps the film was slightly misnamed. It should have been renamed *The Joker meets Batman*, but uh, I know, in fact me and my friends had a big discussion as to why that is, and a big theory going around is that Tim Burton the director made the decision that was cognizant, that was, that everyone would think that Jack Nicholson as the Joker was brilliant casting,

> but a huge amount of the fans sat around and said,
> "Michael Keaton? Mr. Mom? He can't be Batman,"
> and so—

Humphries: He couldn't—

Fan One: I thought he was brilliant, thank you kindly.

Humphries: Well I thought he stank.

Bacon-Smith: (to Fan One) Why did you think he was good?

Fan One: Well, I liked the haunted quality he gave the character.

At this point, the discussion becomes heated, neither side willing to
modify their opinion of Keaton's performance. Since fans regularly stir
up such controversy for the fun of the argument, it becomes impossible
to determine whether the informant believes what he says about Keaton's Batman, or rather, has taken that position for the pleasure of the
debate. It is clear, however, that the informant did enjoy certain aspects
of the film, in particular the setting.[15] When a friend walks by, he too
is invited to join in the debate:

Fan One: (to Fan Two) What did you think of the Batman film?

Bacon-Smith: Yeah, what did you think of it?

Fan Two: All right.

Bacon Smith: All right. What did you expect it—I mean, was it not
as much as you expected?

Fan Two: The characters, well, I didn't know what to expect of
the Batman, you know. Michael Keaton's portrayal—
Well, strike that. I knew that when Michael Keaton
didn't have the costume on, he was going to do a
really good job as—when the costume's not on, either
as Bruce Wayne, walking around, you know, doing
stuff as Batman. But when he put the costume on, I
didn't know what was going to happen. He's not a
physical kind of actor. I didn't know whether or not
he could carry it off. He did a credible job. I mean . . .
I didn't get the impression that this guy was, has
trained all of, I got the impression that this guy was
um, instead of being like a superhero kind of or even—
Superhero capital S, or super hero, separate word like
a Rambo type, I got the impression that this was
really more like a normal guy who had access to high

technology for the time, was wearing a suit and was
using it and was competent in its use.

The newest member of the discussion explicated a clear understanding of the various hero motifs available to genre movies: the hero
defined as superior by his difference from the normal—nonmutated
human—man, by the exaggeration of human strength and cunning, and
by technological virtuosity. He accepts Keaton's Batman as consistent
with the category of the technological virtuoso—more like *Aliens'*
Ripley than Jor-el's son in *Superman,* but finds fault with the movie on
another level:

> But, uh, the thing I guess that was mediocre to me was uh, the story
> itself wasn't compelling. I mean, I mean, Bruce Wayne just sorta got
> rolled out there, and Jack Nics- Nicholson, Joker got rolled out there
> and they threw in this Vicki Vale, and everybody just sorta just rolled
> in and rolled out. . . . There was no story, no driving motivating plot.
> It was all handled so—crummily. That's why I said—It was alright—
> It didn't live up to the hype at all (laughs) but then again nothing
> could've.

As fans process the movie-going experience, they preferentially focused on aspects of particular interest to themselves. If those parts of
the movie work—for the first male informant in the Anime interview,
the setting and the character of the Joker grabbed his attention and held
it—then the fan is willing to accept or rationalize flaws in the rest of
the film. If, on the other hand, the movie happens to fail at a key focus
point—for Sue Humphries, the portrayal of Bruce Wayne's relationships
and his development as a driven crusader —the fan will respond with
anger rather than a willingness to rationalize the film into an acceptable
configuration. For fans like the second male in the interview, a pedes-
trian handling of their interest—in this case, the story—results in a
lukewarm reaction, regardless of the tour-de-force presentation or the
absolute failure of other parts of the film.

The Theaters

By contrast to the elaborate processing of the Anime community, the
immediate response to *Batman* reflected only partial processing of the
film. Immediate attention skipped along the surface of this film: exit
interviews done at separate screenings of the film show that *Batman*
worked best as an event. When interviewed immediately after seeing
the film, audience response was strongly positive, as this group's reac-

tion demonstrates. When asked what they thought of the movie immediately following the 11:00 a.m. showing at the Olde City Cinema, the
group of five White adult males and one White adult woman responded
in language typical of exit responses shown both on local news programs, and on televised "news magazines" such as *Entertainment Tonight:*

> First male viewer: Amazing.
>
> Second male viewer: It was incredible. . . .
>
> Third male viewer: Very, very excellent movie.
>
> Second male viewer: Incredible.
>
> Yarbrough: What did you like about it?
>
> First male viewer: Everything. (group laughs)

A group of Black teen comic book fans leaving the 2:30 showing on
opening day responded with equal enthusiasm:

> Teen: I loved it.
>
> Bacon-Smith: OK. Now, what'd you love about it?
>
> Teen: (pause) I love Batman. Batman, Bruce Wayne, Vicki
> Vale, ah yes, Vicki Vale.
>
> Bacon-Smith: Now I gather from this conversation that you guys
> are comic book fans.
>
> Teen: Yeah . . . Yes . . . Yes we are . . . Wolverine! (group
> laughs, lists other favorites)
>
> Bacon-Smith: So, what did you think of this movie, what was your
> favorite part of the movie?
>
> Teen: Every time the Joker showed up.
>
> (background):   Yeah, the Joker . . . Yeah, the Joker.
>
> Teen: Yeah,'cause he gave him a run for Batman's money.
>
> Bacon-Smith: Well, that's the truth. Now what did you think of
> Batman in this movie?
>
> Teen: He was pretty good.
>
> Teen: I think, I think they, uh . . . they, they matched it up
> with the comic real well. There was nothing that
> was different and nothing was phony about it. It was
> original. Y'know, it was from Bob Kane, it was, it was
> still pretty good.

Bacon-Smith:	Everybody think that?
(unison):	Yeah, yeah . . .
Bacon-Smith:	So the guy who did Batman did a good job?
(together):	Yes . . . yeah . . . Eventually he did.
Bacon-Smith:	Now how 'bout Vicki Vale?
(together):	She played . . . She was fine [good-looking] . . . Kim Basinger . . . (laughs)
Teen:	But Jack Nicholson was a classic as the Joker . . .
(background):	Oh, yeah . . . Yeah, he was . . .
Teen:	. . . nobody, ain't nobody who could top him on that. Nobody.

Immediately after seeing the movie, fan enthusiasm bubbled over, but the focus of the attention was, as always, the Joker. The viewers brought the discussion back to Nicholson's character in spite of the interviewer's efforts to divert it to other characters of the movie. One of the members of this latter group had already seen the film twice, and like the rest of the group, he still seemed high on the experience.

Conclusion

While the two films differ in striking ways, the response of comic book fans to the *Batman* movie compares more closely to that of Star Trek fans when *Star Trek: The Motion Picture* first appeared than to the slow-building cult following of films like *Blade Runner* and *Brazil* to which the reviewers consistently refer. Like the Star Trek film, *Batman* appeared after many years of struggle to make the movie, a struggle in which the fans participated vicariously through the fan and professional press and word-of-mouth. Fans awaited the finished product with equal shares of excitement and forboding—would the producers get it right? Fans (and mainstream audiences) went to the movie in its opening weeks in droves and returned to see the film many times in its first run in spite of serious misgivings many viewers had about some parts of the movie. And fans discussed the movie endlessly, trying to reconcile the conflicting images of the film to the pre-existing model of the characters and settings they already had in their heads.

Ultimately, however, Star Trek fans discarded *The Motion Picture* for the very reasons that Batman fans complain about their film: in reaching for an excess of setting, and relying on special effects and set pieces, the filmmakers failed to build a continuation of the character development and relationships fans already knew. The Star Trek fan community considers the original series episodes, some of the cartoon episodes, and three of the films "real" Star Trek—the canon. *The Motion Picture* (and *Star Trek V*) are not considered part of the ongoing macrotext made up of the other products. Among comic book fans, this same process is already at work with the *Batman* movie. While fans continue to argue the points at which the movie agrees and those at which it diverges from the most commonly held images of Batman, no fans talk about the movie as part of the repertoire of Batman representations accepted as "real" in the community.

For comic books fans, as for Star Trek fans before them, however, the movie serves one vital purpose: it represents them to the outside world. For mainstream audiences to accept the Batman film means that to some extent they accept the comic book fan as well. As long-time fan and professional comic book artist Randy DuBurke explained at the Greenberg comic convention:

> ... [I]t seems to me that a lot of these people [fans] felt like film legitimizes the character—that if it was done on celluloid, y'know, you can say to your friends or family or something, who are telling you that comics are crap, "well, see it can't be bad, it's up on film." And particularly if they see that it's done the way that they want it to be done, so that they see it has a lot of potential—And you know that thing when you feel like you want to share with everybody and also prove to them that "I'm not reading junk?" And so I feel like film legitimizes the character.

APPENDIX A

Sample response chart, AMC Walnut III theatre preview showing of *Batman*

Film Action	Audience Response
Family pushes through crowd— "don't act like a tourist"	laughter
Family gets mugged	restless, inattentive
Batman silhouette on rooftops	some muttered comments
Mugger in doorway, "American Express, don't leave home without it."	laughter, recognition (intertextual, not textual response)
Batman is shot	laughter
Batman gets up	more laughter
"I'm Batman"	first applause of movie

Harvey Dent (Billy Dee Williams) picture at banquet.	recognition laughter, but general restlessness, inattention, movement. Some audience members leave theater, return.
Jack Napier (Nicholson) appears on screen.	ripple of interest, murmur in audience
Nicholson/Hall exchange—to Alicia's flattery, Napier: "I didn't ask"	huge applause, but still seems to be recognition from the promos, not engagement with the film
Eckhardt line about muggers— "Drinking Draino," later, Knox asks about Batman's salary	laughter, but response again seems more to do with incongruous introduction of outside world in film, not engagement
Napier and Eckhardt payoff	quiet, one woman comments, "He [Napier] looks wicked."
Napier, "Better be sure," as sidekick points gun at Eckhardt	laughter
"Have you seen this man?" Kane illustration of bat in three piece suit.	smattering of laughter, no general response
Vicki Vale's first appearance	wolf whistles
Knox "If you want me to pose nude, you'll need a longer lens"	ribald laughter
Vale rejects Knox marriage proposal	laughter
Carl Grissom's first appearance	murmur of questions and recognition—"Who is that? Jack Palance. Oh."
Jerry Hall/Alicia reappears	comments "who is she? Mick Jagger's wife." still reacting intertextually, not textually
Casino scene	audience chats, pays little attention to the screen
Bruce Wayne appears	no widespread response or increase in attention
Knox tips Alfred the butler	mild laughter

Vicki Vale meets Bruce Wayne, doesn't know who hc is	small, conspiratorial titter, but not a lot of attention to screen
Alfred picking up after Wayne	laughter, response picks up
Mayor of Gotham	one voice: "That's Koch, isn't he?" but overall drifting of attention
Vicki and Knox in hall of armor	audience begins to pay attention again, gets quiet. Banter earns small laugh.
Knox about a suit of armor: "King of the Wicker People"	big laugh
Bruce Wayne knows armor is from Japan because that's where he bought it—Knox and Vale realize who he is.	another explosive laugh. Audience shares in the joke on the secondary characters (finally they know more than the people on screen)
Alfred enters to draw Wayne to the command center. Banter about grant	short laugh (comment—"Alfred's on the ball")
Axis Chemical plant fight scene	little attention, comment, "chicken ass" derogatory about the scene, people leave theater, small children in next row talk and ignore movie
Napier pulls a gun	audience stirs, grows somewhat more attentive
Napier to Batman: "Nice outfit."	small laugh
Napier turns away, Batman disappears	small laugh
Napier & Batman fight, Napier falls into vat of acid	audience gasps, general comments, "Oh, my God," etc.
Commissioner Gordon says "Keep a lid on it" (Batman's existence)	conspiratorial laughter
Joker's whitened hand emerges from river	little reaction
Joker's bandages are removed	audience quiet and tense
Wayne Manor appears	interest drops dramatically, audience stirs, talks and

	shushes, leaving and returning, ask "What did I miss?" answer, "Nothing."
Bruce & Vicki seated far apart at table	perfunctory laughter
Bruce Wayne "I've never been in this room before."	Big laugh
Kitchen scene/seduction on staircase	no response, loss of interest
Joker confronts Grissom, speaks from shadows	attention returns to screen, nervous giggles
Joker to Grissom: "As you can see, I'm a lot happier now."	big laugh
Joker shoots Grissom, dancing	big laugh
Joker line, "eh, what a day"	big laugh, and applause
Joker, at Grissom's desk, mugging	low, unsure laugh

Notes

1. This is particularly true of many culture criticism scholars, and Radway's *Reading the Romance*, (Chapel Hill: University of North Carolina Press, 1984) is a good example of this kind of work.

2. The two best known of Dell Hymes' works are *In Vain I Tried to Tell You* (Philadelphia: University of Pennsylvania Press, 1981), and *Foundations in Sociolinguistics* (Philadelphia: University of Pennsylvania Press, 1974). Unfortunately, Hymes has not published much of his most seminal work. My own understanding of his methods and theories comes from working with the Hymeses and their students over many years.

3. Fans of the Honeymooners.

4. Comic book fan term for Spiderman, a favorite character.

5. Comic book fan term for Superman. Fans do not use the nicknames consistently, but as a humorous marker of long-term affection for the book or character.

6. This is the problem Clifford Geertz addressed in his seminal theoretical article, "Thick Description," in *The Interpretation of Cultures* (New York: Basic Books, 1973).

7. Class is a complex concept to define, but for the purposes of this article, is based on property values, educational values (educational levels of adults and per-child spending on public schooling), speech patterns, and other factors.

8. In all, eleven books received two votes.

9. Based on volume, duration and enthusiasm of applause and verbal response, with ten the most enthusiastic, and one being silence.

10. David Bordwell, *Narration in the Fiction Film*, (Madison, WI: University of Wisconsin Press, 1985), p. 45.

11. Bordwell uses cognitive theory and textually extrapolated spectators to describe how audiences learn to anticipate the action in narrative film. Ethnographic methods can be used to observe changes in the nature or amount of ongoing audible or visually kinesic activity in the auditorium as audiences anticipate response. When response anticipates sequence, there is generally some sign of growing expectation—viewing partners nudging each other with the elbow is an obvious example—that is released with an audience reaction not only to the scene, but also to the vindication of the anticipation—viewing partners may look at each other, to follow the previous example—when the action occurs. Similar observations can be made to recognize the lag in response.

12. The two newspapers, produced by the same ownership from the same building, are distinguished by format, and target reading level. *The Daily News* is tabloid style, with a single front page photograph that takes up at least one-half of the page. The large-type headline usually completes the page, with a page reference for the story below the headline. Target reading level is adult at the fifth to seventh grade reading level. *The Philadelphia Inquirer* is large-format (like *The New York Times*), with the major stories of the day presented on the front page. Its target reading level is about adult tenth grade.

13. Gary Thompson, "The Joker is Wild!" *Philadelphia Daily News*, June 23, 1989.

14. All of the interviews quoted here are verbatim transcripts of the spoken record, based on the most rigourous possible ethnolinguistic methods. As ethnolinguistic scholars, we follow the philosophy that to modify the recorded speech of a participant in a culture to norms that we find more aesthetically satisfying does not empower that person, but rather, deprives that person of the dignity of his own way of speaking. Modifying the speech of our informants also performs a disservice to ethnolinguists to come, who may want to study the texts linguistically.

15. A clear marker of the fan's interest in the setting of the film is the wealth of detail he offers to substantiate his opinion, and which detail is lacking in his discussion of Michael Keaton's portrayal of the Batman character.

7

Same Bat Channel, Different Bat Times: Mass Culture and Popular Memory

Lynn Spigel and Henry Jenkins

I don't know about the rest of you,
but I feel the cruelest
nostalgia—not for the past—
but nostalgia for the present.
Andrei Voznesensky

Batmania hit hard in the summer of 1989, bringing with it a wave of nostalgia that superceded the dark postmodern text projected on the nation's cinema screens.[1] As the truly hysterical Joker danced with the Devil in the pale moonlight, Batmania sparked memories of a better world where good guys always finished first, if only through a camp sensibility. *Batman* and the gift shop craze of high-ticket memorabilia provoked fond longings for an innocent world of childish play where kids once gathered on back porches, imitating their favorite TV heroes. This super-commercialized comic book text gave rise to a potent historical fantasy as people reappropriated the past to restructure the present.

Looking backward is a major preoccupation of historians, but it is also something that people do in personal daydreams and everyday contexts as a way to understand their present-day lives. History and memory have traditionally remained separate projects—one highly objective and rational, the other highly subjective and playful. In relatively recent years, historians have questioned this set of "common sense" oppositions by thinking about the interplay between memory and history in a variety of ways. Intellectual and cultural historians, most notably David Lowenthal, have examined how the idea of memory has been used in various historical and cultural contexts, linking the concept of memory to the ways in which historical consciousness has functioned throughout time.[2] Lowenthal's wide-reaching arguments consider literary and historiographical texts as well as recent research in cognitive psychology that studies "real uses of memory in humanly understandable situations."[3] Other historians have examined popular conceptions of the past by using methods of oral history. For example, working within the fields of folklore, anthropology and history, "ethnohistorians" have tied historical methods to anthropological models in an attempt to explain how people from non-literate cultures use oral traditions and storytelling practices in their everyday life.[4] Other historians have concentrated on modern Western cultures, typically using oral sources as a way to do social history or "history from below." These studies incorporate voices of everyday people into the historical narrative, and in a dialogical manner, often give community members opportunities to use their own historical consciousness in politically relevant ways. The community activist work of Britain's History Workshop and America's Massachusetts History Workshop are exemplary of this use of oral sources within an explicitly political activist agenda.[5]

Important as oral history is, it tends to sidestep the question of exactly what these oral utterances represent. Although these histories often ask how oral testimony functions as evidence in an empirical sense (are these memories true or false representations of the past?), they say little about the larger theoretical and historiographical problems entailed. What do oral testimonies tell us about the nature of historical consciousness? How much are these testimonies based on prepackaged and culturally agreed upon notions of the past? Finally, how does the historian give voice to these memories? Are we simply a transparent medium for other people's speech, or does the process of history writing itself tailor these remembrances in specific ways?[6]

Indeed, past experiences, whether academic or personal, can never be directly reclaimed or relived; they can only be comprehended through the construction of narratives that reshape the past in response to current needs, desires and perspectives. As Hayden White has argued, the craft of the historian involves the "emplotment" of past events into familiar narratives that make sense to people in the present. This emplotment necessarily insures that the telling of history is bound by discursive conventions that simplify and reduce the multiplicity of past events.[7] Although accepting White's basic intervention, Dominique La Capra has offered an important caveat when he claims that "White's poetics of historiography stem from a neo-idealist and formalist conception of the mind of the historian as a free-shaping agent with respect to an inert, neutral documentary record. . . . This view tended to obscure both the way people in the past lived, told, and wrote 'stories' and the way the documentary record is itself always textually processed before any given historian comes to it."[8] La Capra's challenge is one that is necessarily unresolvable in any complete way, but it does suggest the need to form a dialogue between historical conventions of writing and the way language is used in everyday life.

For historians interested in the interplay between mass media and audiences, this is particularly important since we are involved in writing historical narratives about people's encounters with storytelling practices of a prior era. Although we will never be able to recapture subjective experiences of the past in any definitive way, it is possible to provide partial pictures by reconstructing dialogues between audiences and texts. Along these lines, George Lipsitz, Colin MacCabe, Roy Rosensweig, and others have considered the way media texts evoke and shape memories of the past.[9] In this essay we would like to build upon this work by looking at the way memories have reshaped the popular myths surrounding a superhero. What interests us particularly about Batman is the way this comic book hero has retained cultural significance since Bob Kane created him for DC comics in 1939. Over the past fifty years the caped crusader has battled crime in the Columbia serials of the 1940s, the TV version and feature length movie of the late 1960s, Frank Miller's *Dark Knight Returns* and other graphic novels of the 1980s, and the 1989 blockbuster movie. Along the way, his image was licensed to toy companies like Ideal and Mego that produced everything from Bat action figures to Bat periscopes. Batman, then, has become part of our culture's popular memory. Why those memories persist and how they function in everyday life presents a fascinating set of questions for cultural historians.

Writing about *Batman* in the summer of 1989, it became difficult to separate the nostalgic memorabilia and TV re-runs from the television *Batman* of 1966 that we sought to explain. For us, like many of our generation, the series evoked vivid images: dime-store heroes and vampish heroines, summer nights with the TV flickering pop art images, children dressed for Halloween, bat toys we never had. In short, *Batman* seemed a point of entry into children's culture of the 1960s, and it also provided a clue to yuppie culture of the late 1980s because these memories seemed to constitute a common heritage of a particular adult generation.

Rather than seeing these subjective and often emotional memories as an obstacle to overcome, we decided to incorporate them into our study by setting up a dialogue between our own historical writing and current recollections of the TV program. Unlike academic history, popular memory is integral to everyday experience; it is memory for the public, and understood as being contingent and open rather than definitive and closed. Popular memories are part of the living culture; they are adopted in ways that make them useful for and relevant to present-day situations.

In addition, popular memory is grounded in notions of personal identity. Unlike historical writing conventions that demand the minimalization of authorial commentary, popular memory is based on the dialectic between autobiography and the description of public events. This autobiographical element continually entwines the past in present-day identities, so that people strive to place themselves in history, using the past as a way to understand their current lives. As John A. Robinson suggests, "There is a generative dimension to remembering that mediates the matching of past and present . . . . Autobiographical memory is not only a record, it is a resource."[10]

The following essay examines how *Batman* was received by television critics and audiences at the time of its initial airing on ABC in 1966–68, and then focuses on the way that present-day people who were children at the time remember *Batman* and use it in their construction of autobiographical history. For this latter section of the essay we interviewed adults who were children at the time of *Batman*'s first run on network TV. Certainly these interviews will not reflect directly how people interpreted *Batman* in their youth; rather they will suggest how people use *Batman* as adults to reconstruct their childhood memories and personal histories. Taken as a whole, the study begins to reveal how the initial critical response to *Batman* differs from long-range memories of it, and more generally it suggests how the reactivation of television in everyday memory might intersect with academic histories of popular culture.

Commercial Into Pop Into Art Into Camp

In 1966, *Mad* magazine asked, "Would a typical red-blooded teenage boy really be happy dressing in some far-out costume and spending all his free time chasing crooks?" In standard parodic prose, the magazine showed the "Boy Wonderful," driven "batty," by his association with the caped crusader, trying to overcome public ridicule by plotting his superior's death. Forced to recognize his ward's embarrassment, the more TV-literate "Bats-man" reminds his earnest sidekick:

> What difference does it make if they laugh, as long as they watch the program! For years TV tried to reach the so-called sophisticates with "Playhouse 90," "The Defenders," etc. But they wouldn't even turn on their sets. Then along came "Bats-man" and the industry made a revolutionary discovery. Give the "in" group garbage—make the show bad enough and they'll call it "camp" and stay glued to their sets!

Grasping the logic of this industry rhetoric, the "Boy Wonderful" shouts, "Holy Nielsen! You mean the swingers are really squarer than the squares?"[11]

This exchange encapsulates the contradictory reception of *Batman* in the 1960s. Like the Boy Wonderful, some critics saw the series as an embarrassing blight on their good taste and cultural standing. Savvy ABC executives were likely to identify with the slick and supercilious attitudes of the jaded "Bats-man" who is willing to sacrifice critical dignity for big money profits. Still others, less idealistic or cynical than either of *Mad*'s two extremes, entered the fray and battled, often with ambivalent attitudes, over the series' uncomfortable position within the traditional canon of television art.

Upon its initial premiere in 1966, *Batman* evoked a series of critical disputes. Influential East Coast critics, who had typically derided Hollywood's half-hour series, were undecided about how to place the program in existing cultural hierarchies. For many of these critics, *Batman* appeared to be an emblematic example of commercial trash with its childish heroes, melodramatic plots, and formulaic structure. *Batman* thus defied the golden rules of "Golden Age" critics who elevated programs that perpetuated TV's "hyperrealism," its complete simulation of real-life events.

Indeed, Golden Age newspaper and magazine critics like Jack Gould, Gilbert Seldes, and John Crosby claimed that television was best when it presented a heightened sense of reality, when it made viewers feel as if they were actually on the scene, watching a performance in a theater. For this reason, critics typically elevated the live broadcast over and above filmed presentations. As Seldes told prospective television writers in 1952, "The essence of television techniques is their contribution to the sense of immediacy . . . they [audiences] feel that what they see and hear [on television] is happening in the present and is therefore more real than anything taken and cut and dried which has the feel of the past." Similarly in 1956, Gould claimed in the *New York Times Magazine* that live television was better than film because it "unites the individual at home with the event afar. The viewer has a chance to be in two places at once. Physically, he may be at his own hearthside but intellectually, and above all, emotionally, he is at the cameraman's side."[12] Critics argued that the immediacy of live presentation was enhanced by slice-of-life stories, characterizations that were drawn with psychological depth, naturalistic acting styles, and shooting strategies that gave the home audience an intimate "box seat" view of the performance.[13] Indeed, for television's first critics this hyperrealist aesthetic with its stress on intimacy, immediacy and presence was the preferred form for television programs. Within this hierarchy, the live anthology drama and reality-based news series like *See It Now* reigned supreme.

By the time of *Batman*'s appearance in 1966, the number of programs that met these criteria had dwindled considerably. After 1955, the networks increasingly replaced their expensive live formats with relatively cheap filmed westerns, sit-coms and adventure shows produced by Hollywood studios. Critics lashed out against these "degraded" texts, often attacking the regulatory and industrial system that allowed television to be invaded by inferior product.[14] In 1961, in response to these developments, Federal Communications Commission (FCC) Chair Newton Minow told the National Association of Broadcasters that television was a "vast wasteland" in need of cultural reform. Minow's reform plans centered around the aesthetic hierarchies of the Golden Age critics, calling for more reality-based, educational programs and fewer game shows, sit-coms and westerns. Meanwhile, the critics adopted Minow's phrase, applying it to the commercially successful and highly popular series that failed to capture the sense of presence and intimacy so crucial to their notions of TV art. From this perspective, the decidedly unrealistic elements of *Batman* placed it in the outer limits of the critical canon. However, in the mid-sixties this kind of criticism was disrupted by the new aesthetic of Popism, which challenged the aesthetic categories of Golden Age discourses. Andy Warhol's Pop creations valorized mass art by appropriating commercial practices for use in high art circles.[15] Beginning in the early sixties, Warhol used the techniques of slide screen projection and stenciling to paint over the comic book outlines of Batman and Superman. He applied similar techniques of photo-screen processing to real life celebrities ranging from movie queens such as Elizabeth Taylor to political leaders such as Chairman Mao, and also used it to mass produce life-like replicas of consumer goods, most notably his Campbell soup cans. By applying mass production techniques to portraiture and by using popular icons as artist's models, Warhol flattened out distinctions between "good" and "bad" art. Art was no longer defined by subjective states of talent, greatness, and beauty. Instead, Pop revelled in cartoonish characters, cheap industrial tools, gimmicky special effects, a flattened-out and exaggerated sense of color, repetitious imagery, and factory-like production.

Not incidentally, all of these aesthetic principles were also part of television's dominant practice, and the striking similarities between Popism and television style were not lost on the East Coast television critics. However, while Warhol and his haute couture followers rejoiced in recycling the low for higher pleasures, the TV critics were uneasy about assigning value to what they traditionally viewed as cultural debris. Indeed, Popism completely disrupted the typical criteria for judging television. Whereas TV critics valorized programs that simulated reality and invited viewers to participate intimately with the "real" event represented on the TV screen, Pop denied this illusionary social relationship between viewer and text. In Pop, the image was the image and the viewer was the consumer, pure and simple. Pop replaced TV's hyperrealism with hypercommercialism. For TV critics who lived through the sponsor boycotts of McCarthyism and the histrionics of the quiz show scandals, this valorization of commercialism must have been particularly hard to take. However, since these critics also travelled in New York art circles, they had trouble ignoring the fact that Popism was the latest thing in museums, fashion magazines, and even in the New York theater where Superman and *Mad* were both adapted for theatrical presentation.

In this context, *Batman* precipitated a questioning of critical hierarchies because it self-consciously placed itself within the Pop art scene. While shows like *Bewitched, Mr. Ed*, and *My Favorite Martian* stretched the limits of TV's realist aesthetic, *Batman* laughed in the face of realism, making it difficult for critics to dismiss the program as one more example of TV's puerile content. *Batman* presented these critics with the particularly chilling possibility that this childish text was really the ultimate in art circle chic. As *Life* claimed in 1966, "Pop art and the cult of Camp have turned Superman and Batman into members of the intellectual community, and what the kids used to devour in comic books has become a staple in avant-garde art."[16]

ABC used the Pop aesthetic as a promotional and publicity vehicle, giving the show cultural status by hyperbolically referring to its Warholian aspects. For the premier episode the network scheduled a "cocktail and frug" party at the fashionable New York discothèque, Harlow's, with Andy Warhol, Harold Prince (director of the League of New York Theaters) and other celebrities attending the event. (Jackie Kennedy, already immortalized in Pop iconography on Warhol's canvas, rejected ABC's invitation.) After cocktails, ABC invited the group to see a special screening of *Batman* at the York Theater, whose lobby was adorned with Batman drawings and stickers that sported slogans proclaiming their status as "authentic pop art." Guests at the York were reportedly unexcited about the show, but in true Pop style, they cheered when a commercial for corn flakes came on the screen. *Batman* was thus promoted as being part of a larger Pop art scene where unlikely mixtures of social elites gathered to celebrate their own celebrity-hood while getting high on mass culture. As one person at the York Theater said, "The real pop art . . . are the people who are attending this party."[17]

Television critics often had trouble reconciling Popism with their own cultural hierarchies and expressed highly ambivalent sentiments. Jack Gould, the veteran television critic for the *New York Times*, admitted that the program was "a belated extension of the phenomenon of Pop Art to the television medium," and as such might "be an unforeseen blessing in major proportions." But with an intonation of sly irony and an acknowledgement of his dubious role as television critic in this case, he also cautioned that Pop art had its own inverted standards, and that *Batman* "might not be adequately bad" when compared to *Green Acres* and *Camp Runamuck*."[18] Similarly one reviewer for the *Saturday Evening Post* claimed:

> The pop-art fad, one of whose twitches is an enthusiasm for old comic books, had made *Batman* almost flopproof. As long as the pop fad lasted there could be no such things as bad pop art. . . . *Batman* is a success because it is television doing what television does best: doing things badly. *Batman*, in other words, is so bad, it's good. . . . *Batman* translated from one junk medium into another is junk squared. But it is thoroughly successful and—this troubles critics for whom good and bad are art's only poles—it can be surprisingly likable.[19]

In this case as elsewhere, the TV critic felt obliged to express his chic understanding of the new Pop aesthetic, even as he mistrusted its ultimate merits.

If Pop presented irresolvable anxieties for the critics, they eased these tensions by shifting their focus to *Batman*'s "camp" qualities. They typically displaced their confusions about the changing status of good and bad art by proposing cultural splits in terms of reception aesthetics. *Batman*, they argued, had two distinct audience groups—adults who understood the program through camp reception practices and children who interpreted *Batman* as a fantasy portrayal of real life.[20] *Time* magazine saw *Batman* as a shift from television's "single-standard" that demanded "simple-minded cartoons for kids [and] simple-minded programs . . . for adults" towards a style of entertainment open to multiple interpretations. While the kids took *Batman* "seriously," the grown ups were "supposed to see Batman as camp." Similarly, *Newsweek* reported that "Adults like him [Batman] as a campy put-on. Children thought of him as a hero." According to one report in the *Saturday Evening Post*, this dual address even created domestic conflicts: "*Batman*-watching families with eight-year-olds in them are torn with dissention because of the 'Daddy, stop laughing' problem."[21]

The camp sensibility gave adult readers, who had previously displayed disdain for mass culture, a comfortable distance from the show's comic book materials because it reworked the aesthetics of Popism in a way more in line with the firmly entrenched "wasteland" critique. Having earned a legitimate intellectual status after Susan Sontag's 1964 essay "Notes On Camp," camp was particularly high cultural capital for television critics at the time.[22] In its earliest years, Popism was virtuous in its appeal to mass culture; the Pop sensibility exalted in a commercial sublime where mass art was experienced with a kind of detached exhilaration.²³ Camp, however, was playful. It reread mass culture through irony. Its appeal was based on laughing at the empty ideals of outworn texts and faded stars, and for some oppressed groups, this ironic pose was a particularly liberating reception practice. Gay men, for example, resurrected stars such as Judy Garland, Joan Crawford and Montgomery Clift, stars whose tragic life-histories threw their romanticized film images into relief. But if camp provided gay men with viewing strategies that expressed their own marginalization from dominant modes of representation, it allowed straight readers to reaffirm their superior position within the critical hierarchy even as they began to embrace elements of mass culture previously disdained.

When discussing his own interpretive strategies, William Dozier, producer of the series, suggested that the camp sensibility was structured into the program for exactly these reasons. By the 1960s, Dozier was firmly entrenched in the canon of Golden Age excellence for having produced *Playhouse 90*, one of the most prestigious and fondly remembered live anthology dramas. Given his status in the cultural elite, Dozier recognized the potentially degrading results of producing a television show based on a comic book hero. Remembering this conflict in a 1986 interview, Dozier admits, "I had never read a Batman comic book; I had never read *any* comic book. When I was growing up I read *David Copperfield*, *Great Expectations*, and the things you are supposed to read." Invited to produce the program, Dozier initially had to familiarize himself with the comic book mythos, resulting in an embarrassing moment when an old associate saw him reading the comics:

> Now I couldn't tell him why a full grown man was sitting there with a lap full of Batman comic books . . . I felt a little bit like an idiot. . . . At first I thought they [ABC] were crazy . . . if they were going to put this on television. Then I had just the simple idea of overdoing it, of making it so square and so serious that adults would find it amusing. I knew kids would go for the derring-do, the adventure, but the trick would be to find adults who would either watch it with their kids, or to hell with the kids, and watch it anyway.²⁴

Dozier's awareness of the polysemic nature of reception worked perfectly for ABC executives seeking to appeal to a cross-section of adults and children who watched TV in the early prime-time hours. By 1966, this was a tried and true strategy for the network, which had already programmed dual address cartoons like *The Flintstones*, *The Jetsons* and *The Bugs Bunny Show* in similar time slots. As one *New York Times* reporter explained about *Batman*, "ABC could not afford to put the show in an expensive time slot if it only appealed to children; they don't have the buying power." Thus, Dozier's polysemic approach potentially allowed the network to appeal to "everyone from the milk to the martini set."[25]

Bat Brats and Innocent Children

Not all observers shared the producer's and sponsors' enthusiasm over the program's dual address. Eda J. LeShan, a child psychologist and New York educator, asked the readers of the *New York Times'* Sunday magazine to consider what happened when camp confronted childhood innocence: "If camp involves a wry sophistication, an adult grasp of subtleties in language and point of view, does it matter that children watching this program take it absolutely literally?" LeShan thought that children's literalization of the program content had brought "a new kind of wildness in the children's play" that erupted in elementary schools and daycare centers where bat brats, clad in homemade capes and cowls, tried to imitate the series' carefully choreographed slug fests: "One kid pushes another, and suddenly, there's Batman in the middle, socking both of them and running off triumphantly." [26] Her article attracted considerable response from concerned parents, who wrote to report similar incidents in their neighborhoods. "My six-year-old and three-year-old have been wild since Batman's appearance on the scene. We're plagued by the dynamic duo," one Massachusetts mother reported. Another mother confirmed that bat play was "rough, disorderly, loud and generally aggressive," expressing her hopes that children would soon "lose their lust for this aggressive fantasy world" and return to the standard children's classics.[27] In these accounts *Batman* embodied the brutal threat that popular culture posed to middle brow sensibilities endorsed by the American educational system. School teachers and concerned parents stood as the last bulwark protecting childhood innocence from the corruption of commercial culture, "at war with Batman," for control over their youngsters' impressionable minds.

LeShan insisted that the program's young viewers were "completely confused" about its moral orientation. More generally, however, the confusion that LeShan ascribes to the child was actually a product of the adult mind that wrestled with ways to understand children's play.[28] Cartoonish illustrations of brawling bat bullies competed for space in magazines and newspapers with cute photographs of children in handcrafted costumes dancing and leaping with youthful vitality. A *New York Times* article on the death of a young British boy who accidentally hung himself while play-acting *Batman* was followed one day later by a report on Adam West and Burt Ward who were dressed in full costume, presenting Junior Good Citizens' awards to worthy children at a Central Park ceremony.[29]

At the center of these debates about *Batman*'s effect on children was the more general ambivalence about the program's status as high or low art. In discussions of children, taste distinctions were transformed into moral dilemmas and social problems. The controversy surrounding the show, of course, was simply a new skirmish in a much older battle to define what constituted appropriate children's entertainment. Mark West has traced this controversy from Anthony Comstock's crusade to regulate the content of dime novels at the turn of the century to the rise of pressure groups in the thirties and forties who were concerned about movies and radio programs to 1950s attacks on the debased nature of rock and roll, TV and comic books.[30] In all cases, childhood was conceived as a never-never-land where sexuality was taboo and violence unwelcome. In accordance with this ideal, social reformers typically prescribed a children's culture of innocence, sweetness and higher morals that conformed to adult aesthetic standards.

As Jacqueline Rose claims, this Peter-Panish version of childhood innocence is so conventionalized in our culture that it has become the reigning fantasy at the heart of children's literature: "Childhood . . . serves as a term of universal social reference which conceals all the historical divisions and difficulties of which children, no less than ourselves, form a part. There is no child behind the category 'children's fiction,' other than the one which the category itself sets in place, the one which it needs to believe is there for its own purposes."[31] For the critics of mass culture, this *tabula rasa* conception of the child was often instrumental in the promotion and enforcement of conventional cultural categories. By evoking the "threat to children," social reformers typically justified their own position as cultural custodians, linking (either implicitly or explicitly) anxieties about violence, sexuality and morality to the mandates of good taste and artistic merit.

Fredric Wertham's *Seduction of the Innocent*, the cornerstone of the 1950s campaign against crime comic books, is a perfect example. The book provided a number of rationales for reform, including the comics' fostering of racial and sexual antagonisms, anxiety over fascistic "might makes right" ideologies, hesitancy about violent and morbid imagery, and appeals to anticommunist and homophobic sentiments.[32] Yet, many of Wertham's frequently repeated claims centered around the low aesthetic status of the comic book and the ways its visual immediacy left children vulnerable to its sordid contents. He described comic books as "a debasement of the old institution of printing, the corruption of the art of drawing and almost an abolition of literary writing."[33] The book's final chapter, "Homicide at Home," placed this antagonism towards comics in a much broader cultural context. Wertham claimed that audiences whose generic expectations were shaped by early and constant exposure to comics demanded similar styles of entertainment from the movies and television. In addition, he feared the commercial success of shows like *Captain Video*, *Sky King*, *Rin Tin Tin* and *Superman* would lead the networks to model children's programing upon the crime comic's sensationalistic themes and crude content.[34]

Wertham's shift of attention towards children's television reflected the increasing public interest in the role that television played in children's social and cultural development.[35] As early as 1949, PTA members voted at their national convention to keep an eye on "unwholesome television programs." In subsequent years, various school boards across the country surveyed TV's affects on youth,[36] while popular magazines cautioned against the "parental dilemma" that TV brought to the home.[37] Such concerns were given legislative credence in the 1954 hearings held by Estes Kefauver's Senate Subcommittee on Juvenile Delinquency and in subsequent hearings chaired by Thomas Dodd, both of which focused on television as one of the major factors contributing to a perceived increase in youth crime. Reform sentiments became even stronger by the end of the fifties. Ron Goulart's *The Assault on Childhood* (1959) and Jules Henry's *Culture Against Man* (1963) directed attention to the ways that advertisers targeted children for commercial exploitation.[38] In 1961, Newton Minow incorporated this view into his "vast wasteland" campaign, claiming that children's television was "just as tasteless, just as nourishing as dishwater."[39]

In the popular press of the 1960s, these reform discourses provided a primary way of thinking about television's relation to young people.[40] Popular magazines like *Saturday Review*, *Reader's Digest* and *Parents* championed a succession of popular programs (*Ding Dong School*, *Romper Room*, *Shari Lewis*, *Captain Kangaroo*, even *Huckleberry Hound*), which better adhered to their own aesthetic criteria and which promised to raise the standards of audiences accustomed to the heroics of Roy Rogers and the low comedy of Pinky Lee.[41] *Parents* magazine published annual reports from the National Association for Better Radio and Television, evaluating all of the network series according to their suitability for young viewers. The organization's critiques suggest that aesthetic hierarchies were at the center of public concerns about media violence and vulgarity. The NABRT promoted the folksy humor and hominess of programs like *The Andy Griffith Show* and *The Patty Duke Show*, while rejecting the grotesquery of *The Addams Family* and *The Munsters*. It celebrated the educational merits of nature documentaries, while condemning the sensationalism of *Flipper*, *Lassie* and *Gentle*

Ben. More generally, the association directed protests against larger-than-life adventure programs such as *Lost In Space, Man From U.N.C.L.E., The Wild Wild West, Voyage to the Bottom of the Sea,* and *Johnny Quest,* whose intensified fascination with crime, suspense, and intrigue were "terrifying to young children" and "unpleasant" to adults.[42]

Batman emerged, then, at the end of nearly two decades of controversy surrounding the quality of children's television and the suitability of comic book adventure programs for young viewers. Some of the critics could trace their activism back to earlier participation in Wertham's anti-comic book campaigns, regarding the series as yet another attempt to televise crime comics. Moreover, the series seemed a composite of all the qualities that the NABRT protested in earlier programs: an exaggerated style of performance, lurid use of colors and graphics, larger-than-life protagonists, cliff-hanger conclusions, the glamorization of criminals and the ridicule of traditional authority. The merchandizing of the series, which amounted to some seventy-five to eighty million dollars in sales in 1966, fueled concerns about the commercial exploitation of child consumers. Not surprisingly, reform organizations expressed skepticism and dismay over the premiere of *Batman. PTA* magazine, for example, warned that children "should not be permitted to watch" *Batman* unless they have "developed antibodies to nightmares by previous exposure to crime-and-horror comics and television programs."[43]

Indeed, the regulation of children was particularly important for critics who were confused about their own cultural authority at a time when critical hierarchies were shifting ground. Popism blurred distinctions between high and low art, but even more importantly, it suggested that the whole enterprise of assigning value to art was itself undemocratic and "un-popular." For TV critics worried about their public appeal, allusions to the innocent child worked to justify their position as cultural custodians. By evoking the "threat to children" they secured (at least temporarily) their own position as arbiters of good taste, giving moral purpose to their tirades against mass culture.

But moral condemnation wasn't the only strategy by which critics positioned themselves as mediators of cultural change. Robert E. Terwilliger, an Episcopal minister, countered this position, arguing in *Catholic World* that *Batman* provided "an American fantasy of salvation for spiritually frustrated people." Similarly, a critic for the *Christian Century* argued that while "there is a danger that this type of parody might lead to a complete cynicism concerning moral judgment and action, a TV series such as *Batman* performs the necessary function in society of profaning the holy. . . . If we do not laugh at ourselves, others will—which, after all, is the moral of the story."[44] Such commentary recognized the changing tides of mass culture and popular taste, embracing, if only by default, the new camp aesthetic as a vehicle for spiritual enlightenment within the more traditional confines of the clergy.

Batman also elicited reactions that were based less on moral-ethical norms than on deeply personalized ideals. These commentators still evoked childhood innocence, but this time they did so by remembering a better mass culture, located somewhere in their autobiographical past. Here, nostalgia worked to transform Minow's dirty dishwater into a sparkling fountain of youth as popular icons disparaged in bygone decades were filtered and purified through romanticized memories. As one writer for the *New York Times* argued, "For the adult viewer dipping into his reservoir of nostalgia it [*Batman*] was probably the best therapy since Lawrence Welk's Champaign Music."[45]

Fredric Wertham had predicted that American teenagers of the 1950s would discard their comic books with shame and revulsion as soon as they reached maturity. Instead, in the 1960s many critics celebrated the revival of Bat-culture as "a deliberate evocation of juvenile fantasy,"[46] an invitation to turn the present into a childhood playground. In this respect, Batman's television incarnation tapped into a wider revival of interest in comic book heroes of the previous decades. In 1965, Jules Feiffer published a book-length elegy to superheroes[47] and, in that same year, college-town theaters revived the 1943 Batman movie serial. One man attending a marathon screening in Illinois confessed, "I saw one episode when I was eleven and wanted to know how it came out."[48] Here as elsewhere, *Batman* reintroduced childhood enigmas, opening a space for childish play and fantasy to reenter adult life. Upon *Batman*'s TV premiere, this kind of childish play found another expressive outlet. *Life*'s March 11, 1966 cover story played on the desire to return to innocence by juxtaposing images of dancing children dressed in bat capes with adults out for the night at Wayne Manor, San Francisco's Bat-motif discothèque.[49] College students at a Connecticut university capered around campus dressed as the daring duo. Even the FCC Chair, E. William Henry, succumbed to childish fun when he appeared at a Washington benefit dressed as the caped crusader.[50]

If these examples present somewhat liminal celebrations of the past, others used nostalgic readings in ways that valorized their adult authority in the present. Here, the once "noxious" comic books were trumpeted as good objects against which the ills of the more contemporary commercial culture could be evaluated. *Batman* was rejected by these critics not because it failed to measure up to "high" TV art, but rather because it betrayed the pulp traditions by turning the larger-than-life

Detective Comics hero into a campy clown. When reviewing *Batman* for the *New York Times*, Russell Baker used Feiffer's idealized memories as a vehicle through which to deride contemporary mass art. He compared the "dim-witted stooges" and "social carnage" of the TV show to the more heroic comic book figure who offered earlier readers the utopian possibility of escaping "the humdrum prison of teachers, parents and block bullies." A *Saturday Review* commentator sounded a similar note, contrasting the new camp crusader with his own boyhood spent leaping from garage rooftops imitating a Batman who "burned with belief."[51] Thus, quite paradoxically, the degraded forms of their childhood days provided the content for satisfying visions of a more perfect world. Indeed, for these critics and their readers the process of remembering was more important that the actual objects upon which memory was fixed. For it was their romantic fantasies of the past that empowered them to police the present.

Nostalgia For the Present

This history of *Batman*'s critical reception in the 1960s is clearly laced with personal memories, evocations of earlier and simpler times. In this respect, our own historiographical account is founded on a series of fantasies about the personal past that permeate the written documents we cite. If traditional historiographers see this as an obstacle to a full objective account of the past, our interest lies precisely in this overlapping between subjective memories and academic history writing. From our point of view, the goal is not to obliterate the "distorted" memories from the historical record, but to account for their construction of historical consciousness. By examining memories of past events, we might better understand the processes by which people shape their past and understand the present.

During the height of this summer's Batman nostalgia wave, we interviewed four groups of adults who were school children at the time of Batman's TV premiere. The groups ranged from two to four participants, mixed by gender, income levels and occupations. Two groups were interviewed in Madison, Wisconsin; one interviewed in Santa Barbara, California; and the last in Cambridge, Massachusetts. Obviously, we did not attempt to gather a statistically representative sample, but rather we sought to provide what Clifford Geertz calls a "thick description" of localized conditions of reception.[52] We tried to get to know the interview participants through a relatively unstructured and lengthy interaction, allowing their interests and memories to determine the direction that the session took. We were as interested in the associative logic by which *Batman* was linked to other aspects of their lives as we were with their interpretations of the program itself.

The interview participants were not compensated for their time; when asked why they had come to the group, they provided various personal interests for talking about *Batman* with others. The *Batman* series gave these individuals a shared set of references and experiences that facilitated warm and animated communication, even among people who had little else in common. As Connie, a Cambridge computer technician, exclaimed at the end of one session, "I get a big smile on my face just thinking about it all." Memories of *Batman* opened up a floodgate of television references as people recalled encounters with television shows and other popular texts of the late 1960s. *Batman* was also a catalyst for a far reaching exploration of the sixties, as people remembered political and social struggles, moving fluidly between memories of a personal and a public past.

It is wise to be cautious about the types of generalizations that we can draw from this data. Memories that are discussed in a group situation are not necessarily the same as internalized memories; the act of telling already involves a restructuring of the remembered material. Despite the interviews' relatively unstructured and undirected approach, the research process and researcher's goals always affect the type of information gathered and the nature of the responses elicited. In addition, as other studies have shown, people's lived experiences, their cultural and social environment, impacts upon the way they interpret texts. Despite our attempt to conduct interviews in distinctive geographical regions and to talk to people from different walks of life, much of this everyday context was not retrievable in the interview situation. Finally, since psychological and historical studies of memory are still at an early and exploratory stage we do not intend to reach firm conclusions. However, this type of study, especially when coupled with the emerging body of literature on the logic and functions of personal memory, does allow us to pose a series of questions and to speculate about the role that memory plays in the reception of popular media.

Memory of past events is necessarily selective and partial. None of us can recall everything that happens to us. Instead, certain moments are selected based on criteria of personal and public pertinence. In David Lowenthal's words, "All memory transmutes experience, distills the past rather than simply reflecting it. . . . Memory sifts again what perception had already sifted, leaving us only fragments of the fragments of what was initially on view."[53] Perhaps, the most persistent complaint that the interview participants expressed was their inability to recall aspects of their personal and public past. Susan, a Madison law student, jokingly suggested that she suffered "total amnesia about everything that ever happened to me." Yet, most people repeatedly resorted to vague descriptions and qualifying terms ("I can't quite recall," "as far as I can remember," "I guess," "It must have been . . .") in order to convey a sense of the forgetting that is inextricably bound to the process of remembering. We might, then, find it productive to direct attention to those aspects of the media past that survive in popular memory, what has been forgotten and what potential criteria govern this selective process of memory and forgetfulness.

Popular memories of *Batman* actively reworked the terms of its original reception, often appealing to a similar logic of nostalgia and cultural custodianship as the sixties critics did, yet defining the terms of the debate in fundamentally different ways. Our respondents shared few of the earlier critics' anxiety about the program's aesthetic status. Most insisted that they could not remember a time when television had not played a central role in their lives. So enmeshed had *Batman* become in their personal life histories that they did not feel compelled or even able to judge its merits. Still, some type of evaluative distance is suggested by the consistency with which people denied any period in their lives when they took the program content seriously or literally. All insisted that they, like the adult spectators constructed by the 1960s critical discourse, had always been 'in on the joke,' had always read the series as camp.

Similarly, any concerns about the suitability of *Batman* for young viewers had vanished from popular memory. Several people expressed astonishment when learning of the 1960s controversy surrounding the program: "Really! *Batman* bad for kids. You've got to be kidding," Lori, a Madison game shop owner, declared. Instead, the program had become emblematic of a purer children's culture against which the offensive features of contemporary mass culture might be judged and condemned. Kate, a Madison commercial artist, contrasted her childhood experience of *Batman* with the consumer-oriented programs preferred by her children: "I can't remember that there even were Batman figures when the show was first on. . . . I don't remember shows at the time being promoted as such a big package deal." Kate's denial of the series' commercialization was shared by other interview participants, most of whom claimed no knowledge or access to Batman spinoff products in the 1960s and saw the commodification of children's television as a relatively new development. While we can not be sure what any of these people might or might not have known about the cultural past, the general pattern of these memories suggests a simplification of historical contradictions in favor of an image of the past as a purer, less complex time, as a place not yet confronted with our contemporary problems. What is remembered works to confirm those suppositions, what is forgotten is often information that might challenge such a picture.

When remembering the *Batman* series, people tended to construct vivid images of themselves watching the program as children:

> Doug: (a Madison graduate student in psychology): We tended to eat dinner later, cause that was when my Dad was going to seminary so he would often get back late. I remember several episodes—I mean—incidents where I was upstairs shoveling down my dinner cause I wanted to get downstairs to turn on the television by 6:30 or whatever, and I was told that was not to be done. I was not to rush through dinner in order to go see some television show.

> Lori: The one scene that stands out in my mind is the third week it was on and the backyard cleared, like that, at 6:25. There was not a kid to be found in the whole neighborhood. Everybody went to their respective houses to watch. . . . In fact, as soon as it was over, we'd go back outside. . . . One kid in the neighborhood could laugh like the Riddler on command. Someone else did the Joker, I guess, I don't remember. . . . As far as I recall we'd just imitate the scenes we liked.

For these and other people, remembering *Batman* brought back a situational context, a scene that painted a rough sketch of places in the house, times of the day, and childhood relationships with family or friends.

As recent work on autobiographical memory has argued, our memory of public events—the Kennedy assassination, say—includes not only the actual event, but also our own relationship to it, the circumstances in which we received this news, where we were, what we were doing, who told us about it.[54] As David C. Rubin and Marc Kozin have shown, even more personal events (car accidents, school days, deaths in the family) tend to be be described through vivid situational contexts.[55]

The degree to which these remembered episodes are actually photographic records of an event is, of course, another question.[56] In describing these past situations, the interview participants seem more likely to have been recasting their memories in terms of a set of shared cultural experiences, rather than merely recounting their own individual past. The degree to which these people relied on shared cultural and social frameworks—family settings, childhood games, school yard contexts—suggests the relational aspects of popular memory, the attempt to use memory in a way that binds the individual to a larger community of ideas. Indeed, *Batman* and an array of other media texts served to evoke a collective past that was discussed in remarkably conventionalized ways. These memories may have differed in details, but their basic narrative form and themes were strikingly shaped by cultural, rather than simply individuated, codes of storytelling.

The narrative elements of long-term memory have been the subject of cognitive psychologists in recent years. Although more interested in the mental schemes and paradigms that govern memory, Ulric Neisser has argued that autobiographical memory tends less to be a record of the past than a composite image of numerous events that occur over time. In his study of John Dean's memory, for example, Neisser shows how Dean's testimony in the Watergate investigation often evoked specific episodes in which he met and spoke with Nixon. However, Dean's memories were rarely accurate in their details; instead they were true to a more generalized conception of the historical past. Neisser thus concludes "What seems to be specific in his memory actually depends upon repeated episodes, rehearsed presentations or overall impressions. . . . The single clear memories that we recollect so vividly actually stand for something else; they are like 'screen memories' a little like those Freud discussed long ago. Often their real basis is a set of repeated experiences, a sequence of related events that the single recollection merely typifies and represents." Neisser describes such memories as "repisodic" rather than episodic, suggesting that much of what we think we remember about our past involves an abstraction of lived experience into something more generic or prototypical, something that doesn't necessarily reflect a single incident as it occurs, but rather preserves the truth of a series of related experiences.[57] Popular memory thus tends to be prototypical and constructive, rather than specific and fixed.

Even when interview participants talked about the program, their accounts tended to be highly generic. Rather than remembering specific episodes, they remembered *Batman* in repisodic ways, expressing fondness for isolated but recurring images (the screeching of the batmobile's tires, the heroes sliding down the batpole, the red glow of the batphone, batrope ascents, zany graphics, hyperbolic voice-overs, and especially, exotic death traps). Often, however, they could not recount specific plots or point towards concrete examples of broader generic elements. Connie confessed at one point, "I don't remember a single death trap he [King Tut] put them through." Similarly, particular character traits—the Joker's laugh, the Catwoman's sensuality, Mr. Freeze's icy personality—had been abstracted from the text. Even when we showed one group a *Batman* episode, the discussion quickly drifted from reflections on specifics towards more generic commentary. What remained in memory was not the single episode, but rather a prototypical text, a repisodic memory that reflected the generic qualities of the series. These prototypical texts bear the marks of the memory process itself— the necessary simplification of the flux of lived experience into terms that can be more readily recalled and comprehended.

In addition to their repisodic nature, popular memories of *Batman* were often highly intertextual and expansive. Here, people recalled the body of other texts they read during the same period or texts which, at later dates, had become associated with their memories of this primary text. For most people, this intertextual framework was in fact a *neces- sary condition* of popular memory; these people drew on matrix of cultural materials in attempts to explain their personal encounters with the series. Our discussions of the Catwoman flowed naturally into considerations of *The Avengers'* Emma Peel; recollections of the open- ing credits merged into memories of *Bonanza's* opening song and map burning sequence; discussions of *Batman's* campy and self-conscious qualities repeatedly invited analogies to *Laugh-in*, *The Monkees*, *Rocky and Bullwinkle*, and *Mad* magazine. As Susan confessed, "I can never keep my series apart."

For some people, the ability to tap into this intertextual grid became a source of pride among peers. Dan, a Boston man, identified supporting performers who had appeared as henchmen on both *Batman* and *Super- man* and spotted athletes behind the monster makeup on *Lost in Space*. Responding to the game that Dan had initiated, other group members also exhibited their skills at citing the instances in which *Batman* villains appeared in other programs and films. Tom, a night janitor in Madison, continually displayed his knowledge of TV lore, boasting at one point, "I seem to remember more TV than everybody." This display of TV literacy was clearly a pleasurable activity, one that seemed to give Tom a sense of personal pride because it marked a difference from his present-day life and otherwise mundane family history. At one point, immediately after recounting his knowledge of stars and pro- grams, Tom drifted off into a melancholy confession about his personal life, telling us that his "parents were always busy working, just like me these days." This admission suggested that his pleasurable TV memories might be a buffer for the more arduous conditions of the work-a-day world. Possibly, as well, since Tom was the only working- class member in this particular discussion group, his display of TV literacy might have provided him with feelings of superiority when talking to white collar professionals.

More generally, people used memories of *Batman* to evoke their own personal identity and explain their particular relationship to the social world. As Lowenthal notes, memory often "converts events into idio- syncratic personal experiences," retaining details about a public past insofar as they serve more personal needs: "Remembering the past is crucial for our sense of identity. . . . Recalling past experiences links us with our earlier selves, however different we may since have become."[58] For our respondents, remembering *Batman* meant remembering themselves, and that dialogue between program and self continually framed the stories they told about the past.

In many conversations, *Batman* seemed to elicit stories that told of transitional moments, rites of passage, through which people moved from child to adult, from family to larger social meanings.

> Jim (a Santa Barbara computer technician): I remember we used to watch, the whole family did. My dad always watched television, period, when he came home. I can remember watching it and being excited when I first started to tune in the advertisements, seeing the Batmobile come screaming out of the cave and over the fence that falls down. I can remember my sister thought it was really cool . . . and she would sit there and watch it with me. She was a young teenager. . . . When she went off to college she became a hippy . . . and completely stopped watching. I was amazed because I always loved the show.

Jim's narrative positions *Batman* as a mediator between his family's personal history and the larger social changes of the 1960s, measuring the counterculture's impact upon his sister via her shifting attitudes toward a cultural product that they once enjoyed together. His story allows him to come to terms with his personal past with his sister while also serving to explain his place in the public past of student protests. Here, as elsewhere, these memories fluidly move from personal to collective consciousness as people weave histories around themselves, while at the same time imbricating themselves into the wider social fabric.

Indeed, this matching of personal and public pasts became a strategy for understanding the relationship of self to society, and within this matching process television memories served a key role. John, a Madison graduate student, summarized his feelings upon reviewing an episode of *Batman*: "When I go back and see something from that long ago, I tend to remember who I was when I first saw it, how I thought the world was." As John suggests, these memories aren't simply the residue of earlier times; instead they are a resource people use to think about the world and their position within it.

Memories of *Batman* often evoked tales in which people took on a liminal status—existing somewhere in between child and adult. Most of the participants invoked some aspects of the general myth of childhood innocence, constructing children as unknowledgeable and presexual. As Rose suggests, this notion of childhood innocence constitutes a universalized category that erases questions of sexual and cultural difference. Yet, these differences resurface in contradictory ways within personal memories that depend for their vividness upon references to gender, sexuality and resistance to adult authorities. In the interviews, memory entitled people to play with the ideological distinctions between child and adult. Childhood memories evoked a pleasure in liminality as people moved fluidly between imagining themselves as children and recognizing their current adult status.

Ambiguities between child and adult surfaced most vividly in discussions of the Catwoman. Several of the male respondents spoke of the Dark Knight's feline foe as one of the first objects of their erotic interest, suggesting that her role in the program invited a greater awareness of sexual difference. As Jim remarked, "I can remember not being interested in any of the female characters until halfway through the series, when suddenly I became exceedingly interested in the Catwoman." Frequently, however, these claims were coupled with a denial of childhood sexuality. Michael, a Santa Barbara computer technician, admitted, "I appreciated the women right from the start, but to me they looked like really great mother figures. I didn't know what they meant at the time." In another discussion group, Lori speculated, "I guess maybe subconsciously I was aware of female-male interactions but they certainly hadn't entered my life yet." Michael and Lori remember themselves at a time before erotic desire entered their lives. Still, as adults they find it important to employ categories of sexual difference as they reflect on their narrative pleasure in *Batman*. What emerges is a complex economy of desire where they invoke their own erotic fantasies while still maintaining the culturally defined differences between child (presexual) and adult (sexual). Moreover, the memory of *Batman* seems pleasurable precisely in its ability to maintain this liminal-in-between-state between knowing adult and innocent child.

For others, Catwoman introduced contradictions surrounding gender. Catwoman's exercise of authority over her gang and her resistance to Batman suggested, for some women, the possibility of feminine power. Yet, simultaneously many of these same women claimed initial disinterest, ignorance or hostility to what they called "women's lib attitudes," which were being debated elsewhere in the 1960s. The women often spoke of their initial ignorance of gender roles even as they evoked their youthful pleasure in resisting or redefining those roles. Susan recalled discussing with her playmates the pleasure they took in Catwoman's antisocial antics: "The Catwoman was having so much fun, and we were discussing the fact that Batman and Robin never had any fun. . . . And, of course, parents would have been appalled hearing this, but we had this discussion. Are we really allowed to draw this moral . . . that the bad girls have more fun? Can we do that?" Here, Susan attributes to adult authorities certain attitudes about childhood innocence while constructing a memory that celebrates the possibilities of feminine resistance to sex-role stereotyping.

As with Susan's account, many of the memories centered around a childhood fantasy of resisting the adult culture. Jim recalled an incident when he used Batman and Robin Halloween costumes to confound adult authorities through an elaborate play with secret identities: "I put on the Batman costume and went trick-or-treating. Then I came home and put on the Robin costume and went trick-or-treating again and hit a lot of the same houses!" While most interview participants remembered their parents as exercising only minimal control over their use of television and other media, those moments when entertainment choices faced parental resistance seemed to be particularly charged memorics. Dan expressed regret that he saw *Batman* mostly on summer reruns since his mother refused to allow him to watch television on school nights. He enthusiastically recalled how he and his siblings conspired to thwart his mother's edicts: "My mother's big thing was she would pull the cord out from behind the back of the TV. . . . So we discovered what she was doing and I figured out how to plug it back in. . . . I was the one who figured out how to fix the TV. And to this day, they always give me the clicker [at family gatherings]. It's like I'm the master of thc TV." Dan treated this incident of childhood resistance to adult control as an origin myth that explains his own particular placement in his family structure.

But these accounts of childhood resistance often gave way to adult anxieties about control and power over youth. Indeed, people seemed to move in the alternate states of child and adult, at once condemning, at once embracing, the social structure that regulates childhood. Doug, for example, remembered how "I wanted to stay up and watch George Pal's *War of the Worlds* . . . and my folks didn't think that would be such a good idea. . . . But finally they caved in. In retrospect, I think they were right. I should have listened to them." Doug's account shifts between two identificatory postions. He identifies with himself as a child controlled by his parents, and then shifts the terms, using memory to accept the rules of the adult culture. In this way, memory works to maintain the ideological construction of adult authority over children, particularly when it comes to policing the media choices of youth. The older Doug now thinks as his parents did ("they were right"), but he still maintains a continuity with his own life history by thinking back to when he resisted adult rules. This tenuous balance between child and adult identificatory positions seems to present Doug with a pleasurable equilibrium, giving him a way of explaining his present-day life while still maintaining a sense of his past.

These fluid transfers between different attitudes and cultural positions suggest the political duality of popular memory, the degree to which reflections on the past can be simultaneously a progressive and a conservative force. On the one hand, memory can assume a utopian quality, offering a fantasy of resistance to adult norms that also provides a basis upon which to criticize contemporary social conditions. On the other hand, memory can assume a more conservative quality, denying cultural and social change and justifying the exercise of custodial authority over contemporary children's culture. Memories of *Batman* assumed both dimensions in our discussions, sometimes inviting regret over the "political apathy" of eighties' culture in contrast to the more activist period when the show was first aired, elsewhere provoking expressions of outrage over the "poor quality" and "shabbiness" of more recent children's programs. Often, the same person expressed both attitudes in the course of the interview, suggesting a range of contradictory emotions and thoughts that emerged when people compared past and present day worlds. These comparisons were indeed endemic to the memory process itself, as all respondents used their recollections to consider the merits and failures of contemporary life.

Some people used their memories of *Batman* to invoke an image of a more politicized past. Recollections of the series were intertwined with memories of sixties' news events where student protests, civil rights riots, and the Vietnam war provoked fond longings for a radical time when the world was full of possibilities. Indeed, since all of the people interviewed were too young to have participated in these events at the time, memories of television broadcasts were the key to historical consciousness. Michael traced his radical political commitments to sixties' television, suggesting that what he learned from *Batman* was "a strong aversion to injustice," and a distrust of authority: "If you're fighting injustice, sometimes you're not necessarily working for the police. Sometimes the police obstruct justice." This fantasy of a more just and more politically righteous past was often compared to the moral confusion and passive acceptance of adult life. Kate confessed, "*Batman* makes me remember the sixties a lot. The confusion, a lot of anger . . . . Suddenly it brings back a lot of those feelings and makes me realize how politically uninvolved I am now." Responding to this, Susan explained that the reason "everything has gotten the way it is now" is because people no longer protest social problems the way they did in the 1960s. The ability to remember the 1960s, if only through its media images, authorized these women to evaluate and condemn contemporary political culture: "There aren't the same kind of questions anymore. . . . All of those things [reforms] are gone because nobody fought for them anymore."

Yet, this logic of nostalgia may just as readily be evoked to justify a more repressive attitude towards contemporary culture. Just like the critics of the 1960s who used their romanticized memories of the *Batman* comics to condemn the TV version, many of the people compared the more wholesome texts of their childhood to the degraded media forms of the present. Most saw television as corrupting childhood innocence, producing a generation that is too "sophisticated" in its understanding of sexual matters, too accepting of media violence and too enamored with the pleasure of overconsumption. As Jim explained, "There's just not that much on television any more that I can consider innocent. . . . I don't want my little kids watching the *A-Team*! It's a lot more violent and a lot less straight forward fun than what we used to watch." This comparison with the past entitled him to boast about his current role as watchful father, making sure to tell us how he had steered his youngsters away from broadcast television and onto books and "videotapes of known quality." Even the acknowledged shortcomings of the sixties series—the cardboard sets, the flabby Adam West, the squealing Robin—were remembered affectionately by the respondents who often claimed that these low production values actually enhanced opportunities for imaginative participation in the program. These responses suggest that children who grew up watching *Batman* had reversed a previous generation's condemnation of the program, yet had retained the same cultural logic upon which the earlier criticism had been founded. Like the sixties' critics, they appealed to a better past to justify their criticisms of contemporary mass culture, to rationalize their exercise of cultural authority and to motivate their construction of a new aesthetic canon.

This conservative mode of popular memory also shaped their own responses to contemporary media. Many of the respondents expressed lack of interest in and sometimes hostility to the new *Batman* movie, holding open little possibility for the 1989 release to duplicate the pleasures they found in the TV series. In Kate's words, "I don't think you could make that series now, I don't think you could make an eighties' version and have it come out the same." Many found the darker tone of the Tim Burton film emblematic of the loss of innocence and playfulness that their childhood texts had once contained. Reflecting on a recent Batman comic book, Connie suggested, "Gotham City used to be a much more fun place." Susan, who had yet to see the film at the time of the interview, compared it to the *Star Trek* films, which she liked best when they were "consistent with a lot of the things in

the original series . . . so you felt like you were in the same place again."
If the merchandizing and publicity materials surrounding the film's
release invited "baby boomers" to return to a prepackaged version of
their childhood, it is clear that many rejected this invitation, desiring
instead to cling to their more "authentic" autobiographical memories
of the series. Perhaps, in fact, it was this pleasurable reconstruction of
a personal past that was really at the heart of their reluctance to accept
a new version of Batman.

Conclusion

We would like to end by returning to the problems entailed in writing
the history of memory and, more specifically, in using memory as a
way to understand people's encounters with mass culture. History,
media texts, and personal memories all share in a common project of
narrativization, although the conventions, desires and mechanisms of
storytelling differ in each case. By forging connections between these
different storytelling practices, we bring into relief not one historical
truth, but rather a set of differences, of separate truths, of versions of
the past that often contradict each other.

This is especially important when we consider the chameleon-like
nature of popular heroes like Batman. These heroes retain their cultural
significance precisely because they are open to reinterpreation by different generations. For the critics of the 1960s, the transformation of the
comic book hero into a campy clown created a series of disputes around
the meanings of *Batman* and, more generally, the status of popular
texts. The anxieties that these critics displayed over the series and their
attempts to divide audience interpretation along generational lines be-
lie their desire to control cultural change, to stabilize meanings and
pleasures in a way that better suits the meanings of the past.

By 1989, the anxieties about the 1960s series had vanished from
popular memory. Instead, the program now presents opportunities for
thinking about a decade that is out of focus but still part of our collective
and autobiographical past. Remembering our own TV histories evokes
powerful, even poignant, moments as we reinvent ourselves and the
times from which we came. Here, memory mediates our present-day
desires and gives the past an imaginary status that strips away closure,
opening it up to personal (although culturally-mediated) fantasies. At
times, in our interviews, these memories seemed to serve a conservative function, as people used romantic visions of a better past to control
and police the often difficult realities of present-day life. At other times,
these memories seemed to have a potentially liberating dimension, as
people imagined themselves in a liminal state, somewhere in between

child and adult, using this indistinction to transgress the rules of normal adult conversations. Memories, in other words, entitled people to think and speak about themselves in opposition to adult authorities and, in more politicized discussions, to imagine a less authoritarian world where peace rallies and Bob Dylan were virtuous and authentic once more.

In all of these discussions, history-making was clearly enjoyable for the group. Indeed, whereas traditional history effaces the pleasure of the text, popular memory is full of self-parody, wit, and laughter. In its own historical context, *Batman* was viewed with a high degree of anxiety over its status as high or low art, but in the 1980s this angst had virtually disappeared from historical consciousness, and *Batman* instead found resonance in satisfying childhood memories and reflections on contemporary struggles. The interview participants were making *Batman* mean something new, and in the process they drew upon shared cultural myths, actively engaged in collective storytelling, and intertwined their own personal histories with the many lives of the Batman.

But within the collective process of making history, where do we, the historians, stand? What function did we serve in this study? Facilitators? Mediators? Authorities? As Alassendro Portelli claims, even while they draw autonomous voices into their texts, oral historians still make "them [the informants] speak; and the 'floor,' whether admittedly or not, is still the historian's." Expanding this, Karl Figlio argues that while the oral historian might have control over the way people express themselves in the interview situation, he or she is always part of a set of relationships that involve at least three groups: "that on which his or her sample gives testimony; that to which the informants and the historian belong; and that made up of the informants, the historian and the audience for the historical project." Figlio thus foregrounds the intersubjective character of history-making and in so doing stresses the collaborative dimension of historical truths.[59]

In the end, perhaps, the historians do still have the floor, but at least the act of speaking about the past has been more of a dialogue than a monologue. The question of how this dialogue with the past can be relevant in the present is one that tortures the texts of modern philosophers and historians, from Marx to Foucault. But rather than look for large scale political relevance behind the memories of ordinary folks, perhaps we need to start with the idea that memories are themselves relevant in the small-scale politics of everyday life. Memories are one of the rare common grounds upon which people think about the present-day world. If mass media texts are now part of our historical consciousness, this is no time to bemoan the passing of a truer, more politically acute historical consciousness, one based on wars, class struggle and other more "authentic" historical experiences. Nor is it useful to fall into a completely nihilistic embrace of postmodern pastiche where history is emptied of all meaning to become pure style, an endless TV re-rerun. Instead, we think, autobiographical memories of media texts can shed light on how people use and reuse media in their daily lives. These memories begin to show how sense is wrestled from the claws of the past, how historical meanings are disengaged and reworked for contemporary purposes.

As the case of Batman so vividly illustrates, we are now encountering popular texts that endure, in transformed states, for multiple generations. These texts provide clues to a shared, collective past that runs parallel to and often intersects with our own life histories. In our study, remembering *Batman* evoked a transitional space where people actively used their previous encounters with mass culture to reshape and understand their relation to larger social practices. Popular memory, then, is the place where private and public pasts meet. At this crossroads we find a mix of personal and collective fantasies that transform the products of mass culture into the tools of everyday life.

Notes

1. We are grateful to Janet Bergstrom, Michael Curtin, Bill Forman, and Cindy Jenkins for reading and improving upon this essay. We also extend thanks to David Bordwell and George Lipsitz for their extremely helpful bibliographical suggestions; to Kevin Glynn, Shelly Happy and Paul Seale for their research assistance; and to Mike Lord and Tom Patterson for watching *Batman* with so much pleasure. Most importantly, to all the people who participated in the interview sessions, thanks for the memories. The authors collaborated equally in the writing of this essay.

2. David Lowenthal, *The Past Is a Foreign Country* (Cambridge and New York: Cambridge UP, 1985).

3. Ulric Neisser, *Memory Observed: Remembering in Natural Contexts* (San Francisco: Freeman, 1982), p. 12.

4. For an introduction see Jan Vansina, *Oral Tradition As History* (Madison: Wisconsin UP, 1985).

5. For good introductions to oral history and the wider implications that it has for engaging people in the process of history-making see James Green, "Engaging in People's History: The Massachussetts History Workshop" in *Presenting the Past: Essays on History and the Public*, ed. Susan Porter Benson, et. al. (Philidelphia: Temple UP, 1986) pp. 339–359; and Linda Shopes," Oral History and Community Involvement: The Baltimore Neighborhood Heritage Project," *Radical History Review* 25 (1981): 27–44, reprinted in *Presenting the Past*, pp. 249–263.

6. For interesting considerations of these problems see Michael H. Frish, "The Memory of History," *Radical History Review* 25 (October 1981): 9–23; Philippe Lejeune, *On Autobiography* (Minneapolis: Minnesota UP, 1989), especially pp. 185–215.

7. Hayden White, *Tropics of Discourse: Essays in Cultural Criticism* (Baltimore and London: Johns Hopkins UP, 1978).

8. Dominick La Capra, *History and Criticism* (Ithaca and London: Cornell UP, 1985), pp. 34–35.

9. See George Lipsitz, "The Meaning of Memory: Family, Class and Ethnicity in Early Network Television Programs," *Camera Obscura* 16 (March 1988): 79–117. Also see his *Time Passages: Collective Memory and American Popular Culture* (Minneapolis: Minnesota UP, 1989); Colin MacCabe, "Memory, Phantasy, Identity: 'Days of Hope' and the Politics of the Past," *Edinburgh Magazine* 2 (1977): 13–17; Roy Rosenzweig, "American Heritage and Popular History in the United States," in *Presenting the Past*, pp. 21–49; Eric Breitbart, "Historical Recreation from the Panorama to the Docudrama," in *Presenting the Past*, pp. 105–117; Henry Jenkins, "Reading Popular History: *The Atlanta Child Murders*," *Journal of Communication Inquiry* 11:2 (Summer 1987): 60–78.

10. John A. Robinson, "Autobiographical Memory: A Historical Prologue," in *Autobiographical Memory*, ed. David C. Rubin, (Cambridge: Cambridge University Press, 1986) p. 23.

11. Mort Drucker and Lou Silverstone, "Bats-Man," *Mad* September 1966: 7–12.

12. Gilbert Seldes, *Writing For Television* (Garden City, NY: Doubleday, 1952), p. 32; Jack Gould, "'Live vs, 'Canned,'" *New York Times Magazine* 5 February 1956, p. 27.

13. For more on golden age aesthetics see William Boddy's important account of Golden Age critical discourses in "From the 'Golden Age' to the 'Vast Wasteland:' The Struggles Over Market Power and Dramatic Formats in 1950's Television," (Ph.D. diss., New York University, 1984), pp. 104–115; for more on hyperrealism and TV aesthetic ideals in the 1950s see Lynn Spigel's "Installing the Television Set: The Social Construction of Television's Place in the American Home," (Ph. D. diss., University of California-Los Angeles, 1988), pp. 293–352.

14. For more on the critic's response to the telefilm see Boddy. For an analysis of critical discourses in relation to industrial and regulatory reforms see James L. Baughman, *Television's Guardians: The FCC and the Politics of Programming, 1958–1967* (Knoxville: Tennessee UP, 1985) and "The National Purpose and the Newest Medium: Liberal Critics of Television, 1958–60," *Mid-America* 64 (April-July 1983): pp. 41–55.

15. Note that we have focused on Andy Warhol in our discussion of Popism because the television critics of the sixties saw Warhol as being synonymous with the Pop movement. Indeed, the critics continually referenced Warhol's work to the exclusion of other Pop artists.

16. "The Whole Country Goes Supermad," *Life* 11 March 1966, p. 23.

17. "Discotheque Frug Party Heralds Batman's Film and TV Premiere," *New York Times* 13 January 1966, p. 79.

18. Jack Gould, "Too Good To Be Camp," *New York Times* 23 January 1966, Section 1, p. 17.

19. John Skow, "Has TV Gasp Gone Batty?" *Post* 7 May 1966, p. 95.

20. This dual-address aspect of the series was also recognized by Fox Domestic Syndication in the summer of 1989. This time, however, the industry based the crossover appeal on the nostalgic, rather than camp, quality of the series: "This show is really

for the yuppies and the baby boomers who grew up with the television show, but I also see a younger generation who will see the series for the first time and love it. It has a cross-generation appeal similar to the kind of product that Disney offers." Cited in "Superhero Comes to Aid of Syndicator," p. 33.

21. *Time* 28 January, 1966, p. 61."Holy Cancellation!" *Newsweek* 5 February 1968, p. 84; John Skow, "Has TV Gasp Gone Batty?" *Saturday Evening Post* 7 May 1966, p. 96.

22. Susan Sontag, "Notes on Camp," in *Against Interpretation* (New York: Farrar, Straus and Giroux, 1966), pp. 275–292.

23. For more on Pop and Camp see Andrew Ross, *No Respect: Intellectuals and Popular Culture* (New York and London: Routledge, 1989), pp. 135–170.

24. Joel Eisner, *The Official Batman Batbook* (Chicago: Contemporary, 1986), pp. 5–6.

25. Judy Stone, "Caped Crusader of Camp," *New York Times* 4 January 1966, p. 15.

26. Eda J. LeShan, "At War With Batman," *New York Times Magazine* 15 May 1966, p. 112.

27. Mrs. B. Cloosin, "What's So Wrong With Batman?" *New York Times Magazine* 5 June 1966, p. 41; Mrs. Helen Heinman, "Batman: Menace or Hero?" *New York Times Magazine* 29 May 1966, p. 40.

28. LeShan, p. 122.

29. "Young Britons Told Not to Copy Batman," *New York Times* 24 August 1966, p. 38; "Wow! Bam! Socko! Seven Thousand Children Greet Batman," *New York Times* 25 August 1966, p. 424.

30. Mark West, *Children, Culture and Controversy* (Hamden, CT: Archon, 1988)

31. Jaqueline Rose, *The Case of Peter Pan Or The Impossibility of Children's Fiction* (London: MacMillan, 1984), p. 10.

32. For a detailed discussion of Wertham's anti-comic book campaign see James Gilbert, *A Cycle of Outrage: America's Reaction to the Juvenile Delinquent in the 1950s* (New York: Oxford, 1986); William Lloyd Oakley Jr., "The Destruction of an Industry: Dr. Wertham, the Henderickson Committee, William Gaines and the Comic Book Controversy of the 1950s," Thesis, Harvard, 1988.

33. Fredric Wertham, *Seduction of the Innocent* (New York: Rinehart, 1953), p. 381. Although he acknowledged, albeit begrudgingly, that the classics often had the same themes of sex and violence, Wertham insisted that their aesthetic qualities and sensitivity more than offset any unsavoriness. Moreover, the effort required in the reading process provided an imaginative buffer for children that protected them from "merging completely with the story," while the visual immediacy of comic books absorbed children completely, making it impossible to separate violent fantasies from real life. "How Movie and TV Violence Affects Children," *Ladies' Home Journal*, February 1960, pp. 58–59.

34. Wertham, pp. 354–397.

35. See for example, Fredric Wertham, "How Movie and TV Violence Affects Children," *Ladies' Home Journal* February 1960, pp. 58–59.

36. PTA reform reported in "Another TV Censor, "*Variety* 5 October 1949, p. 27. For early school board activities see for example, "TV Also Alarms Cleve. Educators," *Variety* 22 March 1950, p. 29; "Students Read, Sleep Less In TV Homes, Ohio School Survey Shows," *Variety* 5 April 1950, p. 38.

37. Lloyd Shearer, "The Parental Dilemma" *House Beautiful* October 1951, pp. 220, 222, 224. For other examples from women's home magazines see Dorothy Diamond and Frances Tenenbaum, "Should You Tear 'Em Away From TV?" *Better Homes and Gardens* September 1950, pp. 56, 239–240; William Porter, "Is Your Child Glued to TV, Radio, Movies, or Comics?" *Better Homes and Gardens* October 1951, pp. 125, 178–179; Ann Usher, "TV. . .Good or Bad For Your Children?" *Better Homes and Gardens* October 1955, pp. 145, 176, 202. As Spigel has argued elsewhere, the debates over television's effects on youth pivoted on the question of adult authority over children, raising parental anxiety about television's effects on their own everyday lives. See Lynn Spigel, "Installing the Television Set," especially pp. 143–165.

38. Ron Goulart, *The Assault On Childhood* (Los Angeles: Shelbourne, 1959); Jules Henry, *Culture Against Man* (New York, Random House, 1963).

39. Newton Minow, "Is TV Cheating Our Children?" *Parents* February 1962, pp. 52–53; "Minow Magic," *Newsweek* 14 August 1963, p. 66.

40. See for example, Benjamin Spock, "Television, Radio, Comics and Movies," *Ladies' Home Journal* April 1969, p. 61; Eve Merriam, "We're Teaching Our Children That Violence Is Fun," *Ladies' Home Journal* October 1964, p. 44; Anna W. M. Woolfe, "TV, Movies, Comics . . . Boon or Bane to Children?" *Parents* April 1961, pp. 46–40; Bruno Bettelheim, "Sex and Violence in Television," *Redbook* May 1964, pp. 60–61.

41. See for example, Jane Kesner Ardmore, "Television Without Terror," *Parents*, July 1962, pp. 42–43; "To Improve TV For Children," *America* 23 April 1955, p. 94; "Culture for Kids," *Newsweek* 21 February 1955, p. 62; "Children's Hour," *Newsweek* 16 January 1956, p. 78.

42. Frank Orme, "TV For Children: What's Good? What's Bad?" *Parents* February 1962, p. 54; "TV For Children," *Parents* February 1966, p. 42–43; "Report On TV For Children," *Parents* February 1967, pp. 63–65; "Best On TV: Choosing Programs For Children," *Parents* February 1968, pp. 58–59.

43. "Time Out for Television," *PTA* April 1966, p. 22.

44. Robert E. Terwilliger, "The Theology of Batman," *Catholic World* November 1966, p. 127; M. Conrad Hyers, "Batman and the Comic Profanation of the Sacred," *Christian Century* 18 October 1967, p. 1323.

45. "TV: Pow! Zap! It's Batman and Robin." *New York Times* 13 January 1966, p. 79.

46. Terwilliger, p. 127.

47. Jules Feiffer, ed. *The Great Comic Book Heroes* (New York: Dial, 1965).

48. "The Return of Batman," *Time* 26 November 1965, p. 60.

49. "The Whole Country Goes Supermad," p. 26.

50. Skow, p. 93.

51. Russell Baker, "Observer: Televison's Bat Burlesque," *New York Times* 8 February 1966: 38; R. L. Shayon, "All the Way to the Bank: Batman," *Saturday Review* 12 February 1966, p. 46.

52. Clifford Geertz, *The Interpretation of Culture* (New York: Basic, 1973).

53. Lowenthal, p. 204.

54. For an important study on this see Roger Brown and James Kulik, "Flashbulb Memories," *Cognition* 5 (1977): 73–99.

55. David C. Rubin and Marc Kozin, "Vivid Memories," *Cognition* 16 (1984): pp. 81–95.

56. See Ulric Neisser, "Snapshots or Benchmarks," in Ulric Neisser Ed. *Memory Observed: Remembering in Natural Contexts*, pp. 43–48.

57. Ulric Neisser, "John Dean's Memory: A Case Study, " *Cognition* 9 (1981): p. 20.

58. Lowenthal, pp. 195, 197.

59. Alessandro Portelli,"The Peculiarities of Oral History " *History Workshop* 12 (Fall 1981): p. 105; Karl Figlio, "Psychoanalysis and Oral History" *History Workshop* 26 (Fall 1988): p. 120.

8

Batman, Deviance and Camp

Andy Medhurst

Only someone ignorant of the fundamentals of
psychiatry and of the psychopatholgy of sex can fail
to realize a subtle atmosphere of homoerotism which
pervades the adventure of the mature "Batman" and
his young friend "Robin."—Fredric Wertham[1]

It's embarrassing to be solemn and treatise-like about
Camp. One runs the risk of having, oneself, produced
a very inferior piece of Camp.—Susan Sontag[2]

I'm not sure how qualified I am to write this essay. Batman hasn't
been particularly important in my life since I was seven years old. Back
then he was crucial, paramount, unmissable as I sat twice weekly to
watch the latest episode on TV. Pure pleasure, except for the annoying
fact that my parents didn't seem to appreciate the thrills on offer. Worse
than that, they actually laughed. How could anyone laugh when the
Dynamic Duo were about to be turned into Frostie Freezies (pineapple
for the Caped Crusader, lime for his chum) by the evil Mr. Freeze?

Batman and I drifted apart after those early days. Every now and then
I'd see a repeated episode and I soon began to understand and share that
once infuriating parental hilarity, but this aside I hardly thought about
the man in the cape at all. I knew about the subculture of comic freaks,
and the new and alarmingly pretentious phrase 'graphic novel' made
itself known to me, but I still regarded (with the confidence of distant
ignorance) such texts as violent, macho, adolescent and, well, silly.

That's when the warning bells rang. The word 'silly' reeks of the com-
placent condescension that has at various times been bestowed on all
the cultural forms that matter most to me (Hollywood musicals, British
melodramas, pop music, soap operas) so what right had I to apply it to
someone else's part of the popular cultural playground? I had to rethink
my disdain, and 1989 has been a very good year in which to do so, because
in term of popular culture 1989 has been the Year of the Bat.

This essay, then, is not written by a devotee of Batman, someone
steeped in every last twist of the mythology. I come to these texts
as an interested outsider, armed with a particular perspective. That
perspective is homosexuality, and what I want to try and do here is to
offer a gay reading of the whole Bat-business. It has no pretension to
definitiveness, I don't presume to speak for all gay people everywhere.

I'm male, white, British, thirty years old (at the time of writing) and all of those factors need to be taken into account. Nonetheless, I'd argue that Batman is especially interesting to gay audiences for three reasons.

Firstly, he was one of the first fictional characters to be attacked on the grounds of presumed homosexuality, by Fredric Wertham in his book *Seduction Of The Innocent*. Secondly, the 1960s TV series was and remains a touchstone of camp (a banal attempt to define the meaning of camp might well start with "like the sixties' *Batman* series"). Thirdly, as a recurring hero figure for the last fifty years, Batman merits analysis as a notably successful construction of masculinity.

Nightmare On Psychiatry Street: Freddy's Obsession

Seduction Of The Innocent is an extraordinary book. It is a gripping, flamboyant melodrama masquerading as social psychology. Fredric Wertham is, like Senator McCarthy, like Batman, a crusader, a man with a mission, an evangelist. He wants to save the youth of America from its own worst impulses, from its id, from comic books. His attack on comic books is founded on an astonishingly crude stimulus-and-response model of reading, in which the child (the child, for Wertham, seems an unusually innocent, blank slate waiting to be written on) reads, absorbs and feels compelled to copy, if only in fantasy terms, the content of the comics. It is a model, in other words, which takes for granted extreme audience passivity.

This is not the place to go into a detailed refutation of Wertham's work, besides which such a refutation has already been done in Martin Barker's excellent *A Haunt of Fears*.[3] The central point of audience passivity needs stressing, however, because it is crucial to the celebrated passage where Wertham points his shrill, witch-hunting finger at the Dynamic Duo and cries "queer."

Such language is not present on the page, of course, but in some ways *Seduction Of The Innocent* (a film title crying out for either D.W. Griffith or Cecil B. DeMille) would be easier to stomach if it were. Instead, Wertham writes with anguished concern about the potential harm that Batman might do to vulnerable children, innocents who might be turned into deviants. He employs what was then conventional psychiatric wisdom about the idea of homosexuality as a 'phase':

> Many pre-adolescent boys pass through a phase of disdain for girls. Some comic books tend to fix that attitude and instill the idea that girls are only good for being banged around or used as decoys. A homoerotic attitude is also suggested by the presentation of masculine, bad, witch-like or violent women. In such comics women are

depicted in a definitely anti-erotic light, while the young male heroes
have pronounced erotic overtones. The muscular male supertype,
whose primary sex characteristics are usually well emphasized, is in
the setting of certain stories the object of homoerotic sexual curiosity
and stimulation.[4]

The implications of this are breathtaking. Homosexuality, for Wertham, is synonymous with misogyny. Men love other men because
they hate women. The sight of women being "banged around" is liable
to appeal to repressed homoerotic desires (this, I think, would be news
to the thousands of women who are systematically physically abused
by heterosexual men). Women who do not conform to existing stereo-
types of femininity are another incitement to homosexuality.

Having mapped out his terms of reference, Wertham goes on to peel
the lid from Wayne Manor:

> Sometimes Batman ends up in bed injured and young Robin is shown
> sitting next to him. At home they lead an idyllic life. They are Bruce
> Wayne and 'Dick' Grayson. Bruce Wayne is described as a 'socialite'
> and the official relationship is that Dick is Bruce's ward. They live in
> sumptuous quarters, with beautiful flowers in large vases, and have
> a butler, Alfred. Batman is sometimes shown in a dressing gown. . . .
> It is like a wish dream of two homosexuals living together. Sometimes
> they are shown on a couch, Bruce reclining and Dick sitting next to
> him, jacket off, collar open, and his hand on his friend's arm.[5]

So, Wertham's assumptions of homosexuality are fabricated out of
his interpretation of certain visual signs. To avoid being thought queer
by Wertham, Bruce and Dick should have done the following: never
show concern if the other is hurt, live in a shack, only have ugly flowers
in small vases, call the butler 'Chip' or 'Joe' if you have to have one at
all, never share a couch, keep your collar buttoned up, keep your jacket
on, and never, ever wear a dressing gown. After all, didn't Noel Coward
wear a dressing gown?

Wertham is easy to mock, but the identification of homosexuals
through dress codes has a long history.[6] Moreover, such codes originate
as semiotic systems adopted by gay people themselves, as a way of
signalling the otherwise invisible fact of sexual preference. There is a
difference, though, between sporting the secret symbols of a subculture
if you form part of that subculture and the elephantine spot-the-homo
routine that Wertham performs.

Bat-fans have always responded angrily to Wertham's accusation.
One calls it "one of the most incredible charges . . . unfounded rumours
. . . sly sneers"[7] and the general response has been to reassert the mascu-

linity of the two heros, mixed with a little indignation: "If they had been actual men they could have won a libel suit."[8] This seems to me not only to miss the point, but also to *reinforce* Wertham's homophobia—it is only possible to win a libel suit over an 'accusation' of homosexuality in a culture where homosexuality is deemed categorically inferior to heterosexuality.

Thus the rush to 'protect' Batman and Robin from Wertham is simply the other side to the coin of his bigotry. It may reject Wertham, cast him in the role of dirty-minded old man, but its view of homosexuality is identical. Mark Cotta Vaz thus describes the imputed homosexual relationship as "licentious" while claiming that in fact Bruce Wayne "regularly squired the most beautiful women in Gotham city and presumably had a healthy sex life."[9] Licentious versus healthy—Dr. Wertham himself could not have bettered this homophobic opposition.

Despite the passions aroused on both sides (or rather the two facets of the same side), there is something comic at the heart of this dispute. It is, simply, that Bruce and Dick are *not* real people but fictional constructions, and hence to squabble over their 'real' sex life is to take things a little too far. What is at stake here is the question of reading, of what readers do with the raw material that they are given. Readers are at liberty to construct whatever fantasy lives they like with the characters of the fiction they read (within the limits of generic and narrative credibility, that is). This returns us to the unfortunate patients of Dr. Wertham:

> One young homosexual during psychotherapy brought us a copy of *Detective* comic, with a Batman story. He pointed out a picture of "The Home of Bruce and Dick," a house beautifully landscaped, warmly lighted and showing the devoted pair side by side, looking out a picture window. When he was eight this boy had realized from fantasies about comic book pictures that he was aroused by men. At the age of ten or eleven, "I found my liking, my sexual desires, in comic books. I think I put myself in the position of Robin. I did want to have relations with Batman . . . I remember the first time I came across the page mentioning the "secret batcave." The thought of Batman and Robin living together and possibly having sex relations came to my mind. . . "[10]

Wertham quotes this to shock us, to impel us to tear the pages of *Detective* away before little Tommy grows up and moves to Greenwich Village, but reading it as a gay man today I find it rather moving and also highly recognizable.

What this anonymous gay man did was to practice that form of bricolage which Richard Dyer has identified as a characteristic reading strategy of gay audiences.[11] Denied even the remotest possibility of supportive images of homosexuality within the dominant heterosexual culture, gay people have had to fashion what we could out of the imageries of dominance, to snatch illicit meanings from the fabric of normality, to undertake a corrupt decoding for the purposes of satisfying marginalized desires.[12] This may not be as necessary as it once was, given the greater visibility of gay representations, but it is still an important practice. Wertham's patient evokes in me an admiration, that in a period of American history even more homophobic than most, there he was, raiding the citadels of masculinity, weaving fantasies of oppositional desire. What effect the dread Wertham had on him is hard to predict, but I profoundly hope that he wasn't 'cured.'

It wasn't only Batman who was subjected to Dr. Doom's bizarre ideas about human sexuality. Hence:

> The homosexual connotation of the Wonder Woman type of story is psychologically unmistakable. . . . For boys, Wonder Woman is a frightening image. For girls she is a morbid ideal. Where Batman is anti-feminine, the attractive Wonder Woman and her counterparts are definitely anti-masculine. Wonder Woman has her own female following. . . . Her followers are the 'Holiday girls', i.e. the holiday girls, the gay party girls, the gay girls.[13]

Just how much elision can be covered with one "i.e."? Wertham's view of homosexuality is not, at least, inconsistent. Strong, admirable women will turn little girls into dykes—such a heroine can only be seen as a 'morbid ideal.'

Crazed as Wertham's ideas were, their effectiveness is not in doubt. The mid-fifties saw a moral panic about the assumed dangers of comic books. In the United States companies were driven out of business, careers wrecked, and the Comics Code introduced. This had distinct shades of the Hays Code that had been brought in to clamp down on Hollywood in the 1930s, and under its jurisdiction comics opted for the bland, the safe and the reactionary. In Britain there was government legislation to prohibit the importing of American comics, as the comics panic slotted neatly into a whole series of anxieties about the effects on British youth of American popular culture.[14]

And in all of this, what happened to Batman? He turned into Fred MacMurray from *My Three Sons*. He lost any remaining edge of the shadowy vigilante of his earliest years, and became an upholder of the most stifling small town American values. Batwoman and Batgirl appeared (June Allyson and Bat-Gidget) to take away any lingering doubts about the Dynamic Duo's sex lives. A 1963 story called "The Great Clayface-Joker Feud" has some especially choice examples of the new, squeaky-clean sexuality of the assembled Bats.

Bat-Girl says to Robin, "I can hardly wait to get into my Bat-Girl costume again! Won't it be terrific if we could go on a crime case together like the last time? (sigh)." Robin replies, "It sure would, Betty (sigh)." The elder Bats look on approvingly. Bat-Girl is Batwoman's niece—to make her a daughter would have implied that Batwoman had had (gulp) sexual intercourse, and that would never do. This is the era of Troy Donohue and Pat Boone, and *Batman* as ever serves as a cultural thermometer, taking the temperature of the times.

The Clayface/Joker business is wrapped up (the villains of this period are wacky conjurors, nothing more, with no menace or violence about them) and the episode concludes with another tableau of terrifying heterosexual contentment. "Oh Robin," simpers Batgirl, "I'm afraid you'll just have to hold me! I'm still so shaky after fighting Clayface . . . and you're so strong!" Robin: "Gosh Batgirl, it was swell of you to calm me down when I was worried about Batman tackling Clayface alone." (One feels a distinct Wertham influence here: if Robin shows concern about Batman, wheel on a supportive female, the very opposite of a 'morbid ideal,' to minister in a suitably self-effacing way.) Bat-woman here seizes her chance and tackles Batman: "You look worried about Clayface, Batman . . . so why don't you follow Robin's example and let me soothe you?" Batman can only reply "Gulp."

Gulp indeed. While it's easy simply to laugh at strips like these, knowing as we do the way in which such straight-faced material would be mercilessly shredded by the sixties' TV series, they do reveal the retreat into coziness forced on comics by the Wertham onslaught and its repercussions. There no doubt were still subversive readers of *Batman*, erasing Batgirl on her every preposterous appearance and reworking the Duo's capers to leave some room for homoerotic speculation, but such a reading would have had to work so much harder than before. The *Batman* of this era was such a closed text, so immune to polysemic interpretation, that its interest today is only as a symptom—or, more productively, as camp. "The Great Clayface-Joker Feud" may have been published in 1963, but in every other respect it is a fifties' text. If the 1960s began for the world in general with the Beatles, the 1960s for *Batman* began with the TV series in 1966. If the Caped Crusader had been all but Werthamed out of existence, he was about to be camped back into life.

The Camped Crusader and the Boys Wondered

Trying to define Camp is like attempting to sit in the corner of a circular room. It can't be done, which only adds to the quixotic appeal of the attempt. Try these:

To be camp is to present oneself as being committed to the marginal with a commitment greater than the marginal merits.[15]

Camp sees everything in quotation marks. It's not a lamp but a 'lamp'; not a woman but a 'woman'. . . . It is the farthest extension, in sensibility, of the metaphor of life as theatre.[16]

Camp is . . . a way of poking fun at the whole cosmology of restrictive sex roles and sexual identifications which our society uses to oppress its women and repress its men.[17]

Camp was and is a way for gay men to re-imagine the world around them . . . by exaggerating, stylizing and remaking what is usually thought to be average or normal.[18]

Camp was a prison for an illegal minority; now it is a holiday for consenting adults.[19]

All true, in their way, but all inadequate. The problem with camp is that it is primarily an experiential rather than an analytical discourse. Camp is a set of attitudes, a gallery of snapshots, an inventory of postures, a modus vivendi, a shop-full of frocks, an arch of eyebrows, a great big pink butterfly that just won't be pinned down. Camp is primarily an adjective, occasionally a verb, but never anything as prosaic, as earth-bound, as a noun.

Yet if I propose to use this adjective as a way of describing one or more of the guises of Batman, I need to arrive at some sort of working definition. So, for the purposes of this analysis, I intend the term camp to refer to a playful, knowing, self-reflexive theatricality. *Batman*, the sixties' TV series, was nothing if not knowing. It employed the codes of camp in an unusually public and heavily signalled way. This makes it different from those people or texts who are taken up by camp audiences without ever consciously putting camp into practice. The difference may be very briefly spelled out by reference to Hollywood films. If *Mildred Pierce* and *The Letter* were taken up *as* camp, teased by primarily gay male audiences into yielding meaning not intended by their makers, then *Whatever Happened To Baby Jane?* is a piece of self-conscious camp, capitalizing on certain attitudinal and stylistic tendencies known to exist in audiences. *Baby Jane* is also, significantly, a 1960s' film, and the 1960s were the decade in which camp swished out of the ghetto and up into the scarcely prepared mainstream.

A number of key events and texts reinforced this. Susan Sontag wrote her *Notes On Camp*, which remains the starting point for researchers even now. Pop Art was in vogue (and in *Vogue*) and whatever the more elevated claims of Lichtenstein, Warhol and the rest, their art-works were on one level a new inflection of camp. The growing intellectual respectability of pop music displayed very clearly that the old barriers that once rigidly separated high and low culture were no longer in force. The James Bond films, and even more so their successors like *Modesty Blaise*, popularized a dry, self-mocking wit that makes up one part of the multifaceted diamond of camp. And on television there were *The Avengers*, *The Man From UNCLE*, *Thunderbirds*, and *Batman*.

To quote the inevitable Sontag, "The whole point of Camp is to dethrone the serious. . . . More precisely, Camp involves a new, more complex relation to 'the serious.' One can be serious about the frivolous, frivolous about the serious."[20]

The problem with Batman in those terms is that there was never anything truly serious to begin with (unless one swallows that whole portentous Dark Knight charade, more of which in the next section). Batman in its comic book form had, unwittingly, always been camp— it was serious (the tone, the moral homilies) about the frivolous (a man in a stupid suit). He was camp in the way that classic Hollywood was camp, but what the sixties' TV series and film did was to overlay this 'innocent' camp with a thick layer of ironic distance, the self-mockery version of camp. And given the long associations of camp with the homosexual male subculture, Batman was a particular gift on the grounds of his relationship with Robin. As George Melly put it, "The real Batman series were beautiful because of their unselfconscious absurdity. The remakes, too, at first worked on a double level. Over the absorbed children's heads we winked and nudged, but in the end what were we laughing at? The fact they didn't know that Batman had it off with Robin."[21]

It was as if Wertham's fears were being vindicated at last, but his 1950s' bigot's anguish had been supplanted by a self-consciously hip 1960s' playfulness. What adult audiences laughed at in the sixties' *Batman* was a camped-up version of the fifties they had just left behind.

Batman's lessons in good citizenship ("We'd like to feel that our efforts may help every youngster to grow up into an honest, useful citizen"[22]) were another part of the character ripe for ridiculing deconstruction—"Let's go, Robin, we've set another youth on the road to a brighter tomorrow" (the episode "It's How You Play The Game"). Everything the Adam West Batman said was a parody of seriousness, and how could it be otherwise? How could anyone take genuinely seriously the words of a man dressed like that?

The Batman/Robin relationship is never referred to directly; more fun can be had by presenting it 'straight,' in other words, screamingly camp. Wertham's reading of the Dubious Duo had been so extensively aired as to pass into the general consciousness (in George Kelly's words, "We all knew Robin and Batman were pouves"[23]), it was part of the fabric of *Batman*, and the makers of the TV series proceeded accordingly.

Consider the Duo's encounter with Marsha, Queen of Diamonds. The threat she embodies is nothing less than heterosexuality itself, the deadliest threat to the domestic bliss of the Bat-couple. She is even about to marry Batman before Alfred intervenes to save the day. He and Batman flee the church, but have to do so in the already decorated Batmobile, festooned with wedding paraphernalia including a large 'Just Married' sign. "We'll have to drive it as it is," says Batman, while somewhere in the audience a Dr. Wertham takes feverish notes. Robin, Commissioner Gordon and Chief O'Hara have all been drugged with Marsha's 'Cupid's Dart,' but it is of course the Boy Wonder who Batman saves first. The dart, he tells Robin, "contains some secret ingredient by which your sense and your will were affected," and it isn't hard to read that ingredient as heterosexual desire, since its result, seen in the previous episode, was to turn Robin into Marsha's slobbering slave.

We can tell with relief now, though, as Robin is "back in fighting form" (with impeccable timing, Batman clasps Robin's shoulder on the word 'fighting'). Marsha has one last attempt to destroy the duo, but naturally she fails. The female temptress, the seductress, the enchantress must be vanquished. None of this is in the least subtle (Marsha's cat, for example, is called Circe) but this type of mass-market camp can't afford the luxury of subtlety. The threat of heterosexuality is similarly mobilized in the 1966 feature film, where it is Bruce Wayne's infatuation with Kitka (Catwoman in disguise) that causes all manner of problems.

A more interesting employment of camp comes in the episodes where the Duo battle the Black Widow, played by Tallulah Bankhead. The major camp coup here, of course, is the casting. Bankhead was one of the supreme icons of camp, one of its goddesses, "Too intelligent not to be self-conscious, too ambitious to bother about her self-consciousness, too insecure ever to be content, but too arrogant ever to admit insecurity, Tallulah personified camp."[24]

A heady claim, but perhaps justified, because the Black Widow episodes are, against stiff competition, the campest slices of Batman of them all. The stories about Bankhead are legendary—the time when on finding no toilet paper in her cubicle she slipped a ten dollar bill under the partition and asked the woman next door for two fives, or her whispered remark to a priest conducting a particularly elaborate service and swinging a censor of smoking incense, "Darling, I love the drag, but your purse is on fire"—and casting her in Batman was the final demonstration of the series' commitment to camp.

The plot is unremarkable, the usual Bat-shenanigans, the pleasure lies in the detail. Details like the elderly Bankhead crammed into her Super-Villainess costume, or like the way in which (through a plot detail I won't go into) she impersonates Robin, so we see Burt Ward miming to Bankhead's voice, giving the unforgettable image of Robin flirting with burly traffic cops. Best of all, and Bankhead isn't even in this scene but the thrill of having her involved clearly spurred the writer to new heights of camp, Batman has to sing a song to break free of the Black Widow's spell. Does he choose to sing "God Bless America?" Nothing so rugged. He clutches a flower to his Bat chest and sings Gilbert and Sullivan's "I'm Just Little Buttercup." It is this single image, more than any other, that prevents me from taking the post-Adam West Dark Knight at all seriously.

The fundamental camp trick which the series pulls is to make the comics speak. What was acceptable on the page, in speech balloons, stands revealed as ridiculous once given audible voice. The famous visualized sound effects (URKKK! KA-SPLOOSH!) that are for many the fondest memory of the series work along similar lines. Camp often makes its point by transposing the codes of one cultural form into the inappropriate codes of another. It thrives on mischievous incongruity.

The incongruities, the absurdities, the sheer ludicrousness of Batman were brought out so well by the sixties' version that for some audience there will never be another credible approach. I have to include myself here. I've recently read widely in post-sixties Bat-lore, and I can appreciate what the writers and artists are trying to do, but my Batman will always be Adam West. It's impossible to be sombre or pompous about Batman because if you try the ghost of West will come Bat-climbing into your mind, fortune cookie wisdom on his lips and keen young Dick by his side. It's significant, I think, that the letters I received from the editors of this book began "Dear Bat-Contributor." Writers preparing chapters about James Joyce or Ingmar Bergman do not, I suspect, receive analogous greetings. To deny the large camp component of Batman is to blind oneself to one of the richest parts of his history.

Is There Bat-Life After Bat-Camp?

The international success of the Adam West incarnation left Batman high and dry. The camping around had been fun while it lasted, but it hadn't lasted very long. Most camp humour has a relatively short life-span, new targets are always needed, and the camp aspect of Batman had been squeezed dry. The mass public had moved on to other heroes, other genres, other acres of merchandising, but there was still a hard

Bat-core of fans to satisfy. Where could the Bat go next? Clearly there was no possibility of returning to the caped Eisenhower, the benevolent patriarch of the 1950s. That option had been well and truly closed down by the TV show. Batman needed to be given his dignity back, and this entailed a return to his roots.

This, in any case, is the official version. For the unreconstructed devotee of the Batman (that is, people who insist on giving him the definite article before the name), the West years had been hell—a tricksy travesty, an effeminizing of the cowled avenger. There's a scene in *Midnight Cowboy* where Dustin Hoffman tells Jon Voight that the only audience liable to be receptive to his cowboy clothes are gay men looking for rough trade. Voight is appalled—"you mean to tell me John Wayne was a fag?" (quoted, roughly, from memory). This outrage, this horror at shattered illusions, comes close to encapsulating the loathing and dread the campy Batman has received from the old guard of Gotham City and the younger born-again Bat-fans.

So what has happened since the 1960s has been the painstaking re-heterosexualization of Batman, I apologize for coining such a clumsy word, but no other quite gets the sense that I mean. This strategy has worked, too, for large audiences, reaching its peak with the 1989 film. To watch this and then come home to see a video of the 1966 movie is to grasp how complete the transformation has been. What I want to do in this section is to trace some of the crucial moments in that change, written from the standpoint of someone still unashamedly committed to Bat-camp.

If one wants to take Batman as a Real Man, the biggest stumbling block has always been Robin. There have been disingenuous claims that "Batman and Robin had a blood-brother closeness. Theirs was a spiritual intimacy forged from the stress of countless battles fought side by side"[25] (one can imagine what Tallulah Bankhead might say to *that*), but we know otherwise. The Wertham lobby and the acolytes of camp alike have ensured that any Batman/Robin relationship is guaranteed to bring on the sniggers. Besides which, in the late 1960s, Robin was getting to be a big boy, too big for any shreds of credibility to attach themselves to all that father-son smokescreen. So in 1969 Dick Grayson was packed off to college and the Bat was solitary once more.

This was a shrewd move. It's impossible to conceive of the recent, obsessive, sturm-und-drang Batman with a chirpy little Robin getting in the way.[26] A text of the disturbing power of *The Killing Joke* could not have functioned with Robin to rupture the grim dualism of its Batman/Joker struggle. There was, however, a post-Dick Robin, but he was killed off by fans in that infamous telephone poll.

It's intriguing to speculate how much latent (or blatant) homophobia lay behind that vote. Did the fans decide to kill off Jason Todd so as to redeem Batman for unproblematic heterosexuality? Impossible to say. There are other factors to take into account, such as Jason's apparent failure to live up to the expectations of what a Robin should be like. The sequence of issues in which Jason/Robin died, *A Death in the Family*, is worth looking at in some detail, however, in order to see whether the camp connotations of Bruce and Dick had been fully purged.

The depressing answer is that they had. This is very much the Batman of the 1980s, his endless feud with the Joker this time uneasily stretched over a framework involving the Middle East and Ethiopia. Little to be camp about there, though the presence of the Joker guarantees a quota of sick jokes. The sickest of all is the introduction of the Ayatollah Kohomeini, a real and important political figure, into this fantasy world of THUNK! and THER-ACKK! and grown men dressed as bats. (As someone who lived in the part of England from which Reagan's planes took off on their murderous mission to bomb Libya, I fail to see the humor in this cartoon version of American foreign policy: it's too near the real thing.)

Jason dies at the Joker's hands because he becomes involved in a search for his own origins, a clear parallel to Batman's endless returns to *his* Oedipal scenario. Families, in the Bat-mythology, are dark and troubled things, one more reason why the introduction of the fifties versions of Batwoman and Bat-Girl seemed so inappropriate. This applies only to real, biological families, though; the true familial bond is between Batman and Robin, hence the title of these issues. Whether one chooses to read Robin as Batman's ward (official version), son (approved fantasy) or lover (forbidden fantasy), the sense of loss at his death is bound to be devastating. Batman finds Robin's body and, in the time-honored tradition of Hollywood cinema, is at least able to give him a loving embrace. Good guys hug their dead buddies, only queers smooch when still alive.

If the word 'camp' is applied at all to the eighties' Batman, it is a label for the Joker. This sly displacement is the cleverest method yet devised of preserving Bat-heterosexuality. The play that the texts regularly make with the concept of Batman and the Joker as mirror images now takes a new twist. The Joker is Batman's 'bad twin,' and part of that badness is, increasingly, an implied homosexuality. This is certainly present in the 1989 film, a generally glum and portentous affair except for Jack Nicholson's Joker, a characterization enacted with venomous camp. The only moment when this dour film comes to life is when the

Joker and his gang raid the Art Gallery, spraying the paintings and generally camping up a storm.

The film strives and strains to make us forget the Adam West Batman, to the point of giving us Vicki Vale as Bruce Wayne's lover, and certainly Michael Keaton's existential agonizing (variations on the theme of why-did-I-have-to-be-a-Bat) is a world away from West's gleeful subversion of truth, justice and the American Way. This is the same species of Batman celebrated by Frank Miller: "If your only memory of Batman is that of Adam West and Burt Ward exchanging camped-out quips while clobbering slumming guest-stars Vincent Price and Cesar Romero, I hope this book will come as a surprise. . . . For me, Batman was never funny. . . ."[27]

The most recent linkage of the Joker with homosexuality comes in *Arkham Asylum*, the darkest image of the Bat-world yet. Here the Joker has become a parody of a screaming queen, calling Batman "honey pie," given to exclamations like "oooh!" (one of the oldest homophobic cliches in the book) and pinching Batman's behind with the advice, "loosen up, tight ass." He also, having no doubt read his Wertham, follows the pinching by asking, "What's the matter? Have I touched a nerve? How is the Boy Wonder? Started shaving yet?" The Bat-response is unequivocal: "Take your filthy hands off me . . . Filthy degenerate!"

Arkham Asylum is a highly complex reworking of certain key aspects of the mythology, of which the sexual tension between Batman and the Joker is only one small part. Nonetheless the Joker's question "Have I touched a nerve?" seems a crucial one, as revealed by the homophobic ferocity of Batman's reply. After all, the dominant cultural construction of gay men at the end of the 1980s is as plague carriers, and the word 'degenerate' is not far removed from some of the labels affixed to us in the age of AIDS.

Batman: Is He or Isn't He?

The one constant factor through all of the transformations of Batman has been the devotion of his admirers. They will defend him against what they see as negative interpretations, and they carry around in their heads a kind of essence of batness, a Bat-Platonic Ideal of how Batman should really be. The Titan Books reissue of key comics from the 1970s each carry a preface by a noted fan, and most of them contain claims such as "This, I feel, is Batman as he was meant to be."[28]

Where a negative construction is specifically targeted, no prizes for guessing which one it is: "you . . . are probably also fond of the TV show he appeared in. But then maybe you prefer Elvis Presley's Vegas years or the later Jerry Lewis movies over their early stuff . . . for me, the definitive Batman was then and always will be the one portrayed in these pages."[29]

The sixties' TV show remains anathema to the serious Bat-fan precisely because it heaps ridicule on the very notion of a serious Batman. *Batman* the series revealed the man in the cape as a pompous fool, an embodiment of superceded ethics, and a closet queen. As Marsha, Queen of Diamonds, put it, "Oh Batman, darling, you're so divinely square." Perhaps the enormous success of the 1989 film will help to advance the cause of the rival Bat-archetype, the grim, vengeful Dark Knight whose heterosexuality is rarely called into question (his humorlessness, fondness for violence and obsessive monomania seem to me exemplary qualities for a heterosexual man). The answer, surely, is that they needn't be mutually exclusive.

If I might be permitted a rather camp comparison, each generation has its definitive Hamlet, so why not the same for Batman? I'm prepared to admit the validity, for some people, of the swooping eighties' vigilante, so why are they so concerned to trash my sixties' camped crusader? Why do they insist so vehemently that Adam West was a faggy aberration, a blot on the otherwise impeccably butch Bat-landscape? What *are* they trying to hide?

If I had a suspicious frame of mind, I might think that they were protesting too much, that maybe Dr. Wertham was on to something when he targeted these narratives as incitements to homosexual fantasy. And if I want Batman to be gay, then, for me, he is. After all, outside of the minds of his writers and readers, he doesn't really exist.

Notes

1. Fredric Wertham, *Seduction Of The Innocent* (London: Museum Press, 1955), p. 190.
2. Susan Sontag, "Notes on Camp," in *A Susan Sontag Reader* (Harmondsworth: Penguin Books), p. 106.
3. Martin Barker, *A Haunt Of Fears* (London: Pluto Press, 1984).
4. Wertham, p. 188.
5. Wertham, p. 190.
6. See, for example, the newspaper stories on 'how to spot' homosexuals printed in Britain in the fifties and sixties, and discussed in Jeffrey Weeks, *Coming Out: Homosexual Politics in Britain* (London: Quartet, 1979).
7. Phrases taken from Chapters 5 and 6 of Mark Cotta Vaz, *Tales Of The Dark Knight: Batman's First Fifty Years* (London: Futura, 1989).
8. Les Daniels, *Comix: A History of Comic Books in America* (New York: Bonanza Books, 1971), p. 87.

9. Cotta Vaz, pp. 47 and 53.

10. Wertham, p. 192.

11. Richard Dyer, ed., *Gays and Film*, 2nd Edition (New York: Zoetrope, 1984), p. 1.

12. See Richard Dyer, "Judy Garland and Gay Men", in Dyer, *Heavenly Bodies* (London: BFI, 1987) and Claire Whitaker, "Hollywood Transformed: Interviews with Lesbian Viewers," in Peter Steven, ed., *Jump Cut: Hollywood, Politics and Counter-Cinema* (Toronto: Between the Lines, 1985).

13. Wertham, pp. 192–3.

14. See Barker.

15. Mark Booth, *Camp* (London: Quartet, 1983), p. 18.

16. Sontag, p. 109.

17. Jack Babuscio, "Camp and the Gay Sensibility", in Dyer, ed., *Gays and Film*, p. 46.

18. Michael Bronski, *Culture Clash: The Making of Gay Sensibility* (Boston: South End Press,), p. 42.

19. Philip Core, *Camp: The Lie That Tells The Truth* (London: Plexus), p. 7.

20. Sontag, p. 116.

21. George Melly, *Revolt Into Style: The Pop Arts in the 50s and 60s* (Oxford: Oxford University Press, 1989 (first published 1970)), p. 193.

22. "The Batman Says," *Batman #* 3 (1940), quoted in Cotta Vaz, p. 15.

23. Melly, p. 192.

24. Core, p. 25.

25. Cotta Vaz, p. 53.

26. A female Robin is introduced in the *Dark Knight Returns* series, which, while raising interesting questions about the sexuality of Batman, which I don't here have the space to address, seems significant in that the Dark Knight cannot run the risk of reader speculation that a traditionally-male Robin might provoke.

27. Frank Miller, "Introduction," *Batman: Year One* (London: Titan, 1988).

28. Kim Newman, "Introduction," *Batman: The Demon Awakes* (London: Titan, 1989).

29. Jonathan Ross, "Introduction," to *Batman: Vow From the Grave* (London: Titan, 1989).

9

Batman: The Movie,
Narrative: The Hyperconscious

Jim Collins

Perhaps the best way to introduce the difficulties involved in trying to specify the distinctive features of the Batman narrative in its various incarnations is to begin by relating what occurred when I began my field work for this article.[1] Entering a mall bookstore, I was faced with a massive Batman display that held the following texts: the novelization of Tim Burton's film *Batman*, the graphic novels of Frank Miller, *The Dark Knight Returns* and *Batman: Year One*, another graphic novel (in format at least) entitled *Batman's Greatest Adventures*, which promised to be the best of the original comic books, a traditional small format paperback, *The Further Adventures of Batman*, in which authors such as Isaac Asimov, Max Collins, Robert Silverberg, Joe R. Landsdale and Stuart Kaminsky constructed still more narratives that promised to take Batman into genres hitherto unexplored, and the *Batman Role-Playing Game*, which allows individual readers/players to assume Bat identities and construct their own narrative adventures as "participants." At the local comic shop I found the current Batman comic books (standard format), as well as a compilation of one of the most popular of the recent series of comics, bound as the graphic novel *A Death in the Family* and Alan Moore's special format comic, *Batman: The Killing Joke.*

The array presented multiple narrativizations of the same figure produced over a fifty-year period, appearing as simultaneous options, a simultaneity made more complicated by the fact that these narratives were not just continuations of an Ur text, but, in the case of the *Batman* film and *Batman: Year One* very ambitious attempts to re-construct the beginnings of the Batman story, re-inventing, as it were, the point of origin for the seemingly endless re-articulations. This array of texts could obviously generate any number of narrative analyses that might concentrate on consistent or inconsistent plot functions, significant alterations in the configuration of characters, the use and abuse of certain topoi, etc. I cannot hope to do justice to all these possibilities in an essay of this length, so I will concentrate on what I consider the distinguishing feature of recent popular narrative,[2] namely its increasing hyperconsciousness about both the history of popular culture and the shifting status of popular culture in the current context.

That popular texts demonstrate an awareness of their antecedents and their rivals in the marketplace is itself not a new development. John Cawelti, in his overview of the genre films of the sixties and seventies, focused on their "generic transformation" of the mythology of popular culture according to four different perspectives: the burlesque, demythologization, the evocation of nostalgia, and affirmation of myth for its own sake.[3] I have argued elsewhere[4] that popular texts construct quite elaborate intertextual arenas at every stage of their development, not just in a post-classical decadent stage—e.g. that even within the classic period of British detective fiction in the thirties, texts were already situating themselves very self-consciously in relation to earlier forms of the detective novel, as well as the Great Tradition of the British novel. The hyperconsciousness of popular narrative in the eighties is not a matter of popular culture "suddenly" becoming self-reflexive. Like their forebears, popular texts in the eighties acknowledge the force of what Umberto Eco (1987) calls "the already said,"[5] but rather than simply rework conventions within the confines of a specific genre (as do, say, *Chinatown* (1974), *The Wild Bunch* (1969), *All That Jazz* (1979), etc.), texts like Tim Burton's *Batman* (1989), Frank Miller's *The Dark Knight Returns* (1986), and Alan Moore's *Watchmen* (1986), re-configure that "already said" by moving across genres, mixing different forms of discourse as well as different media, which by extension alters their traditional modes of circulation.

This reconfiguration involves the inversion of specific generic conventions, but more importantly, it depends upon the amalgamation of disparate narrative and visual codes. Joe R. Landsdale's short story, "Subway Jack: A Batman Adventure,"[6] for example, is constructed from a number of fragments that feature different narrative modes—journal entries, case files from the Bat computer, first person narration from Batman and Commissioner Gordon's perspectives, third person narration from the authorial voice, and so forth. This combination of fragments is not especially new or unique, since epistolary novels like Bram Stoker's *Dracula* (1895), for instance, feature exactly such a mixture. Landsdale's story is set apart by the introduction of comic book panels into this series of fragments, at which point the prose of the "short story" gives way to the visual narration of the comic book. In these panels, Landsdale describes in minute detail not the action as such, but the representation of the action within the panel, for example:

Series of Panels, Rich in Shadow and Movement

1)Batcave—Interior

Background: Blue black with stalactites hanging down from the cave roof like witch fingers. There's enough light that we can see the wink of glass trophy cases. Their interiors, except for two—once containing a sampling of the Penguin's umbrellas and another containing Robin's retired uniform—are too dark for us to make out their contents. But we can see the larger. . .[7]

The juxtaposition of different media underscores the inseparability of the action from its codified representation; it acknowledges, very explicitly, the complexity of current popular culture in which the negotiation of the array (of the "already said") forms an essential part of the "action" of the narrative for both author and audience. In a recent *Dr. Strange* comic,[8] for example, the cover appears to be that of a tabloid rather than a comic, entitled *Now*, self-consciously modeled after the *National Inquirer*. This cover promises "A Special Bound-to-be-Controversial New-Book Excerpt about Dr. Strange—The Man—The Myth—the Magic," as well as a "Startling Interview with Dr. Strange Author Morgana Blessing," and another story in which Janet Van Dyne (a.k.a. The Wasp of *Avengers* fame) tells Princess Di to "Keep your hands off my man, Princess!" The first page of the "comic" shows an enraged Dr. Strange throwing down this copy of *Now* in disgust, followed by two pages of comic book panels in which Strange discusses this outrage with his colleagues. On the following page, the comic gives way to the tabloid excerpt, an extended prose section featuring "photographs" of Dr. Strange (his high school graduation picture—"Portrait of the Sorcerer as a Young Man—his mansion on Bleeker Street, his meeting with Moebius on a recent trip to Paris), file photos of the actual locations of his adventures, artist's conceptions of the author Blessing's description of those adventures, stills from a short-lived TV show, a series of photos and drawings of "the Drac Pack," a vampires-through-the-ages composite. This section is followed by the interview with the author, after which the comic panels return and then give way to a "Guest Editorial" by J. Jonah Jameson (editor of *The Daily Bugle*, featured in *Spiderman* and other Marvel comics), "reprinted" from *Now* magazine, in which Jameson questions the validity of the excerpts and discusses plans for their publication and circulation.

This hybridization of popular narrative does not destabilize the already said as much as it reveals its fluidity, the absence of any kind of unseen hand or unitary hierarchy that might still delimit the appropriate subject matter, function, and audience for different forms of cultural production. In their seminal study of the Bond phenomenon,[9] Tony Bennett and Janet Woollacott make the key point that Bond is a "mobile signifier," subject to "multiple activations" which adhere to the texts like so many encrustations, thereby undermining any notion of the "text itself" or the "original" text. The figure of the superhero, especially Batman, has clearly become such a mobile signifier, but the activations of Batman by Burton, Miller, and company in the later eighties are differentiated from the redefinitions of Bond in the sixties and seventies by the degree of hyperconsciousness the former display concerning their own status as mobile signifiers, subject to further rearticulation as they circulate throughout disparate cultures, or more accurately, different micro-cultures. The focus of this essay will be this hybridization, this narration by amalgamation that is a response to the ways that the superhero has been already activated, an attempt to re-tell the story of Batman that recognizes full well that re-telling the story is impossible without reconfiguring the encrustations that have become as inseparable from the "text" as any generic convention or plot function.

Gaudi Knight: Calling Up and Cutting Up the Past

Just as we can no longer imagine popular narratives to be so ignorant of their intertextual dimensions and cultural significance, we can no longer presuppose that the attitude toward their antecedents, their very "retro" quality will be in any way univocal. Divergent strategies of re-articulation can be discerned not only between different "retro" texts, but even more importantly, within individual texts that adopt shifting, ambivalent attitudes toward these antecedents. Burton's *Batman* depends on two such conflicting strategies, and the differences between them are perhaps best understood by comparing the scenes in which Batman and the Joker actively play with images. Throughout the film we see both figures watching television and manipulating images. That the struggle between them is in large part a televisual one becomes most obvious when the Joker, seeing that Batman has gained greater coverage on the local news program, asks what kind of world he lives in "when a guy in a Bat suit can steal my press" then smashes his set in disgust. The destruction of the image here is part of a series of image deformations that the Joker engages in throughout the film. In his hideout we see the Joker producing "cut-ups" out of the photographic images which surround him, and then in the later scene at the museum he defaces one masterpiece after another, either by painting over the original or writing his name over its surface. This hijacking of signs is most obvious in his seizure of the television signal and his replacement of scheduled programming with his own gruesomely parodic advertisements.

Batman's manipulation of images, on the other hand, operate according to an altogether different dynamic. Like the Joker, Batman is shown watching television a number of times in the film, and like his adversary, he appears to be surrounded by images that he controls for his own purposes. Just as the Joker appears to be practically engulfed by the images he cuts up, the first shots of Batman in the Batcave show him before a bank of video monitors, surrounded on all sides by the images of his guests that his hidden cameras have been recording, and which he *calls up* rather than *cuts up* in order to bring back a reality that he has somehow missed. Where the Joker's manipulation of images is a process of deformation, Batman engages in a process of retrieval, drawing from that reservoir of images which constitutes "the past." This tension between abduction and retrieval epitomizes the conflicting strategies at work in this film, a text which alternately hijacks and "accesses" the traditional Batman topoi.

The tension between these two opposing yet intermingled strategies of rearticulation is especially prominent in the climactic confrontation between the pair atop the cathedral. The scene's function within the plot could hardly be more traditional—Batman and archvillain face-off in a final battle conducted in an outrageously oversized, artificially isolated location with Batman using his physical prowess and his utility belt to conquer his opponent. In providing the expected narrative closure, the film unproblematically calls up the appropriate narrative topoi. But the work of the narration here is not restricted to completing the plot, the syntagmatic axis of the narrative. The layering of intertexts that occurs simultaneously deforms those same topoi by re-situating them along a paradigmatic axis of antecedent representations of suspense, horror, etc., making explicit connections that were traditionally unstated, as well as introducing juxtapositions that are "foreign" to the Batman myth. As for the former, the choice of the cathedral, complete with gargoyles, is the culmination of the Gothic citations that pervade the text, citations which represent the medieval, Romantic, Modernist, and Post-Modernist incarnations simultaneously—e.g. the explicitly Gothic dimension of the cathedral's ornamentation and interior, as well as the Wayne Mansion and the chemical plant that resembles a Gothic castle more than a factory, the *mise en scene* that visualizes Batman as a menacing figure from "the darkness," the suggestion that he is a blood-drinking vampire, the doppelganger relationship between the hero-villain, the use of the woman (specifically the control of the woman's body) as the embodiment of their conflict, the very self-conscious invocation of Gaudi's Sagrada Familia Cathedral in Barcelona.

But the cathedral scene in *Batman* is not simply a filmic equivalent of Gaudi's design. The former is differentiated from the latter by both the simultaneous presence of the multiplicity of Gothic incarnations as well as the introduction of other citations not so explicitly associated with the Gothic. The narration of the film, the very formation of the *mise en scene*, depends upon a process of calling up the Gothic, but it also "steals" specific shots from classical Hollywood films just as self-consciously. The high angle shots of the seemingly endless flights of stairs is reminiscent of *Vertigo* (as is the basic deployment of characters—woman at the top of the stairs, hero working his way up to save her), and the alternation of high angle and low angle shots between the Joker and Batman and Vicky Vale as they hang from the side of the Cathedral is explicitly taken from the conclusion of *North by Northwest* (as well as the climactic confrontation scene in *Blade Runner*). The invocation of texts as different as *Dracula*, Notre Dame de Paris, the Sagrada Familia, and *Vertigo*, as well as all the antecedent comic and graphic novel versions of Batman produces an eclecticism that is in many ways even more complicated than Gaudi's Cathedral, which Post-Modernist architects consider one of the high temples of eclecticism. Where Gaudi's Cathedral is a repertoire of architectural styles, the narrative structure of Batman is founded on a hybrid repertoire, calling up and/or abducting motifs from cinematic and non-cinematic texts alike—comic books, Hollywood films, nineteenth-century novels, medieval architecture, etc.

In his article "*Casablanca:* Cult Movies and Intertextual Collage" (written well before Burton's *Batman* went into production), Umberto Eco argues that *Casablanca* remains a cult favorite because "Forced to improvise a plot, the authors mixed a little of everything, and everything they chose came from a repertoire that had stood the test of time. When only a few of these formulas are used, the result is kitsch. But when the repertoire of stock formulas is used wholesale, then the result is architecture like Gaudi's Sagrada Familia: the same vertigo, the same stroke of genius."[10] The relevance of the quote to this scene in *Batman* is obviously uncanny, but I introduce it here in order to distinguish between the intertextual narration of *Casablanca* and *Batman*. Although both rely on repertoires of what Eco has referred to as "the already said," the uses of that repertoire reflect quite different negotiations of their semiotic environments. Where the former might well be a surplus that suggests pastiche, the latter reflects a meticulously constructed *intertextual arena* in which the text positions itself within its own invented array.[11] Eco himself acknowledges that *Casablanca* and a film like *Raiders of the Lost Ark* involve different contexts regarding both their production and reception, insisting that "It would be semiotically uninteresting to look for quotations of archetypes in *Raiders* or in *Indiana Jones.* They were conceived within a meta-semiotic culture, and what the semiotician can find in them is exactly what the directors put there. Spielberg and Lucas are semiotically nourished authors working for a culture of instinctive semioticians."[12] One could easily add Tim Burton, Anton Furst, and company to that list of artists, and *Batman*'s audience must certainly be as instinctively semiotic in their orientation. But Eco seriously underestimates the "interesting-ness" of meta-semiotic cultures, and his preference for the naiveté of *Casablanca* (and its authors and audiences) seems like badly misplaced nostalgia that fails to specify when a semiotic sophistication somehow corrupted the innocent pleasures of popular culture. What Eco fails to pursue here is just when this semiotic nourishment began, or when audiences became "instinctively" something other than they were before. What factors produced such awesome and all-pervasive changes in just four decades?

Answering that question has everything to do with specifying the distinctive features of contemporary popular narrative, but it is answerable only if we begin by rejecting the notion that texts are "interesting" semiotically only when they can be decoded/re-encoded by an analyst capable of exposing the hidden textual mechanisms. The foregrounding of the citations, the explicitness of the calling-up/cutting-up process reflects a different dynamic in the exchange between producer and audience, one based on the sophistication of both parties, each possess-ing knowledge formerly (and allegedly) accessible only to the semioti-cian. The hyperconsciousness of both sides of the "communication exchange" results from the persistence of the repertoire of antecedent representations, which continue to live in both the various institution-alized reservoirs of images (the comics industry, television, etc.), and by extension in the cultural memory of the audiences that have refused to treat popular texts as disposable commodities. The intertextual nar-ration in a film like *Batman* does indeed depend on a kind of meta-semiotic environment, and as such it is a shining example of meta-popular culture. The emergence of this "meta-pop"[13] in the eighties is due to a number of interconnected factors, but its all-pervasiveness in so many different media cannot be fully accounted for by the usual explanation that "retro" culture is simply "late" capitalism's way of recycling old merchandise as new for guaranteed audiences, an explana-tion that carries with it the usual one-dimensional indictment of nostalgia. This explanation has its obvious merits: the Batman "phenomenon" that began to gather force even before the release of the film represents contemporary capitalism at its most sophisticated. (Eileen Meehan's essay in this collection effectively details these operations.) But to attribute the growing popularity of Batman in the past few years to the force of advertising doesn't explain its attraction to quite diverse audiences, especially the audiences of the comic and graphic novels, which until quite recently enjoyed virtually no advertising support, and were seldom seen in mall bookstores where they are now so prominently displayed. The fact that Miller's *Batman: Year One* is now offered by the Quality Paperback Book Club as part of a full page advertisement in *The New York Times Book Review* suggests that the popularity of Batman goes well beyond the sort of people who will use Batman lunch boxes.

The meta-pop phenomenon of the eighties may be unimaginable outside of corporate capitalism, but its emergence and continuing popularity is attributable to another set of factors in which nostalgia is conceived not in terms of merchandising, but cultural memory. The hyperconsciousness of contemporary popular narrative depends upon a simple realization on the part of both the producer and the audience: popular culture has a *history*; earlier texts do not simply disappear or become kitsch, but persist in their original forms as well as diverse reactivations that continue to be a source of fascination for audiences, providing pleasure in the present and forming a fundamental part of cultural memory (which has everything to do with that current pleasure for some audiences). The relationship between any text and its audience may of course be said to depend on the appeal to a shared body of assumptions, values, etc., which may be maintained or violated by senders or receivers of a given text. What characterizes the meta-pop texts of the eighties is their appeal to a body of popular texts which are now seen as inseparable from those cultural values since those texts have been the most forceful vehicles for their transmission and/or contestation.

Eco's apparent dismissal of this meta-semiotic environment is perhaps due to his belief that the mass media may be "genealogical," in that "every new intention sets off a chain reaction of inventions, produces a sort of common language." But they "have no memory because, when the chain of imitations has been produced, no one can remember who started it, and the head of the clan is confused with the latest great grandson." Eco goes on to compare Wenders's *Hammett* to Huston's *The Maltese Falcon*, arguing that despite the technical sophistication of the former, the latter "will always enjoy a certain ingenuousness that in Wenders is already lost."[14] The issue of ingenuousness hides the crucial question: why did Wenders want to make a film about Hammett in the first place? The fascination for the antecedent/originary text is part of a complicated process that distinguishes meta-pop culture—the ad hoc construction of "traditions" within popular culture, operating outside the realm of the academy (and the traditional mechanism responsible for the canonization of privileged works). Do the various Batman narratives in their various formats really indicate a lack of memory, a purposeful confusion of themselves and their antecedents as somehow indistinguishable from each other? Alan Moore's *The Killing Joke* and Frank Miller's *Batman: Year One* both attempt to invent new origins for stock characters of the Batman saga, but in so doing they reintroduce the original comics and invest them with the power of any originary narrative. In Moore's work we learn the origin of the Joker, a failed stand up comic who turns to a life of crime only after the tragic accidental death of his adoring wife. While Moore "invents" this aspect of the Batman narrative, he also depends heavily on the original comic book version of the Joker's origins as the infamous Red Hood who jumps into a vat of toxic waste. The end result is both an acknowledgement and an extension, re-introducing the Red Hood narrative while inventing a still earlier back story.

How Many Ways Do We Watch the Watchmen?

The graphic novels of Frank Miller and Alan Moore epitomize the hyperconsciousness of contemporary popular culture in their sophisticated invocation/re-articulation of the historical tradition of the comic book, and the forms of visual narration they have developed (along with artists Klaus Janson, Lynn Varley, and Dave Gibbons) represent a meta-semiotic re-envisioning not only of the world of the superhero, but also of the cultures which consume those narratives. What differentiates this visual narration from earlier comics is their extension of the spatial and temporal dimensions of the narrative well beyond the "action" of the diegesis. The producers of *Dark Knight*[15] and *Watchmen*[16] orchestrate textual space and time, but in doing so they also emphasize (through different, but related means) that to envision textual space is to envision at the same time the cultural space surrounding it, specifically the conflicting visual traditions that constitute those semiotic environments.

The most striking feature of *Dark Knight*, for example, is the radical heterogeneity of its images in regard to their scale, framing and stylistic tradition. Miller's work is often labeled "cinematic," and in many ways the alternation of image scale does resemble the shift between establishing shots and close-ups in a film narrative. But such analogies are also potentially misleading, because they fail to do justice to the juxtaposition of the disparate images that appear within the single page or two page unit that constitutes the "tableaux" of the graphic novel. *Mise en scene* in film depends upon sequential replacement of one image with another, but the *mise en scene* of the comic depends upon simultaneous co-presence on the page. In the traditional comic form, from classical Batman back to the *Images d'Epinal* broadsheet narratives of fairy tales, the consistency of the size and arrangement of the images (respecting the same left-to-right arrangement of print narratives) de-emphasized simultaneity, the chronological succession of narrative incident producing a sequential processing of the images in which the preceding images did not disappear, but were pushed back by the forward thrust of the narrative. But the juxtaposition of different sized frames on the same page, deployed in constantly changing configurations, intensifies their co-presence, so that the entire page becomes the narrative unit, and the conflictive relationship among the individual images becomes a primary feature of the "narration" of the text, a narration that details the progression of the plot, but also the transgression of one image by another. The end result is a narration that proceeds syntagmatically across and down the page, but also forces a paradigmatic reading of interrelationships among images on the same page or adjacent pages, so that the tableaux moves the plot forward but encourages the eye to move in continually shifting trajectories as it tries to make sense of the overall pattern of fragmentary images.

A number of different visual strategies are used throughout *Dark Knight* to intensify this double movement that projects the story forward frame-by-frame at a relentless pace, but also arrests the strict linear movement of the image (and the eye) through the invention of the fragmented tableaux that draws relationships between images that are non-successive, but co-present. In the concluding two pages of Book I, the top third of each page is a single image with a cluster of smaller images composing the middle third, and another single image filling out the bottom third. The similarity in configuration makes the two pages read as three bands of images, the spatial continuity intensified in the top band by the use of lighting and angles in the background, so that the two images which follow each other in time appear to form the same spatial/temporal unit, the lines of the Venetian blinds seeming to lead back to the same vanishing point. The middle band develops in a more linear fashion on each page since contiguous images constitute a spatial and temporal continuity, but only up to a certain point. The contiguous clusters of images in the left hand side of the middle band follow the action in a continuous fashion, but they differ drastically in image size and image scale, "cutting" between long shots and extreme close-ups, followed by a page-wide image in the bottom third band, which breaks this pattern in reference to size and in the sudden introduction of color. The right hand side of the bottom third panel resembles only the top panel, so that the top and bottom bands of the tableau appear to form one unit, and the middle bands two more. While this subdivision of tableaux into units which move the eye in different rhythms and trajectories all over these pages, the fragmentation is counter-balanced by the use of other visual paradigms which serve to interrelate the disparate units so they might still be conceived as an overall tableau. The consistency in regard to color—the stark contrasts between dark and white with yellow introduced only in the images of a massive explosion, the symbolic face of the bat, and the balloons of one dialogue exchange—serves to coordinate (rather than unify) the fragments, just as the top and bottom bands provide a frame for the conflictive relationships within. The construction of tableaux as units of visual narration, then, operates according to two sets of opposing imperatives, to move forward and sideways, to fragment and coordinate the pieces at the same time.

The conflictive relationships among images in *Dark Knight* are further sharpened by the combination of images that reflect very different discursive/institutional sources. In addition to the traditional comic, complete with balloons and panels of written text, the individual images in *Dark Knight* at times take on the function of the Eisensteinian "montage cell," especially in Batman's flashback to the murder of his parents on pages 14–16, Book I, where the size and scale are both extremely regular and the sequence is "done silent." But at other points in the narrative, this regularity is not only broken, but very self-consciously "shattered." After three pages of these regularized cells, the pattern is internalized and foregrounded within the first image at the top of the next page, in which a window frame in the foreground splits the plane in exactly the same pattern as the top three bands of images on the page, a pattern reiterated by the shadow of that window frame pattern on the floor of the first frame and in the foreground of the fourth image. The framing of those window frames begins to change in the second and third row of images, with close-ups of the intersection of the frame bars now set off-kilter, emphasizing their "cross" formation, which are then seen in shadows "across" the close-ups of Batman's face. This movement away from symmetry is further emphasized by the appearance of the bat, first within the window frame and then in extreme close-up across the frame bars, forming a strong diagonal slash across the image, so that the diagonal slashes across Batman's face in the next frame appear to be the shadows of the bat wings more than the window frame. The progression toward increasingly tighter close-ups within symmetrical frames is then literally and metaphorically smashed in the bottom quarter of the page where the bat crashes through the window, shattering its frames as well as the symmetrical grid of the page itself. This shattering process could hardly be more self-conscious, and it epitomizes this text's determination not only to invoke/re-articulate the figure of the superhero, but also the conventions of visual narrative through which those figures were envisioned—the content of the myth being inseparable from its "framing."

Where the use and misuse of traditional comic cells and montage techniques represent one aspect of the narration of *Dark Knight*, at other points in the narrative individual images become television images in beveled frames, deployed in successive but not contiguous frames usually on a white background with "voices" appearing below the image. These television images are ubiquitous throughout the narrative, providing a visual and ideological counterpart to the images of the "real world" that surround them. At other points in *Dark Knight* we are presented with full page images that dwarf the adjacent images, resembling classic book illustrations or posters. These oversized images (often referred to as "splash" pages) function as a sequence of composite images, forming their own paradigm of Batman as Cultural Icon, alternately depicted as muscle-bound superhero or old, demonic-looking pallbearer of the psychotic American military, or the crazed cowboy on horseback leading his private army of street punks. The latter typifies the composite nature of these images, which feature the same kind of layering of iconography coming from different genres and periods (the costumed superhero of the modern comic book, the cowboy of the nineteenth century, and the punk costumes of the Post-Modern city) that was prevalent throughout Burton's *Batman*. Throughout the text these different image functions/conventions are combined within the same tableau. On page 14–15 of Book II, for example, the tableau consists of a full-page unframed "illustration" on the left, and a combination of comic and television frames on the right-hand page (the former including dialogue and interior monologue in balloons or boxes within the frame, the latter accompanied by text below the set). The juxtaposition of these different types of images, each with their own narrational function, bringing with them their respective conventionalized contexts and associations, produces a hybrid tableau which accentuates the different discursive registers of those images by their very proximity. This sort of juxtaposition separates *Dark Knight* from earlier experiments in frame variation like those of Windsor McKay and George Herriman. Where the radical variation of frame size and placement in *Little Nemo* and *Krazy Kat* were tableau-oriented, the discursive framework of each image remained consistent, resulting in visually dazzling, but homogeneous tableaux. *Dark Knight*'s juxtapositions of disparate forms of visual discourse constitute heterogeneous tableaux which may be considered chaotic according to traditional notions of the well-made plane, but nevertheless operate systematically, according to their own logic, i.e. that textual space, like the actual space it depicts (and through which it will circulate as a text), is envisioned according to different institutionalized modes of image-making that were formerly separate, but are now thoroughly intertangled, a world of fragmentary images that might produce some kind of provisional "big picture," but only when read in aggregate in all their simultaneity.

In Alan Moore's and Dave Gibbon's graphic novel *Watchmen*, the narration by amalgamation is made still more heterogeneous by the inclusion not only of other visual discourses, but also an entire range of non-visual discourses representing different articulations of the superhero as cultural artifact. At the level of the individual page, the development of images in *Watchmen* follows a standard grid with only slight alteration until the series of oversized splash pages at the beginning of Chapter XII. The profoundly intertextual nature of the narration is elaborated on a frame-by-frame basis within that grid, its very regularity emphasizing the co-existence of antecedent text and current incarnation. Beginning in Chapter II, *Tales of the Black Freighter*, a comic from the early sixties is introduced into the narrative of *Watchmen*. It begins rather simply as a comic-within-a-comic conceit, with a young man reading this comic as he sits next to the newsstand operator. After the initial establishing shots of this figure reading the comic, with the rolled "parchment" text panel from *Freighter* appearing over his image as a kind of misplaced "voice-over" narration, an over-the-shoulder shot shows the actual pages from the comic he reads, then gives way to actual panels from *"Freighter,"* now inserted within the grid, replacing the *Watchmen* images, and then set in varying patterns of alternation throughout the next three chapters, the movement between the two narratives usually accomplished through "graphic matches" (nearly identical compositions with character substitutions). The intertextual frame here could hardly be more explicit, *Freighter* becoming quite literally an intertext of *Watchmen*, with its images interrelated on a frame-by-frame basis, enjoying the same visual status as the *Watchmen* narrative.

The significance of the *Tales From the Black Freighter* is explained by the long excerpt reprinted from the *Treasure Island Treasury of Comics* that appears at the end of Chapter V. This explanation does not comment directly on the insertion of this comic within the diegesis of *Watchmen*, but it does insert *Watchmen* in the history of the comics, contextualizing both *Black Freighter* and *Watchmen* in relation to that historical continuum, which is intensified by those intertextual connections. The explanatory "reprint" is one of several such inserts, placed between the chapters of *Watchmen*, which function as another chain of "intertexts." Where the *Black Freighter* images are interrelated within the narrative world of *Watchmen*, the non-comic inserts comment directly on the various ways superhero narratives are contextualized, expanding the intertextual dimensions of the text still further. These inserts include extracts from the published memoirs of a superhero, academic studies on the significance of superheroes and vigilantism, fan letters to superheros, and letters from a superhero to his employees regarding the successful marketing of himself and his colleagues as Fully Posable Action Figures. *Watchmen* presents not only a highly sophisticated rearticulation of superhero narrative, but a fully fictionalized set of encrustations that constitute the actual "text" of *Watchmen*, which consists of the comic panels, but also the various forms of discourse which it either generates and/or circulates through. This sort of hyperconsciousness, then, is a far more elaborate form of self-reflexivity than that which characterizes the meta-fictional texts of the sixties because it shifts the focus away from the agonies of personal expression, stressing instead the intertextual dimensions of both textual production and textual circulation. Texts like *Watchmen*, *Batman*, and *The Dark Knight Returns* are paradigmatic examples of contemporary popular culture, where texts now evidence a highly sophisticated understanding of their semiotic environments, thereby collapsing the moments of production and eventual circulation so that the former appears inseparable from the latter.

That the cultural terrain of the contemporary crime fighter can be adequately envisioned or "imaged" solely by this assemblage of conflicting images suggests a great deal about the nature of that terrain and the narratives which represent it. Kevin Lynch's notion of "imageability" of certain environments[17] (that particular cities are more "legible" than others because they may be more easily imaged by their inhabitants, i.e. that certain urban environments produce strong, holdable images) is especially relevant, but only if we revise his terminology somewhat. The terrain of *Dark Knight* and *Watchmen* appears endlessly "imageable" in that it can be envisioned any number of ways. It becomes *legible* — comprehensible, manageable—not in one totalizing picture, but in a cluster of images that reveal its discursive discontinuity. The imaging of contemporary environments, then, must begin by recognizing the ways in which it already has been framed; the terrain consists of a set of physical characteristics as well as a set of frames in which our successful negotiation of the former depends entirely on our developing a "competence" in understanding the latter.

The hybridization of popular narrative that is a response to this cultural terrain which comes to us already framed by different genres, different discursive frameworks, and the divergent ways of seeing they entail necessitates a reconsideration of "genre" as a category of narrative. In other words, where "genre" depends on the relative stability of its distinctive characteristics that make possible its recognizability as a style for both the producers and consumers of those texts, the hybrid texts discussed above are aggressively destabilizing, retaining extremely familiar conventions, but juxtaposing them in ways that undermine the purity or integrity of genre as a category. Rick Altman, in his pivotal article on the semantic and syntactic approaches to genre film,[18] argues that the former approach concentrates on primary elements (iconography, location, stock characters, etc.) that define a genre and make it recognizable as such, while the latter defines genericity in regard to the syntactic bonds which set the relationship between those elements. According to Altman, "Just as individual texts establish new meanings for familiar terms, only by subjecting well known semantic units to a syntactic redetermination, so generic meaning comes into being only through the repeated deployment of substantially the same syntactic strategies."[19] But hybrid popular narratives are distinguished by their adoption of those well-known semantic units, deployed according to substantially *different* syntactic strategies. More precisely, hyperconscious popular narrative adopts or appropriates diverse semantic units which, by this point in the development of popular culture, are always already encrusted with one or more sets of syntactic associations that are inseparable from those individual units. The composite splash page in *Dark Knight*, where Batman races through the city on horseback, trailed by an army of street punks, involves not just the combination of different semantic elements, different types of iconography, but the juxtaposition of hitherto divergent syntactic relationships between heroism and villainy, civilization and savagery, order and disorder, etc., which invest those icons with such different semiotic and ideological values.

This hybridization could be seen as the development of a second order "meta-syntax" that sets new relationships between minimal units that are already bundles of syntactic relationships. While such a description might begin to account for the effect of the simultaneity of the "array" on the structure of genre narrative, it presupposes: a) that such a meta-syntax could be constructed out of the heterogeneous, ever-shifting, ever rearticulated "already said"; b) that individual texts like *Dark Knight, Watchmen, Batman, Blade Runner, Road Warrior, The Adventure of Buckaroo Banzai, Earth Girls are Easy*, etc., are still committed to producing even ad hoc versions of such a meta-syntax, that they have any interest in codifying or "setting" new relationships that might encourage audiences to interpret them the same way they do traditional genre works that have been reconfigured by those very texts. In other words, these graphic novels and films resist any kind of easy "re-genrefication." Though they are composed entirely of generic material that remains clearly marked as such within these texts, their very hybrid nature works at cross purposes with the accepted notion of genre as a recognizable, coherent set of formulae that audiences may read predictively. Eco, in his own analysis of the Bond phenomenon, contended that the enjoyment of the generic text comes from precisely that stability that allows predictability, comparing the Bond text to a Harlem Globetrotter game. "We know with absolute confidence that the Globetrotters will win; the pleasure lies in watching the trained virtuosity with which they delay the final moments, with what ingenious deviations they reconfirm the foregone conclusion."[20] The hybrid texts purposely frustrate both that stability and that predictability through a process of reconfiguration that precludes the construction of new syntax—not only do we no longer know the inevitable outcome (to say that the conclusions of *Dark Knight* and *Watchmen* are not predictable is understatement of the first order), but we no longer know if it is really the Globetrotters we are watching, or a group of borderline psychotics dressed in the same costumes, playing a similar game, but driven by entirely different motivations that might push them over the edge at any moment.

In their frustration of the homogeneity and predictability considered the prerequisite for "genericity," these hybrid popular narratives could be considered "post-generic" insofar as they resist syntactic stabilization, but are still composed of what, at this point, must be considered generic artifacts. The trendiness of the "post" prefix makes the choice of the term dubious, but it describes this seemingly paradoxical situation, in which we encounter texts composed entirely of generic materials that contradict, as an assemblage, the function of genre as the coordinator of narrative convention and audience expectation. These texts remain generic, but only if we recognize that "genericity" is now a matter of rearticulation and appropriation of semiotic categories, no longer just the ritual confirmation of deeply held community beliefs, nor the secret agenda of Hollywood as "dominant ideology." "Genericity" in this context is not a form of myth, but a feature of hyperconscious discourse, which might still present itself as "myth," but only in quotation marks, as the citation of antecedent texts rather than the innocent, direct expression of transcendent values.

Texts like *Batman: The Movie, The Dark Knight Returns*, and *Watchmen* which feature narration by amalgamation suggest the emergence of a new type of narrative which is neither a master narrative that might function as a national myth for entire cultures, nor a micro-narrative that targets a specific subculture or a sharply delimited semiotic community. The popularity of these texts depends on their appeal not to a broad general audience, but a series of audiences varying in degrees of sophistication and stored cultural knowledge (i.e. exposure and competence). As *aggregate narratives,* they appeal to disparate but often overlapping audiences, by presenting different incarnations of the superhero simultaneously, so that the text always comes trailing its intertexts and rearticulations. The significance of the superhero can be ascertained, to borrow a phrase from A. J. Greimas, only in terms of an encyclopedia rather than a dictionary, as an assemblage of intertextual representations rather than a set definition. The simultaneity of the array, then, produces a form of narrative which is itself an array of narrative and visual codes that tells the story of the superheroes, but also tells in the process the history of their cultural significance.

In cultures which are incessantly imaged or framed according to conflicting exigencies of different media, genres, and institutions, our notion of narrative "action" can no longer be restricted to character adventure. The rearticulation of the already said, the ways in which narrative conventions are hybridized and forced to account for a quite different cultural terrain become another type of "action" that has become a central feature of popular entertainment. At this point, distinctions between the telling and the told, the narration and the narrative, the diegetic action and the extra-diegetic intertextual references become not only difficult to make, but decidedly misleading. In the hyperconscious narrative, the intertextual arena can no longer be confined to the realm of the extra-diegetic, nor can the conditions of the narrative's eventual circulation be considered somehow "outside" the text. Both now form part of the "action" generated by the text, and in the process narrative pleasure become a process of negotiating the array for both the creators and audiences of those texts.

Notes

1. I would like to thank Greg McCue for his invaluable suggestions while I was completing this article.

2. Given the conflicted nature of the term "popular" culture, I should explain my choice of that term. I use popular here, first because my argument is that while the hyperconsciousness that I attribute to these texts has been all-pervasive in the "high arts" of the Modernist/Post-Modernist era, we now encounter it in texts found most often in multiplex cinemas and grocery store book racks. Here I opt for "popular" as opposed to "mass" because of the Frankfurt school presuppositions surrounding the latter (i.e. the Culture Industry cranks out homogeneous texts and subjects).

For a more detailed explanation of why I find these presuppositions ideologically repugnant (as well as quaint), see Chapter One of my *Uncommon Cultures: Popular Culture and Post-Modernism* (New York: Routledge, 1989).

3. John Cawelti, "*Chinatown* and Generic Transformation in Recent American Films," *Film Theory and Criticism*, ed. Gerald Mast and Marshall Cohen (New York: Oxford Univ. Press, 1985), pp. 503–520.

4. Collins.

5. Umberto Eco, *Postscript to The Name of the Rose* (New York: Harcourt Brace, 1984).

6. Joe R. Landsdale, "Subway Jack: A Batman Adventure," *The Further Adventures of Batman*, ed. Martin H. Greenberg (New York: Bantam, 1989), pp. 103–138.

7. Landsdale, p. 109.

8. Roy Thomas, Dann Thomas, and Jackson Guice, *Dr. Strange, Sorcerer Supreme*, Vol. 1, No. 9, November 1989.

9. Tony Bennett and Janet Woollacott, *Bond and Beyond: The Political Career of a Popular Hero* (New York: Methuen, 1987).

10. Umberto Eco, "*Casablanca:* Cult Movies and Intertextual Collage," *Travels in Hyperreality* (New York: Harcourt Brace, 1987), p. 202.

11. For a more detailed explanation of this term, see Collins pp. 43–64.

12. Eco, p. 210.

13. For further discussion of this term see Jim Collins, "Appropriating Like *Krazy:* From Pop-Art to Meta-Pop," *Ideas of Cultural Modernity*, ed. James Naremore and Patrick Brantlinger (Bloomington: Indiana Univ. Press, forthcoming).

14. Eco, p. 146.

15. Frank Miller, *Batman: The Dark Knight Returns* (New York: DC Comics, 1986).

16. Alan Moore and Dave Gibbons, *Watchmen* (New York: DC Comics, 1986).

17. Kevin Lynch, *The Image of the City* (Cambridge: MIT Press, 1960).

18. Rick Altman, "A Semantic/Syntactic Approach to Film Genre," *Cinema Journal*, 23, no. 3, Spring 1984, pp. 6–17.

19. Altman, p. 16.

20. Umberto Eco, "Narrative Structures in Fleming," *The Poetics of Murder*, ed. Mast and Stowe (New York: Harcourt Brace, 1983), p. 113.

10

"I'm Not Fooled By That Cheap Disguise"

William Uricchio and Roberta E. Pearson

The Floating Signifier

A colony of small, bright-yellow, vaguely bat-like objects floats in a pool of white.[1] A spoon dips into the bowl, scooping up more of the "crunchy bat shapes, with natural flavors of honey-nut."[2] On the breakfast table stands a black cereal box, a familiar black bat in a yellow oval prominently emblazoned on all six sides.

During the summer of 1989, this bat-logo permeated American culture, appearing on candy, boxer shorts, leather medallions, earrings, baseball caps, night lights, sterling silver coins—in short, on any item capable of bearing the trade-marked image (or unlicensed likenesses thereof). The bat-logo's omnipresence diffused its meaning, reducing the wearing of a black bat in a yellow oval to a mere gesture of participation in a particular cultural moment. While the intended meaning of that participation may have varied greatly, and while many bat-logo purchasers might have had very little knowledge of the Batman mythos, the logo, at the very least, carried the connotation "Batman" and thus indicated the purchaser's acknowledgement, however minimal, of the character.

One of the more bizarre consumable expressions of bat-mania, the crunchy bat breakfast cereal pointedly referenced the *character* of the Caped Crusader, the box copy using such terms as "terrifying," "obsession," "death," "killed," and "evil doers." Though these terms may have constituted a potentially distasteful connotative frame for the tasty bat shapes, the side panel containing them sucessfully summarized most of the salient characteristics of the Dark Knight.

His name was The Batman. A dark, mysterious character of the
night, stalking the streets, defying criminals with the intelligence,

athletic prowess, and state of the art gadgetry, terrifying enemies who dare cross his path.

The Batman had a secret identity, that of Bruce Wayne™, wealthy playboy. At a very young age his parents were killed on the streets of Gotham City™. Later, he used his inheritance to travel around the world, seeking masters of justice and the martial arts, honing his body to perfection. A man with an obsession for justice. When he was ready, he returned to Gotham City™ as The Batman, ready to terrorize the evil doers of the city and to avenge the death of his parents.[3]

This copy suggests the minimal components of the Batman character which have circulated for fifty years in various media and among different publics; film-goers, television viewers, comic book readers, etc. The Dark Knights's identity has fluctuated over time and across media as multiple authors and fan communities competed over his definition.

The tensions in the character's identity became clearly apparent in the bat-hyped summer of '89 when a myriad of Batmen simultaneously vied for the cape and cowl—in the blockbuster film and its numerous tie-ins, the syndicated television series, the ongoing runs of *Detective* and *Batman* comics as well as in graphic novels, *The Killing Joke* and *The Dark Knight Returns* most prominent among them. The highest profile Batman, the latest site of fifty years of bat-hype, appeared in the Warner Bros. film. The scriptwriter, Sam Hamm, claimed that the pervasiveness of this particular Batman granted him automatic authenticity. "What you wind up doing when you're putting an existing character in a major Hollywood film is you're essentially *defining* that character for a whole generation of people; and most people have certainly heard of Batman, but they are probably not that familiar with it. So what you're doing becomes sort of *ipso facto* canonical."[4] The film's director, Tim Burton, similarly asserted the canonicity of the Warner's Batman, arguing that his leading man, Michael Keaton, possessed the correct attributes for the role. The Batman "is the one comic book hero who is not a superhero but a human being. Since Michael is hardly a big he-man, but looks just like a regular guy off the street he was perfect for the role."[5]

Others disagreed. Science fiction writer Harlan Ellison believed that the choice of Keaton made little sense. "Michael Keaton truly contravenes the whole point of Batman. Here's the only prominent superhero without special powers; here's one of the very best detectives who ever lived, and he's being played by a scrawny comedian in plastic armor. That, in a capsule, is the kind of erroneous thinking that dooms films."[6] Indeed, the Keaton casting had produced such widespread disappointment that the *Wall Street Journal* ran a front page article speculating

about the film's financial prospects in the face of fierce bat-fan disaffection.

The report deeply disturbed Jon Peters, co-producer of the film. "Every
analyst I knew sent that to me the day it came out. It just deflated everybody. . . . Nobody wanted Keaton. . . . We were ostracized by the Bat-
community. They booed us at the Bat-convention."[7] Tim Burton seemed
less solicitous of fan reaction. "There might be something that's sacri-
lege in the movie. . . . But I can't care about it. . . . This is too big a budget
movie to worry about what a fan of a comic would say."[8]

This debate over the "real" Batman replicated that surrounding the
sixties' television program and reflected an ongoing series of character
transmutations. Bob Kane, "creator" of the Batman, described the potential audience for the 1989 film. "Every ten years, it [Batman] changes,
you see. Right now there are two factions. There are the baby boomers
who know the TV show; they *don't* know the dramatic comic book
prior to that, so they think the movie is probably going to be a comedy.
Then there are readers who *know* the roots from which he came, that
he is a vigilante, mysterious, a loner."[9]

The years since the publication of Miller's *The Dark Knight Returns*
have seen the greatest array of character transmutations and violations
of heretofore sacrosanct canonicity. The "miscasting" of the Warner's
film constituted one of its lesser heresies. Greater transgressions included the establishment of a continuing (sexual) relationship with and
the revealing of his secret identity to Vicki Vale as well as making the
Joker the killer of Bruce Wayne's parents and then killing him. *The
Dark Knight Returns* featured a fifty year old Batman and a female
Robin. *Gotham by Gaslight* set the Batman characters and locations in
the late 1880's, where the Batman encountered Jack the Ripper. In *Son
of the Demon*, the Batman married the daughter of an arch villain and
even had a son.

This moment in the last decade of the twentieth century, then,
represents the most divergent set of refractions of the Batman character.
Whereas broad shifts in emphasis had occured since 1939, these changes
had been, for the most part, consecutive and consensual. Now, newly
created Batmen, existing simultaneously with the older Batmen of the
television series and comic reprints and back issues, all struggled for
recognition and a share of the market. But the contradictions amongst
them may threaten both the integrity of the commodity form and the
coherence of the fans' lived experience of the character necessary to the
Batman's continued success.

Who is the Batman?

The very nature of the Batman's textual existence reveals an impulse
toward fragmentation. Since his creation in 1939, numerous editors,

writers, artists, directors, scriptwriters, performers and licensed manufacturers have continually "authored" the Batman, with the specificit-
ies of various media necessitating the selective emphasis of character
qualities. Unlike some fictional characters, the Batman has no primary
urtext set in a specific period, but has rather existed in a plethora of
equally valid texts constantly appearing over more than five decades.
This has freed him from temporal specificity. The Batman remains
untouched by the ravages of time, an eternal thirty year old, with only
a very selective accruing of canonized historical events.[10]

Neither author, nor medium, nor primary text, nor time period defines the Batman. In the absence of these other markers, character, that
is, a set of key components, becomes the primary marker of Batman
texts: the key components of the Batman character have constituted the
sine qua non for any Batman narrative in any medium. This exclusive
emphasis on the primacy of key components distinguishes the Batman
from other series/serial fictional heroes, where character figures prominently but not exclusively among the defining elements.

Consider, for example, Sherlock Holmes, James Bond and Philip Marlowe. Despite these characters' appearances in films, and even their
continuation in literary form beyond their creators' deaths, their central
identity resides in a series of literary urtexts penned by single authors
and set in single time periods. Hence, were one seeking to define Sherlock Holmes, one would turn not to the latest in a series of numerous
pastiches but would turn to the fifty-six short stories and four novels
of Sir Arthur Conan Doyle written between 1887 and 1927. Indeed, the
fan community in this case tenaciously valorizes these texts as the
single canonized repository of Holmes' character, extrapolating from
them the key components of the Master's identity. While a set of
key components centrally identifies the Batman, the bat-fan has no
authoritative repository of these key components to turn to but is faced
instead with an ongoing and potentially endless stream of new texts.

By contrast, other fictional characters such as Bugs Bunny and
Mickey Mouse, though similar to the Batman in being multiply authored and not bound to a particular medium, urtext or period, differ
from the Batman in that they function as actors/celebrities rather than
as characters.[11] Bugs Bunny can appear in an opera, a Western, a Sher-
wood Forest adventure, a science fiction film, or even, as "himself" at
the Academy Awards. In each case, he plays a role within the narrative
as well as constantly remaining Bugs Bunny, in similar fashion to such
flesh and blood counterparts as Groucho Marx.

Like Holmes, Bond and Marlowe, and unlike Bugs Bunny and Mickey
Mouse, the Batman's set of key components brings with it a particular
generic form, in the Batman's case, crime fighting.[12] The latest batbible,
written by *Batman* and *Detective* editor Dennis O'Neil as a character

guide for DC writers, states: "*Everything* with the exception of his friends' welfare is bent to the task he knows he can never accomplish, the elimination of crime. It is this task which imposes meaning on an existence he would otherwise find intolerable."[13]

What then are the key components of the Batman and how did we go about identifying them, given the lack of authoritative texts and the non-accruing nature of events? Of the many components that constitute the Batman at any one time, we have privileged the lowest common denominator of long lasting and recurrent components that often seem to appear in self-conscious and reductionist articulations of the Batman character such as the cereal box side panel. Even at this moment of multiple and competing Batmen, the character remains a rich man who dresses in an iconographically specific costume (cape, cowl and bat-logo). Because of the murder of his parents, he obsessively fights crime, using his superb physical abilities in combination with his deductive capacities. He maintains his secret identity of Bruce Wayne, who lives in Wayne Manor in Gotham City. He is surrounded by a supporting cast of friends and foes.

Five key components constitute the core character of the Batman: traits/attributes; events; recurrent supporting characters; setting and iconography. We briefly adumbrate these components here.

1). *Traits/Attributes.* Put most succinctly, the Batman might be said to have four central traits/attributes: wealth; physical prowess; deductive abilities and obsession. The batbible provides a more detailed breakdown of these central traits/attributes: the Batman is "tough but not brutal;" "probably the best martial artist alive, and one of the best gymnasts;" "strong and athletic;" "smart with an IQ comfortably in the genius numbers;" "trained, an autodidact;" "obsessed . . . but in the fullest possession of his mental and moral faculties;" "celibate;" and "compassionate." He is also the "heir to a large fortune, estimated at nearly 100 million dollars."

2). *Events.* Two different kinds of events constitute this component: fixed and accruing events, such as the origin story, and iterative, that is repetitive, non-identical and non-accruing events, most of which involve crime fighting.[14] The central fixed event, the origin story, is the source of many of the Batman's traits/attributes, which play themselves out in the iterative events.

Until recently, the fixed and accruing and hence, canonized, events have been few in number: the origin; the appearance of Robin and some few other central characters; and the cases related to the Bat-cave trophies. In the present moment of extreme character refraction, canonized events seems to be proliferating with implications for character continuity and containment. The iterative events, that is, incidents of obsessive crime fighting, display the Batman's traits/attributes, constitute the dominant generic form and embody the character's hegemonic function, as we shall discuss later.

3). *Recurrent Characters.* The Batman's interactions with the good guys and bad guys around him help to define him. Characters such as Commissioner Gordon, Robin I (Dick Grayson), Alfred, and the Joker all entered the Batman's world by the early forties and have maintained a constant, though sporadic, presence. Though we use these characters here to define the Batman, these characters could themselves be defined along many of the same parameters as the Caped Crusader. For example, the Joker has traits/attributes (rhetorical mode and whimsical approach to crime), fixed and iterative events (an origin story and obsessive criminal activities), recurrent characters (Batman and Robin), setting (Gotham City) and iconography (green hair, white face, bright red mouth set in a permanent grin).

4) *Setting.* Batman/Bruce Wayne lives in Gotham City, which has the same symbiotic relationship with him as the recurrent characters. As the Riddler put it, "When is a man a city?" "When it's Batman or when it's Gotham. I'd take either answer. Batman is this city. . . . That's why we're [the Riddler and other costumed villains] here. That's why we stay. We're trying to survive in the city. It's *huge* and contradictory and *dark* and funny and threatening."[15] The fluctuating image of Gotham City relates to the fluctuating nature of crime in the Batman's world and has implications for the playing out of the Batman's hegemonic function.

5) *Iconography.* The Batman's costume serves him well in his endless war against crime. The colors which permit him to lurk unseen in the shadows and the invocation of a terrifying creature of the night both enable him to seize the psychological element of surprise from Gotham's criminal element.

While various artists have redesigned elements of the costume (shortening the ears or adding a yellow circle to the chest emblem), the basic elements of cape, cowl, gauntlets and logo have remained easily identifiable, as one would expect in primarily visual texts. Taking the cue of costume and cognomen, bat-like shapes, like the bat-prefix, abound in the Batman's world. The batmobile, the batcopter, the batarang and the bat-etcs. all serve as repositories of the bat-look: black, shiny, with a bat-wing design incorporated where possible.

Without the presence of all five key components in some form, the Batman ceases to be the Batman, yet the primarily series nature of the character permits fairly wide variation in the treatment of these components across time and media. The elasticity of the components allows for great stretching, but in this moment of extreme character refraction, the Batman may be stretched thin to the point of invisibility.

Gritty—Graphic—Grown-up

A DC advertisement in the same issue of *Rolling Stone* that featured a cover story interview with Michael Keaton declared that the company's gritty, graphic and grown-up comics had come of age. "You outgrew comics, now they've caught up with you!"[16] The advertisment touted the current four most divergent comic book Batmen: *The Killing Joke* by Moore/Bolland, *The Return of the Dark Knight, The Greatest Batman Stories Ever Told,* and *The Batman Movie Adaptation* by O'Neil/Ordway. The simultaneous presence of these divergent Batmen, together with the advertising venue, the appeal to adult readership, and the marketing of graphic novels and special format (high-priced) reprints all signal a major shift in the comic book marketplace.[17]

In the first three decades of the Batman's existence, Bob Kane, now cited in every narrative expression as the character's "creator," took credit for the production of the majority of bat-texts. In actuality, a crew of uncredited ghostwriters and ghost-artists, all expected to subordinate their styles to the dominant Kane look, worked on the books. As Kane said, "I feel a ghost's job is to emulate the cartoonist, as near as you can, instead of recreating what he already did in his own style."[18] In this period, comic book authorship was not valorized as an expressive act and comic artists had low visibility.

During the mid to late sixties, bat-fans began to exhibit great interest in questions of authorship, using the letter columns as a forum for speculation about the identities of writers, pencillers and inkers and as a means for communicating with each other about these matters. By 1968, a fan complained, "Figuring out the authors of stories really isn't much fun now. The fad should soon be dying out because it's getting too easy." DC, replying to the letter, announced a new policy: ". . . the author-guessing fad has run its course. From now on we're giving author (and artists) credit along with each story."[19]

This new crediting of writers and artists reflected increased valorization of comic book authorship, further encouraging the fans to take an auteurist perspective of the production process. Much as film fan discourse in the sixties began to revolve around directors, comic fan discourse increasingly centered on the importance of writers and artists. As a letter column correspondent put it in 1980:

> . . . you're going to have to change your entire attitude towards "putting out" material. Unless you do so, sales will continue to plummet.

> You will have to produce, on a regular basis, "special" material by
> special people that will make your public *want* to buy your magazines.
> In the case of BATMAN, this will be like the following: stories by
> Archie Goodwin, Steve Englehart, and . . . artists like: Jim Starlin,
> Alex Toth, Marshall Rogers, . . . and similar talented, but "different,"
> "special" people.[20]

Today, a substantial portion of published fan correspondence concerns authorship issues. The attendance of comic book authors at comic
conventions both reflects and enhances their status within the fan
community. Those within the industry assert that the names of well-
known writers such as Alan Moore, Frank Miller, Dennis O'Neil, and
John Byrne and well-known illustrators such as Brian Bolland and Bill
Sienkiewicz on a cover guarantee greater sales. The emergence of the
direct distribution system, which permitted more accurate tracking
of individual title sales, further augmented comic-book auteurism by
giving rise to a royalty system now used by both the major comic book
companies, DC and Marvel. Hence, a system which effaced authorship
and insisted upon conformance to the house style has given way to one
which relies upon individual authorship as a criterion of quality and
marketability.

This economic incentive prompts authors/writers toward maximum
differentiation within the standardization imposed by the key components of the Batman character. Differential treatment of the key components can identify a writer/artist with a particular version of the Batman. Thus, we refer to Miller's Batman or Moore's Batman, further
boosting their stock with fans and industry but also further exacerbat-
ing the tendency toward fragmentation of the character's identity.[21]

The language of artistic self-consciousness, however, veils raw economic reality. Since credits, royalties and other recognition have altered
the fundamental relationship between the writer/artist and his[22] work,
the industry can now, to some extent, accomodate employees' aspirations to create "art." This leads to the production of such specialized
permutations of the Batman as the recent *Arkham Asylum*, written by
Grant Morrison and illustrated by Dave McKean. The hard cover, 120-
page graphic novel self-consciously constructs a fragmented, postmodern narrative relayed by overlapping and conflicting narrative voices
and expressed in an evocative melange of artistic styles.

But *Arkham Asylum* and similiar books result not only from the
artists' economic incentives and creative desires but also from DC's
need to expand its market through product differentiation, both from
other companies and within its own output. DC now produces standard
format books, new format books, deluxe format books, prestige format

books, graphic novels and collected editions, differentiated by price
(from one dollar to $29.95), length, ink and paper quality, as well as the
maturity of the content and the mode of representation. This differentiation not only expands the market, but gains the industry an unaccus-
tomed measure of respectability. As the Associated Press said about
The Dark Knight Returns, it "is not like most comic books. Its printing
is deluxe, its artwork is complex, and its mood is nightmarish and
somber."[23]

DC publisher Jenette Kahn addressed the new marketing strategy in
her monthly column.

> Of course, no one could be more aware than you, our readers, of the
> extensive changes in comics during the past six years. We began to
> publish at different price points in a variety of formats with a wide
> range of artistic effects and verbal story-telling. The diversity in the
> content of the comics gave rise to an equal diversity in marketing
> techniques, advertising, and avenues of distribution.[24]

While one might take issue with Ms. Kahn's causality, one cannot
deny the relationships she draws among marketing, distribution and
"diversity in the content." The structural incentives for "diversity"—
"creativity" and an expanding market—speak precisely to the tension
between, on the one hand, the essential maintenance of a recognizable
set of key character components and, on the other, the increasingly
necessary centrifugal dispersion of these components.

"Everything is exactly the same, except for the fact that it's all totally different."

In 1953, *Detective Comics* #195 ran a story titled, "The Original
Batman."[25] Gotham City suddenly has two Batmen: the familiar Caped
Crusader and a competitor, wearing a similar costume—wings instead
of cape, no chest logo, bat logo on belt. The Batman decides that "This
town isn't big enough for both of us," and it seems as if the Gotham
authorities will back him up. After all, Gotham City has passed a law
forbidding anybody to pose as the Batman. The competitor, however,
turns out to have a prior claim to the name. He had performed as a
circus acrobat wearing the bat-costume and calling himself Bat-man.
Gotham City attorneys confirm this fact and conclude that the Batman
"no longer has a right to the name." The competing Bat-man eventually
forbids our hero to wear his costume any longer, effectively ending his
crime fighting career. Things look bleak until Robin learns from his
old circus friends that Bat-Man never performed inside the Gotham

City limits, a fact which invalidates his claim to the name and the costume.

The challenging of the Batman's identity threatened Gotham City with the loss of a crime-fighter, but threatens DC with the loss of a profit-maker, a far more troublesome prospect. The company has good reason to be concerned about the the the Dark Knight's character, particularly since he has experienced a number of major shifts in emphasis during his fifty year existence. Mike Gold, in an introduction to *The Greatest Batman Stories Ever Told*, offered a succinct summary.

> The past fifty years of Batman stories could be divided into at least five distinct eras: the earliest days—the creation of the series through the World War II years; the larger-than-life days of big clocks and surrealistic yet existential buildings; the monster days of aliens, gimmick costumes and weirdos; the short-lived "new look" Batman that stressed the more detective-like aspects of the character; the regretable and, as far as comic books were concerned equally short-lived television era; and the Darknight Detective era which, oddly, has been the longest and most enduring of them all.[26]

DC's editorial offices form one of the two central bastions of character identity, the other being the legal, licensing and rights departments of both DC and Warner Bros. While the importance of the latter has ebbed and flowed with the Batman's cultural currency at a particular moment, the former has served as the main agent of continuity, canonization and containment throughout the character's entire history.[27] At this current moment of divergent expressions of the Batman in several media, the editor of the main Batman comic books must simultaneously safeguard the key components of the character and accomodate variant expressions.

The current Batman editor, Dennis O'Neil, ensures consistent depiction of the character in the DC Comics. O'Neil oversees the *Batman* and *Detective* titles and clears Batman's guest appearances in other titles. The batbible, quoted above, constitutes the clearest expression of character maintenance through editorial guidelines. The manuscript gives a profile of the character's history, attributes and appropriate behavior, assuring continuity despite turnover in writers. DC has recently decided to impose further continuity on the Batman by linking two of the three bat-titles more closely. As publisher Kahn explained, "Another concern of Denny's [O'Neil] and mine was to make sure that next year Detective and Batman reinforced each other. . . . We weren't looking for the totally intense continuity that characterizes the Superman books; we just wanted to make sure that if Alfred has a broken arm in Batman, he's still nursing that broken arm in Detective."[28]

This editorial process has enough flexibility to accomodate some of the most divergent expressions of the Batman, at least, that is, those within the comic book and graphic novel realm. Recently, this flexibility has manifested itself in the self-consciously ambiguous constructions of some of the supporting cast. As the Joker said of his origin in *The Killing Joke*, "sometimes I remember it one way, sometimes another . . . if I'm going to have a past, I prefer it to be multiple-choice! HA HA HA!"[29] The Riddler, like the Joker, refused to specify his origins, suggesting numerous possibilities. "I've always been the Riddler. I always will be . . . maybe it started by cheating in a school history test, photographing a jigsaw puzzle . . . maybe I was a carnival barker, E. Nigma, the Puzzle King, Conundrum Champion, Wizard of Quiz . . . maybe I decided to turn my talents to crime, maybe I wanted to match wits with . . . with Batman, for the glory . . . the fame . . . the buck$."[30] This strategy of accomodation delimits the realm of possibilities for character construction: a writer may tinker with aspects of the Joker's origins but a colorist may not give him purple hair.

The strategy of containment which complements the strategy of accomodation derives from DC's editorial offices and from fan response as well. The industry used to assume a total readership turnover every three years, making continuity fairly unimportant.[31] The rise of the direct distribution market, the proliferation of comic specialty shops, and the targeting of adult audiences have given rise to a more stable readership than in the past. Elements of this new readership exhibit an almost fanatical interest in continuity issues, constantly writing to question, complain or suggest resolutions of apparent contradictions. This fan pressure coupled with the co-existing divergent expressions of the character have even necessitated explicit editorial statements about the canonical and non-canonical.

> 1) By the way, the BATMAN movie (as well as the BATMAN MOVIE ADAPTATION), IS NOT a part of Batman continuity.
> 2) . . . the tale told in BATMAN: THE KILLING JOKE is NOT the definitive origin of the Joker. It's simply one of many POSSIBLE origins. . . .
> 3) Since it is set about 20 years in the future, BATMAN: THE DARK KNIGHT RETURNS is also NOT considered to be a part of normal continuity. It is a POSSIBLE future for Batman, one which may or may not happen. We're NOT saying that it couldn't happen, but it would be a shame to limit the Batman's future to this one story.[32]

Despite the deliberate ambiguity concerning the Joker's origins, a Who's Who Entry for the Joker in *Detective Comics Annual 2* incorporated the *Killing Joke* origin, while accompanying illustrations referenced this story as well as *A Death in the Family* and "The Laughing Fish."[33] This Who's Who Entry again accomodated change yet reveals the containment strategy and self-appointed canonical authority of the DC editorial staff.

While *The Killing Joke* origin may or may not be canonical, the Batman film has been declared conclusively non-canonical, indicating that the DC staff, at least, believes that the comic books truly define the character. The explicit disavowal of the Warner Bros. film appears even in the comic book adaptation written by O'Neil, the Batman editor, and published by DC. The initial splash page shows a strip of film, bearing key frames drawn from the Batman movie, superimposed over an audience in a movie theatre. In the first dialogue balloon on the page, an audience member says ". . . it's just a movie, for Heaven's sake."[34] The back cover also features a film strip design with further scenes from the movie. Editor/writer O'Neil said that he intended these film strips to bracket the adaptation and distinguish it from DC's continuity.[35]

From a legal perspective, the DC staff is right about their canonical authority—their company and not Warner Bros. holds the trademark for "Batman and all related characters, the distinctive likenesses thereof and all related indicia. . . ." as every Batman comic states. DC has gone to great lengths in protecting bat-expressions through trademarking. *The Batman Role-Playing Game* lists 174 trademarked names for people, devices and places, ranging from Batman specifics such as Batcomputer, Batmobile, Bat-shuriken, and Bat team, to bat-specific locations and characters such as Gotham City, Gotham Institute of Technology, Gotham Tennis Hall of Fame, to more general locations and names such as Chelsea and Elizabeth Powell. These 174 trademarked names, of course, include only those used in the game, not every DC trademark.[36]

The DC legal department, then, serves to safeguard character identity through trademark and copyright registration and enforcement. The licensing and rights departments also protect character identity, granting permission to use Batman images on products or in other publications. This protection ensures a uniformity of iconographic and narrative depictions of the Batman and prevents dilution of the trademark. While for fans, canonicity and thus character identity resides in the editorial staff's control of the comic books, for the larger public, character identity resides in the legal department's control of commodity circulation of the Batman and related indicia. The floating signifier of the bat-logo is essentially a legal rather than a narrative evocation of the character.

"I shall become a *bat!*"

Long term DC artist and editor Dick Giordano explained the importance of Batman's origin story.

> Let's talk about Batman's origin and why I believe it is intrinsic to his belicvability, popularity, and longevity. The Batman was born in a few, brief, violent moments in which a young Bruce Wayne was forced to watch the brutal murder of his parents at the hands of a street thief. . . . We can all understand Bruce's grief . . . and we all can understand his need to do something to avenge the deaths of his parents. The origin of the Batman is grounded, therefore, in emotion. An emotion that is primal and timeless and dark. The Batman does what he does for himself, for *his* needs. That society gains from his actions is incidental. . . ."[37]

The first recountings of the origin, appearing in *Detective #33* (1939) and restaged in *Batman #*1 (l940), set out the minimal elements of a story since subjected to compulsive recountings and variations. In the 1940 version, as Bruce and his parents walked home from a movie, a nameless thug attacked them. Attempting to steal the mother's necklace, the hoodlum shot and killed both mother and father when the latter attempted to resist. A traumatized Bruce swore to take vengeance through a war on criminals. He spent several years and some of the family fortune preparing, becoming a master scientist/detective and an amazing athlete. Seeking both disguise and psychological advantage he decided that "I shall become a bat." "And thus is born this weird figure of the dark . . . this avenger of evil. The *Batman."*

Writers have repeatedly returned to the scene of the crime and restaged the origin much as it "happened" in 1940. Though the basic events remain sacrosanct, certain details have varied. In subseqent expansions and reworkings, the Batman identified the nameless thug as Joe Chill, tracked him down and brought him to justice. A few years later, he discovered that Chill had actually been employed by Lew Moxon, whom he also tracked down and brought to justice. Such details as the film the family had seen and the cause of the mother's death (gunshot or heart attack) may vary from version to version, but the reiteration of the basic origin events holds together otherwise divergent expressions of the Batman.

The fixed events of the origin serve two rather paradoxical functions: 1) they provide the motivation for the endless iterative events necessitated by the character's series nature and 2) they help to contain the character while also containing the traits/attributes that contribute to his elasticity. The origin explains the character's continuous crime-fighting. Though, in elaborations of the origin, the Batman avenges his parents' murder by apprehending the actual perpetrators, the metaphoric perpetrators they represent (the faceless thugs, the brutal hirelings, the crime bosses) still blight the urban landscape. Every encounter with a criminal, then, raises the spectre of that original encounter.

Justice-seeking becomes an endless process, with the Batman a Gotham Sisyphus who can never reach the crime-free summit of the mountain. Just as Sisyphus may roll the rock up a different path each time but not achieve his goal, the Batman may combat different criminals with different methods but not achieve his goal. This endless repetition accounts for the non-accruing nature of most of events.

Sisyphus and Batman are primarily defined by their iterative actions: Sisyphus is the man who pushes the rock; Batman is the man who fights crime. The origin thus accounts for the predominant genre of the Batman narratives. Similarly, it accounts for the character's relationship to authority and property rights. His childhood trauma stemmed from an incident in which attempted resistance to a petty violation of property rights (the theft of a necklace) gave rise to a capital crime (murder). Bruce Wayne's father was willing to give his life to defend property and uphold the law. The son followed in his father's footsteps. To compound the irony, the successful theft of the necklace would have deprived the Waynes of a mere fraction of their millions, the inheritance of which enabled Bruce to enter upon his Sisyphean task as the Batman.

Since many of the character's traits/attributes have their origin in the Batman's origin, further examination of the birth of the Dark Knight permits us to explore the primary locus of the character's elasticity. The origin story establishes the four central attributes/traits of the character: obsession; deductive abilities; physical prowess; and wealth. In the 1940 origin, the four panel sequence following the "terror and shock" of his parent's death, shows 1) young Bruce kneeling by his bedside, saying "And I swear by the spirits of my parents to avenge their deaths by spending the rest of my life warring on all criminals." 2) an older Bruce stands in a smoke filled laboratory peering into a test tube. The caption reads, "As the years pass Bruce Wayne prepares himself for his career. He becomes a master scientist." 3) Bruce holds a massive barbell in one hand. The caption reads, "Trains his body to physical perfection until he is able to perform amazing athletic feats." 4) Bruce sits in front of a huge portrait which hangs above a fireplace. He says, "Dad's estate left me wealthy. I am ready . . . But first I must have a disguise." The sequence is completed when the bat flies in the window and Bruce derives his inspiration.

Over the years, a process of uneven accentuation and development has selectively foregrounded or downplayed certain aspects of the key components. This process accounts for both the character's containment and refraction, the elastic treatment of the character's key components allowing his narrative undulations and, thus, his longevity. The current divergent forms of the character represent an ever more articulate and conscious reworking of the character's original capacities rather than the addition or subtraction of key components. This holds true even for that bat-text most often touted as reconfiguring and thus revitalizing the Batman, *The Dark Knight Returns*. Alan Moore realized that Frank Miller had not created a new Batman, but had rather differentially emphasized some of the key traits/attributes. "Depicted over the years as, alternately, a concerned do-gooder and a revenge-driven psychopath, the character as presented here [*The Dark Knight Returns*] manages to bridge both those interpretations quite easily while integrating them in a much larger and more persuasively realized personality."[38]

The constant repetition of the basic origin events has turned them into the central touchstone of the character, which can be and frequently are reduced to one sentence summaries. For example, in *Batman Annual* #13, the narration states "He is a man at war. An intense, obsessed soldier fulfilling an oath he'd made a lifetime ago while standing over his parents' grave."

The merest reference to the origin events activates an intertextual frame which insists upon the Batman's motivation and key traits/attributes while permitting for variant elaboration, as such recent restagings in *Gotham by Gaslight, Arkham Asylum, Legends of the Dark Knight* #1 and *Batman: The Movie* attest. *Gotham by Gaslight*, for example, tells a Batman story set in the nineteenth century, but assures that the reader understands that this Batman is indeed *the* Batman. The first two pages retell the origin with nineteenth century trappings: the Wayne family rides home in a carriage from an evening in town and is accosted by a highwayman who murders the parents. This cues the reader to expect the other key components of the Batman character, which are indeed trotted out: Alfred and Commissioner (then Inspector) Gordon; Gotham City; etc. *Arkham Asylum* emphasizes young Bruce's subjectivity. Bruce, frightened by the film he has just seen, annoys his mother with his crying. She threatens, "If you don't stop crying and act like a grown-up, I'm leaving you right here." She does indeed leave him, as the mugger immediately appears and enacts the ritual murders. This subjectivized version, foregrounding Bruce's insecurity and terror, and focusing on his mother rather than his father, resonates throughout the highly psychologized narrative.

Menage a Trois

Television static within a blazing white bat logo followed by a tracking shot through folds of luminous material to reveal a bat-costumed dancer. Chorus lines of Batmen and Jokers in choreographed tussles.

Prince garbed as half-Batman, half-Joker. Vicki Vale—Batman tattoo on her thigh and a Joker tattoo on her back. Fragments of dialogue sampled from the film.

The multiple bat-dancers of the Prince "Bat-Dance" video most clearly epitomize the multiplicity of Batmen currently proliferating in comics and other media. Which of these dancers is the "real" Batman? Which of the proliferating Batmen is the "real" Batman? "Bat-dance," establishing identity only through iconography and a recurrent character, provides a succinct answer: "real" Batmen wear bat-costumes and fight with Jokers. As Tim Burton put it, the movie the Prince video promoted was about "a man who dresses up like a bat vs. a man who has literally become a clown."[39]

The video presents us with multiple embodiments of the Batman as well as Prince's schizophrenic Batman/Joker and constitutes a clear expression of both the current fragmentation of the Batman character and the symbiotic relationship between him and the Joker. Yet the undulations of the chararacter over his fifty year history have always entailed simultaneous undulations in the presence/absence and depictions of the recurrent characters. In the past few years, the proliferating Batmen in various media present multiple personalities of the Batman, whose psychological make-up crucially relates to the presence/absence and depictions of the two (currently) most important of the recurrent characters: the Joker and Robin.

Both the Joker and Robin characters are defined within many of the same parameters as the Batman, but the parallels between the Batman and the Joker make the Clown Prince of Crime an equal but opposite, an evil doppelganger, while those between the Batman and Robin make the Boy Wonder a dependent reflection, a son/student. The Joker's crazed opposition to the Batman sets up a narrative tension which pulls the Batman's persona to extremes, driving him to the edge of dissolution, whereas Robin's vulnerable reliance tends to reinforce his more "human" dimensions, containing him within his traditional bounds. Thus, the tension between do-gooder and revenge-driven psychopath that Alan Moore noted can be seen as a tension between the shifting depictions and the presences/absences of Robin and the Joker.

The Joker, the oldest of the Batman's continuing antagonists, has enjoyed a great deal of popularity. Between his inception in 1940 and the imposition of the Comics Code, he surfaced nearly every month in one of the two Batman titles. Portrayed by Cesar Romero in the sixties television series, he tied with the Penguin for most guest villain slots, each featured in eighteen episodes. Recently, his popularity has waxed again: the graphic novels, *The Dark Knight Returns*, *Arkham Asylum*, and *The Killing Joke* all feature him in key roles as does the Warner's film. DC has recently issued a companion volume to *The Greatest Batman Stories Ever Told*, *The Greatest Joker Stories Ever Told*. The film has generated Joker ephemera which accompanies the Batman merchandise—toys, tee shirts, hats, etc.

His longevity and the frequency of his appearances establish his centrality to the Batman mythos, reinforcing the key components of his character. The Joker's origin story, in whatever variation, accounts for his motivation and his iconography. In "The Man Behind the Red Hood" (*Detective* #168 (1951)), The Joker bungles a million dollar heist from The Monarch Playing Card Company and escapes the clutches of the Batman by diving into a catch basin for noxious chemicals. The chemicals transform him from garden variety thief into the familiar Clown Prince of Crime. The Joker tells the Batman about looking at himself in the mirror after the accident. Voice over narration: ". . . I looked at myself with growing horror." Panel dialogue:—"That chemical vapor—it turned my hair *green*, my lips *rouge-red*, my skin *chalk-white!* I look like an *evil clown!*" Voice over: "Then, I realized my new face could terrify people."

Both the Batman and the Joker have their origins in cruel twists of fate. Just as the Batman responded to his tragedy by dedicating himself to justice, the Joker responded to his by dedicating himself to perverse, absurdist crime. Both singlemindedly pursue their goals, the Batman striving to impose order on an unjust universe and the Joker doing his best to enhance the chaos of a meaningless world. Just as the Batman adopts a distinctive costume which enables him to blend with the shadows of the night and to strike terror into cowardly, superstitious criminals, the Joker makes the most of his deformity by adopting a jester-like outfit to strike terror into his victims. Both acquire endless accessories based on their names and costumes, the Joker striving to keep up with the Batman with his Joker-mobile, his own utility belt, etc.

Sometimes the characters themselves address their symbiotic relationship. A panel in *A Death in the Family* alternates medium shots of the Joker and Bruce Wayne, as the latter thinks, "We've been linked to each other for so long, neither of us truly understanding the bond." The Joker, too, recognizes the bond that links them together, though, typically for him, speaks of it as a game. In a story where the Joker knocks out the Batman, he stands over his unconscious body musing, "His life is mine. . . . I can crush the breath out of him . . . *effortlessly!* I can, at last, *triumph!* But such a *hollow* victory—! . . . I've always envisioned my winning as a result of *cunning* . . . at the end of a *bitter struggle* between *the Batman* and myself—him using his *detective skills* and me employing the divine gift men call *madness! No!* Without the *game* that *the Batman* and I have played for so many years, winning is *nothing!*[40]

DC publisher Jenette Kahn agreed with the Joker that his game with the Batman must continue, since the hero and villain complement each other so perfectly.

> The Joker is out of control, and in this way neither Batman's powerful mind or strength can surround him. . . . Thus the Batman and the Joker form a Yin/Yang duality, the Joker needing the Batman (for who else could appreciate the bizarre genius of his acts?) and the Batman needing the Joker (for who else, truly, could test him?) It is a world of passionate, binding opposites.[41]

The Batman and the Joker have needed each other throughout their fifty year relationship, performing a bat-dance pas de deux in which each partner measures his step to the other. The Joker started his career as a smiling killer who murdered for profit, countered by an uncomplicated, no-nonsense, vigilante Batman. In the fifties and sixties, the Joker became a relatively harmless merry prankster countered by an uncomplicated, good-natured, boy scout Batman.

Today, an increasingly out-of-control Joker is a raging madman who kills 206 people for pleasure (*The Dark Knight Returns*), shoots Commissioner Gordon's daughter and photographs her nude body to drive her father mad (*The Killing Joke*) and eludes justice by becoming the Iranian ambassador to the United Nations, where he tries to gas the entire General Assembly (*A Death in the Family*). The Batman frequently captures the Joker and incarcerates him with the rest of the recurring villains in Gotham City's home for the criminally insane, Arkham Asylum. The graphic novel of that name features the most psychotic Joker of them all, who is so insane he may be sane. A psychotherapist explains the Joker's case to his long-time adversary.

> . . . we're not even sure if he can be properly defined as insane. . . . It's quite possible we may actually be looking at some kind of supersanity here. A brilliant new modification of human perception. More suited to urban life at the end of the twentieth century. Unlike you and I, the Joker seems to have no control over the sensory information he's receiving from the outside world. He can only cope with that chaotic barage of input by going with the flow. That's why somedays he's a mischievous clown, others a psychopathic killer. He has no real personality.[42]

While this may make the Joker the ideal postmodern cult figure, it has troubling implications for the more conventional Batman, who

continually strives to make sense of that urban chaos which so fundamentally altered his life. If the randomness of late twentieth-century
existence has driven the Joker into the asylum, then the Batman, who
shares so much with his adversary, may belong there too, enabling the
long-time partners to continue their dance in the proper setting. Indeed,
the Joker offers the Batman refuge. "We want you in here. With us. In
the madhouse. Where you belong." Batman, not thoroughly convinced
that he doesn't belong there, admits to Commissioner Gordon: "I'm
afraid the Joker may be right about me. Sometimes I . . . question the
rationality of my actions. And I'm afraid that when I walk through
those asylum gates. . . when I walk into Arkham and the doors close
behind me . . . it'll be just like coming home."

While the novelty of a totally obsessed and even crazed Batman may
appeal to readers who can afford $24.95 for *Arkham Asylum*, this degree
of mental deterioration erodes the character, and may threaten his
function as the series hero of an ongoing line of comics. The increasing
speculation about the character's sanity over the past few years has
generated DC insistence upon the Batman's clean bill of health.

> It's fashionable these days to claim that the Batman is, in his own
> way, as crazy as the Joker. . . . Everyone whose life has ever been
> touched by random, tragic chance has come away from it changed,
> in some way: some transfigured by rage, others by love, some by
> randomness itself. Bruce Wayne was touched by chance and transfig-
> ured by rage; but he's not crazy. And he never has been.[43]

The assertion of the character's sanity forms one of the central premises of the batbible. "First, let us agree that Wayne/Batman is not
insane. There is a difference between obsession and insanity. Obsessed
the man surely is, but he is in the fullest possession of his mental and
moral faculties."

The mental deterioration of the past few years has correlated directly
with the comings and goings of various Robins. The first of the Boy
Wonders entered the bat-world in 1940, the writers needing a foil for
their hero—a bat-Watson to serve an expository function.[44] But Robin
served another equally important function. No shadowy creature of the
night, this lad, his sunny disposition matching his brightly colored
costume. Robin tempered the Batman's grimness, the parallel tragedy
of Dick Grayson's parents' senseless death at the hands of criminals
making him, in some respects, a younger version of the Caped Crusader.
Robin thus shared with his mentor and surrogate parent not only a
bond of sympathy but acted as a continual reminder of the vulnerable
youngster Bruce Wayne had himself once been.

With the late sixties and early seventies return to the Dark Knight image, Robin/Dick Grayson, now more of a liability than an asset, was packed off to college. Making occasional guest appearances in his old pal's comics, Dick then went into the superhero business for himself, adopting the disguise of Nightwing and leading the Teen (subsequently the New) Titans. Yet even one of the most divergent articulations of the Batman, *The Dark Knight Returns,* incorporated a (female) Robin. Frank Miller explained why. "I had always thought that Robin was a real pain-in-the-ass, but I now realize what a brilliant creation it was, because it really does give a human context to Batman's character."[45] The writers of the regular series themselves also felt the need of a Robin, which Batman himself articulated after the death of Jason Todd (Robin II). "It's just that I felt so adrift when I lost Dick Grayson as a partner. The Batman needed a Robin."[46]

The Joker's murder of the second Robin precipitated a severe deterioration of the Batman's mental state, as the Batman, wracked by guilt, refused to come to terms with his grief. Two 1989 serial stories, *Batman: Year Three* and *A Lonely Place of Dying* centered around the Dark Knight's increasingly bizarre behavior, as the balance between physical violence and ratiocination which he (and his writers) had maintained shifted in favor of the former. Both Alfred and Dick Grayson express serious doubts about their friend's mental health, constantly reiterating that he has failed to come to terms with Jason's death, and that his violent and brutal responses negate everything that he stood for. As Alfred says, "I distinctly remember when . . . you said, 'We're not *brutalizers.* We've got to think with our heads, not with our fists.' Since Master Jason's death you've changed. It seems, sir, that you now do *all* your thinking with those sadly bruised and battered knuckles."[47]

The death of Robin and the subsequent profound psychologization of the Batman provoked intense fan debate, much centering around the Batman's mental state. A typical letter stated:

> His lack of reaction to Jason's death could destroy him. We all need to grieve, and a failure to do so is catastrophic, emotionally and psychologically, for the grieving person. Maybe Dick can heal the rift and, at the same time, help Bruce through this difficult time. But first Bruce must acknowledge these differences. It isn't easy for the Batman to show emotion, as it's a human weakness. If he bottles it all up, however, it will eventually explode, and he himself will suffer most of all.[48]

Only the introduction of yet another Robin could halt the Batman's decline. The mysteriously knowledgeable lad who first appears in *Bat-*

man #440 insists that Dick Grayson revert from Nightwing to Robin
and pull his friend back from the brink of psychosis. In *The New Titans*
#61, he holds out the old Robin costume to Nightwing. "Dick, please—
take this. It belongs to you! . . . He needs a partner again. Someone to
care about . . . Someone who cares about him." By *Batman* #442, Tim
Drake has inherited Robin's cheery costume and fights crime side-by-
side with the Caped Crusader.

But the last panel of the comic, showcasing the new Robin, contains
an extreme close-up of a grinning, bright-red mouth. ". . . Easy come,
easy go! HA HA HA HA. . . ." Evidently, the menage-a-trois will continue. The Joker has already dispensed with one Robin; the Batman's
evil doppelganger fittingly killing off the sunny presence which ensures
the Batman's psychic balance. How will the newly well-balanced Batman and his new Robin fare when they inevitably encounter the Clown
Prince of Crime? We suspect that Robin will survive, for DC has learned
a hard won lesson: as Batman himself said, "Batman and Robin. Maybe
they *have* to be a team."[49]

"...Batman only works if the world really sucks."

Who pays Batman's salary? Bruce Wayne, of course.[50] And Bruce's
money is old money, as the trappings of his existence reaffirm. A recent
Diet Coke commercial, at the head of the Warner Bros. video release of
the Batman movie, features "stately Wayne Manor," decorated in old-
fashioned opulence and serviced by a British butler, the Coca-Cola
theme scored for harpsichord reinforcing the dignified ambience. Just
as the Coke advertisement juxtaposes "old world" elegance with a sales
pitch, Wayne himself combines his inherited old money with savvy
new investment strategies, holding vast amounts of prime Gotham real
estate as well as profiting from Wayne Industries and Wayne Tech. He
even has a tax shelter, the Wayne Foundation, which makes substantial
contributions to charity. He's privileged, he's powerful—and, in recent
years, he has increasingly shed his dilettante playboy image for that of
good citizen.

Bruce's income as the source of Batman's salary metaphorically encapsulates several parallels between the day-time millionaire and his
night-time alter ego. Bruce Wayne is a pre-eminent citizen, particularly
through his charitable works, while the Batman is a pre-eminent state
functionary. Wayne's vast inheritance places him largely outside the
constraints of capitalist accumulation. Batman's vigilante brand of justice places him largely outside the constraints of the legal process.
Bruce is a super-citizen, the Batman is a super-cop and both strive to

make Gotham City a better place to live, that is, to make it accord with their own values.

While Batman/Bruce Wayne, like much of popular culture, obviously supports the status quo, not so obvious is the centrality of this support to the character's identity. The particular relationship to property and the state which Bruce/Batman embodies is embedded in his origins, manifested in the iterative events and reinforced by the other key components. His inheritance and his obsession both stem from an attempt to defend property—a mere necklace—against violation. The obsession causes him to engage in his Sisyphean reenactment of that original encounter. The recurrent supporting characters of criminal ilk and the setting activate the traits/atributes and put into play the iterative events which permit him to give rein to his obsession. All these crucially define the nature of crime in the Batman's world, which, in turn, crucially defines the relationship of the Batman to the social order.

Hence Batman to be Batman *must* fight crime, *must* protect property and *must* support the status quo. Other popular heroes such as Sherlock Holmes and Superman may support the status quo, but doing so does not constitute their *sine qua non*. Holmes, for example, dealt with many cases involving no legally defined wrong-doing. But Batman cannot be Batman without crime and criminals.

The "bad" recurrent characters fall into two categories: the highly individualized costumed villains and the endless array of interchangeable criminals in mufti who recur as types, not as individuals. As we have suggested above, one of the narrative functions of the costumed villains is to provide suitable opponents for the Batman. Every crime-fighting hero must have his Moriarty. But the costumed villains do not conform to the psychological profile of ordinary criminality: they steal not because they want the jewels (the money, the gold, etc.) but because the challenge of grappling with the Batman reaffirms their identity. The Batman similarly reaffirms his own identity by grappling with them. Property becomes a kind of McGuffin and both parties, the costumed villains and the Batman, play the game for the game's sake. While the costumed villains do pose a threat to property and the social order, they do so only incidentally—their primary purpose and narrative function being to match wits with the Batman.

When the Batman contests with the costumed villains, his actions to some extent disconnect him from the social order, but his class position remains firmly fixed by his alter ego, while the villains' lack of class position further exacerbates their disembodiment from the social order. Most of their crimes involve grandiose attempts to steal high visibility items from the wealthy or the state but arise from no political purpose or social need. Instead, the villains are inexorably drawn to capers which provide the greatest challenge and fit their *modus operandi*. The Penguin, for example, could not resist a Maltese Falcon while Two-Face would have to steal a statue of the Roman God Janus.

The highly idiosyncratic and personalized nature of the costumed villains' crimes relates to their psychological instability—the villains are always highly abnormal individuals whose crimes result from mental imbalance rather than more systemic social or political causes. Recently, the villains have been written with greater depth, more in accord with the canons of psychological realism. *Secret Origins Special* #1, for example, grounds the Penguin's compulsive criminal activity in childhood trauma. *The Killing Joke* similarly attributes the Joker's motivation to personal tragedy. The Joker had been an out-of-work comic unable to support his pregnant wife. Driven to desperation, he had agreed to participate in a robbery. Even after his wife's accidental death, the gangsters forced him to go through with the crime, during which he tried to escape into a severely polluted waterway. This "deglamorization" of the costumed villains transforms them from flamboyant madmen into pathetic losers but still insists upon the highly personal nature of their criminal activities and connects them no more closely to the social fabric.

Henri Ducard, one of the Batman's former mentors, summed up the relationship between the Caped Crusader and his costumed antagonists:

> [The Batman] . . . functions as a *lightning rod* for a certain breed of *psychotic*. They specialize in absurdly grandiose *schemes*, and whatever the ostensible rationale—their *true agenda* is always the same: to cast *Batman* in the role of *nemesis*. . . . He *always triumphs*. If he failed, they'd be *bereft*. The pas de deux would have no *point*. Like naughty children, who tempt the wrath of a stern, demanding *father*, they seek only to *shock* him by the *enormity* of their *transgressions*. It's the moment of *acknowledgement* they crave. Thus "good" conquers "evil." *True* evil seldom *announces* itself so *loudly*.[51]

Does true evil announce itself less loudly through the countless criminals in mufti who plague the great metropolis of Gotham City? Not really. In the universe of the Batman artists, phrenology and allied "sciences" have never lost their explanatory power. The nameless thugs seem driven to crime by anatomy. To paraphrase Jessica Rabbit, these criminals aren't really bad, they're just drawn bad. This "badness" extends to their apparel, which classifies them as outside respectable society.

In a very self-conscious restaging of the origin event, the Batman rescues a yuppie couple and their son from three instantly identifiable bad guys, muggers with broken or hooked noses, cauliflower ears, and low brows.[52] Each conforms to the stereotype of a different marginalized subculture: Mansonesque biker/hippy; fifties crew-cutted, leather-jacketed hood and contemporary punk. By contrast, the light hair and "clean" good looks of the yuppie family suit them to modeling the jogging suits they wear. These potential victims, like others throughout the bat-texts, resemble the Waynes, Graysons, Todds and Drakes, with their blue eyes, firm chins, straight noses, noble brows, and Anglo names much more than the nameless, though often clearly ethnic, thugs.

The three street punks who attack the yuppie family typify not only the appearance of their countless colleagues, but also their modus operandi. Most of Gotham City's nameless criminals, the lineal descendants of the initially nameless thief who murdered the Waynes, engage in similar thefts and malefactions. Much like local television newsmen, the Batman expends most of his energy on crimes of violence with visual potential, ignoring the visually boring crimes of political grafters, polluters and slum landlords. In Batman's universe, those criminals necessarily embodying a critique of the system remain ignored while the violent criminals whom he fights remain divorced from the social fabric which produces them.

The transiency of these violent criminals usually, of course, prevents any detailed elaboration of their motivation or their social origins. But even one of the most fully elaborated and intermittently reappearing of these bad guys remains largely separate from the social fabric. Boss Anthony Zucco, indirectly responsible for the deaths of Dick Grayson's parents, curiously enough experienced a childhood trauma similar to both the Batman's and Robin's. His father was killed by hoodlums for refusing to pay protection money. Young Anthony grew up in the same orphanage as young Dick Grayson, but then their paths crucially diverged—Anthony becoming a crime boss and Dick a crime fighter. The crucial difference: "Zucco was brought up with hatred, and that's what he returned to the world. Richard Grayson was brought up with love—and not even Zucco's act of murder could change that."[53] Dick is good because his parents were good, and Zucco is bad because his parents were bad, explanation for wrong-doing again being cast in highly personal terms.

Despite the fact that the perpetrators of crime have highly personalized motivations which place them outside a socio-economic context, the site of crime is paradoxically depicted as the very type of urban wasteland which would seem to provide a socio-economic context for crimes of violence. Gotham has in the past been presented as a light and cheery playground (resembling Superman's Metropolis) for the merry pranks of the costumed villains. Of late the emphasis has been on urban decay. Commissioner Gordon recently said, "When I first came to Gotham I thought this city couldn't sink any *lower*. Every day proves me wrong!"[54] If Commissioner Gordon knew how the batbible describes his city, the word lower might take on a whole new meaning for him. "Gotham is a distillation of everything that's dark, moody and frightening about New York. It is Hell's Kitchen. The Lower East Side. Bed Stuy. The South Bronx. Soho and Tribeca off the main thoroughfares at three in the morning."

Gotham certainly looks "dark, moody and frightening," with its deserted warehouse districts, garbage strewn alleys, lurking shadows, dilapidated buildings, abandoned construction sites, and tiny people lost in dark, deserted streets loomed over by grotesquely embellished skyscrapers. As a line from the Batman script, repeated endlessly in the film's publicity, put it, Gotham City looks "as if hell had erupted through the sidewalks."[55] This representation of Gotham certainly gives a compelling image of late twentieth-century urban decay, as any New Yorker can attest, and the astute reader will certainly see these conditions as a causal factor in the high Gotham City crime rate. Yet, like the criminals, Gotham is largely removed from a socio-eocnomic context. The narratives deal with the crime rate, but not the unemployment rate; they deal with criminal brutality, but not brutalizing slum landlords; they deal with the greed of petty theft but not poverty and hopelessness—in short, they deal with the trangressions of the underclasses but not the conditions that give rise to these transgressions.

The terrifying reality of the depiction, however, tends to obscure causality while enhancing the Batman's motivation.

As Frank Miller said, ". . . Batman only really works as a character if the world is essentially a malevolent, frightening place."[56] The depiction of Gotham helps Batman to work as a character by persuading the reader to empathize uncritically with the hero's actions. Let us return to our yuppie family blithely jogging their way through the urban blight. The polarity between good and evil manifested in the innocent victims and the overarmed, oversized robbers, the dread invoked by the empty, litter-strewn streets, the unfair odds of three armed thugs against one lone, unarmed avenger of the night, all compounded by the deliberate reinvocation of the Batman's own origin/obsession, encourage the reader to urge the Batman to retributive punishment. The final panel leaves the exact nature of this retribution to the reader's imagination.

In this instance, as in any of the iterative events, the Batman fights crime, and thus serves as an agent of political domination, safeguarding property relations and enforcing the law. Extratextually, the character and the bat-texts serve to gain consent for political authority and the system of property relations it enshrines, and thus support the dominant hegemonic order. Again we ask, who pays the salary of this agent of political domination and this supporter of the hegemonic order? One who has a great stake in the maintenance of the status quo, Bruce Wayne. This may initially appear to be a deconstructive instance of political domination: a rich man devoting his life to vigilante justice. But the Batman's origin/obsession provides an overarching route of emotional identification even for readers who might have qualms about vigilante justice. Young Bruce's witnessing of the violation of property rights—in the fullest sense of human life—both motivates him within the text and, more importantly, wins the readers' consent to a political position: the inviolability of property relations and the justification of their defense by any means necessary (short of death). The divorce of crime from larger social issues and its embodiment in crazed costume villains or brutal gangsters reinforces the acceptance of this political position.

"I'm not fooled by that cheap disguise.
I *know* what you are."

The crazed shrink of Arkham Asylum believes the Batman to be the metaphoric bat that has driven him to madness.[57] We harbor no such delusions. We know that the Batman is neither Dr. Cavendish's fiendish bat nor the upright defender of the weak and innocent that he himself might claim to be. We know that he functions textually as an agent of political domination and extra-textually as both supporter of the hegemonic order and a commodity form. Does the recent fragmentation of his identity that we have discussed threaten any of these functions?

The Batman's hegemonic postion seems unassailable, triply reinforced by his definition as an obsessive crime fighter, his superhero status and the narrative centrality/authority granted him.

1). *Obsessive Crime Fighter.* Addressing the recent refractions of the Batman character, novelist Eric Van Lustbader claimed ". . . the Batman remains essentially the same, which speaks volumes about his lasting power as a symbol both of elemental fear and of protean protector against the encroachment of night's dread anarchy."[58] Lustbader here identifies that component we believe most centrally defines and contains the character—protection against night's dread anarchy, that is, against crime as presented in the bat-texts. For Lustbader, the Batman should symbolize elemental fear only to anarchy's agents. We believe that he may, in fact, symbolize an even greater fear to those

whom he might claim to aid and protect. As James Gordon said in
Batman #7, "Yes—he works 'outside the law,' as you call it, but the
legal devices that hamper us are hurdled by this crimefighter so he may
bring these men of evil to justice. . . ."[59] This policeman's willingness
to use any means necessary, even "extra-legal" ones, to defend the
"law" provides a particularly clear, if chilling, expression of the Batman's role as as an agent of political domination. Nonetheless, his
obsession, as we have explained above, serves to disguise his extra-legal
dimension and gain support for the hegemonic order.

2). *Superhero Status.* Commentators on the bat-texts constantly
refer to that which sets the Batman apart from other superheroes: he
has no superpowers. As he himself has said, "I . . . I'm a man."[60] As
editor O'Neil has said, it is the quality of human perfectibility which
makes the Batman so attractive to readers, many of whom may secretly
believe that they too could become a bat (with sufficient motivation
and lots of training).[61] *Christianity Today* (of all publications!) addressed this utopian dimension of the Batman's character. "But while
God is conspicuously absent from this universe, Batman appears to
scale the heights to which a mere man can pull himself by his own Bat-
boots. It is difficult to believe that, apart from God's grace, personal
tragedy and suffering can be turned to such an advantage."[62]

But the Batman deliberately cultivates a non-human image to aid
him in his crime fighting—he became a bat, after all. And the image
seems to work. One of the cornered street punks who had attacked the
yuppie family, exclaims, "You're not people! Nothin' like you can be
human! You ain't human, so *nothing* can stop you—man, that ain't
fair."[63] This non-human dimension frees him from the standards of
evaluation applied to lesser mortals. To quote Frank Miller again, "I
think that in order for the character to work, he has to be a force that
in certain ways is beyond good and evil. It can't be judged by the terms
we would use to describe something a man would do because we can't
think of him as a man."[64]

Though he might be different from his supercolleagues, the Batman
is still more superhero than ordinary guy and this status implicitly
endorses his actions. Just as superheroes' superpowers transcend those
of ordinary individuals, so does their supermorality. The Batman's intertextual construction as superhero reinforces his hegemonic function.

3). *Narrative Structure.* While narrative can be construed broadly
enough to include the above two points, specific narrative devices may
foster further reader acceptance of the Batman's hegemonic function.
The bat-texts clearly focalize around the Batman. *Batman Comics*, of
course, foreground the hero in the title, but the covers of both *Batman*
and *Detective* always feature images of the Batman or at least his

distinctive iconography. The stories, in addition to granting him narrative centrality, often cede him narrative authority through point-of-view frames, first person narration, and other devices similar to those film scholars often argue create identification with a character. While we would prefer to deal with actual rather than textually extrapolated readings, dominant cultural constructions of narrative encourage us seriously to consider the implications of these narrative devices.

The bat-texts' intertextual resonance with the larger genre of detective fiction (very broadly defined) also elicits support for the Batman's activities. Though we earlier differentiated the Batman from such other series heroes as Holmes, Marlowe and Bond, he does, in fact, have a generic affiliation with them, proclaimed by the very title of his longest running comic, *Detective.* Indeed, the cover of the fiftieth-anniversary issue of this title consciously references the Batman's lineage, showing him and Sherlock Holmes together. The detective genre has traditionally privileged the hero and encouraged reader identification with him and his exploits.

Unassailable as the Batman's hegemonic function may seem, given the above three factors, some recent bat-texts may have widened incipient fissures in the Batman's construction. Miller's *The Dark Knight Returns,* the opening salvo in the Batman's high-end marketing offensive, departed from the Batman mythos by, as we have said, featuring a fifty-year-old Batman with a female Robin. But his outlawing by the Gotham City police force, his resistance of presidential authority and his fighting with Superman severely questioned the Batman's role as an agent of political dominantion and actually constituted far more significant departures. His new outlaw position caused him to reappraise his analysis of the social order and ultimately to ally with elements of the underclass he had initially struggled to contain. Significantly, however, this alliance took the form of protecting property as the Batman, at the head of the mutant gangs, prevents middle-class rioters from looting a supermarket. *The Dark Knight Returns* problematizes the Batman's role within a dominant political order depicted as irredeemably corrupt and bankrupt, and challenges a political system which could continually re-elect Reagan president while outlawing the Batman, but reaffirms the Batman's role as lone vigilante striving for a higher justice. Society may be corrupt but the Batman's honor and vision remain above reproach in this libertarian tract.

Significantly, the next texts to exploit potential fissures in the Batman's facade did so not by taking up Miller's political critique but rather by exploring the nature of the Batman's obsession. *Arkham Asylum* calls the Batman's motivation into question, showing that the Batman himself suffers from serious doubts about his sanity. *The Kill-*

ing Joke draws explicit parallels between the Joker's trauma and the Batman's, as the Joker urges his nemesis to succumb to a justifiable madness. *Batman: Year Three* and *A Lonely Place of Dying* show the Batman becoming as brutal as the thugs he fights, ignoring his deductive abilities while relying on his physical prowess to punish malefactors.

While all these texts challenge his motivation, they don't question his role as agent of political domination. Both *Arkham Asylum* and *The Killing Joke* stage confrontations between the Batman and costumed villains in isolated settings—an asylum and an abandoned fairground—environments which reflect and justify the character's extremis and thus serve to contain the broader social implications. And in both narratives, the Batman emerges intact, if not exactly triumphant, from his trial. *Batman: Year Three* and *A Lonely Place of Dying* raise doubts not about his role as agent of political domination, but about his performance of that role. If he becomes too overtly brutal neither the supporting characters (Alfred and Dick Grayson) nor the reader can contine to give him their consent.

Some recent texts, significantly in the regular titles, however, have begun to exhibit a certain self-conscious awareness of the Batman's hegemonic function, questioning the most central component of the Batman's identity—the nature of crime and his relation to it. "Anarky™ in Gotham City," (*Detective* #608–609), potentially redefines crime to include industrial polluters and real estate speculators. A twelve-year-old boy, calling himself Anarky and dressed in superhero-like garb, kills a chemical manufacturer with the supposedly "safe" sludge he is dumping into the river, and attempts to demolish a bank being built on the site of a community of homeless persons. Batman can not utterly condemn Anarky's actions or his definition of crime, but seeks to distinguish himself from his fellow vigilante. "His cause may be just—but his methods certainly *aren't*." Alfred interjects, "Really, sir?" Batman responds. "I know, I know—my own methods aren't always legal, either. But there *is* a difference, Alfred. . . . I only use violence when it's absolutely necessary, not as a form of punishment . . . not lately anyway!"[65]

The Batman writers have presented an even blunter reappraisal of their hero's cosmology, permitting Henri Ducard to question the Batman's entire *raison d'être*. "While Batman busies himself with petty thieves and gaudy *madmen*, an *abyss of rot* yawns ever wider at his feet. He's a *band-aid* on a *cancer patient*. I am of course no *moralist*, but this Batman I think, has a very poor understanding of the *world*."[66]

While this kind of questioning seems to represent a fairly minor component of the bat-texts and has yet to be valorized by inclusion in a more expensive format, it nonetheless constitutes the gravest threat to the character's identity amongst the centrifugal forces we have enumerated. Yet the ™ following the name Anarky raises the issue of whether even this seemingly substantial critique will undermine the character or be incorporated as another marketing technique, for the Batman's circulation in commodity form is as important as his support of the hegemonic order. The contradictions of capitalism would thus permit the commodification of criticisms as long as they resulted in profits.

Yet the endless possibilities of containment and refraction inherent in the Batman character result in tensions, all of which act as potential time-bombs. By contrast, that expression of the character which has the widest cultural currency remains unthreatened either by textual challenges to the Batman's role as agent of political domination/supporter of political hegemony or by the centrifugal forces of commodification—valorization of authorship, market diversification. The bat-logo constitutes an expression of corporate presence/control, a point of minimal contact with the character for non bat-fans, and a magnet for discretionary income. Paradoxically a clearer manifestation of private property and the dominant hegemonic order protecting it than the character it signifies, the bat-logo floats untouched, above criticism. A resident of Gotham City recently stated, "I've lived in this city for fifty years and I've never seen any of those creeps [costumed villains]. Or Batman."[67] But he has surely seen the bat-logo.

Notes

1. The title of the chapter is taken from Grant Morrison, *Arkham Asylum* (New York: DC Comics, Inc., 1989), n.p.

2. Box side panel, Batman™ Cereal (St. Louis, MO: Ralston Purina Co., 1989).

3. Box side panel, Batman™ Cereal.

4. "Writer: Sam Hamm," *Comics Interview* 70 (1989), p. 17.

5. John Marriott, *Batman: The Official Book of the Movie* (London: Bantam Books, 1989), p. 39.

6. Howard A. Rodman, "They Shoot Comic Books, Don't They?" *American Film*, May 1989, p. 38.

7. Bill Barol, "Batmania," *Newsweek*, June 26, 1989, p. 72.

8. Simon Garfield, "Batman Versus Hollywood," *Time Out: 20/20*, July 1989, p. 54.

9. "Artist: Bob Kane," *Comics Interview* 70 (1989), p. 49.

10. The Batman's mortality, of course, gives him the potential for aging, though *The Dark Knight Returns* is so far the only text to activate this potential.

11. We are indebted to Henry Jenkins, III for this insight.

12. This is not to assert that Batman has never done anything but fight crime. In *Batman*

#156 (1963) he even fights a pink space monster, but most fans and writers view this and similar science-fictional episodes as aberrant.

13. Dennis O'Neil, "A Brief Batbible: Notes on the Dark Night Detective," unpublished manuscript, April, 1989, n.p.

14. We use the term "iterative" in Umberto Eco's, not Gerard Genette's, sense. Eco defines the iterative as follows: "a series of events repeated according to a set scheme (. . . in such a way that each event takes up again from a sort of virtual beginning, ignoring where the preceding event left off). . . ." Umberto Eco, "The Myth of Superman," in *The Role of the Reader: Explorations in the Semiotics of Texts* (Bloomington, IN: Indiana University Press, 1979) p. 117.

15. Neil Gaiman, "When is a Door. The Secret Origin of the Riddler," *Secret Origins Special* #1 (1989).

16. *Rolling Stone*, June 29, 1989, p. 43.

17. For a discussion of the rise of the direct distribution network, we refer the reader to the Parsons' essay in this volume (Chapter 5).

18. "Artist: Bob Kane," *Comics Interview* 31 (1986), p. 17.

19. *Batman* #206 (November 1968).

20. Letter from Greg W. Myers, "Batcave," *Detective Comics* #495 (October 1980).

21. This recent reconfiguration of authorship in the comics industry accords with the authorship function as described by Michel Foucault. See "What is an Author?" *Language, Counter-Memory, Practice* (Ithaca, NY: Cornell University Press, 1977).

22. The masculine pronoun reflects the current dominance of males at the two major companies.

23. Advertisement for DC Comics in Dennis O'Neil, *The Batman Movie Adaption* (New York: DC Comics, 1989).

24. Jenette Kahn, "Don't Call Me Chief!" *The New Titans* #61 (December 1989).

25. The quotation in the heading of this section is taken from Alan Moore, "The Mark of Batman," in *The Complete Frank Miller Batman* (Stamford, CT: Longmeadow Press, 1989) n.p.

26. Mike Gold, "Our Darkest Knight," *The Greatest Batman Stories Ever Told* (New York: DC Comics Inc., 1988), p. 14.

27. For thirty-five of his fifty years, two men, Jack Schiff and Julie Schwartz, edited the Batman titles. Most of the editors since Schwartz's retirement had worked with him as writers or artists.

28. Jenette Kahn, "Don't Call Me Chief!" *Legends of the Dark Knight* 3 (January 1990).

29. Alan Moore, *Batman: The Killing Joke* (New York: D.C. Comics, 1988) n.p.

30. Neil Gaiman, "When is a Door. The Secret Origin of the Riddler," *Secret Origins Special* #1 (1989).

31. Interview with Dennis O'Neil, see Chapter 2 in this volume.

32. "Batsignals," *Batman* #442 (1989), n.p.

33. "Who's Who," *Detective Comics Annual* #2 (1989).

34. Dennis O'Neil, *Batman: The Official Comic Adaptation of the Warner Bros. Motion Picture* (New York: DC Comics Inc., 1989).

35. Personal Conversation with Dennis O'Neil, September 29, 1989.

36. *The Batman Role-Playing Game* (Niles, IL: Mayfair Games, Inc., 1989).

37. Dick Giordano, "Growing Up With the Greatest," *The Greatest Batman Stories Ever Told* (New York: DC Comics Inc., 1988), pp. 7–8.

38. Moore, "The Mark of Batman," n.p.

39. Batman Card #238, Second Series, The Topps Company, 1989.

40. Dennis O'Neil, "The Joker's Five-Way Revenge," *Batman* #251 (September 1973).

41. Jenette Kahn, "Tribute," *Detective Comics* #599 (April 1989).

42. Morrison.

43. Alan Brennert, "Tribute," *Detective Comics* #600, (May 1989).

44. Bob Kane saw both narrative and other reasons for a Robin. "... I think it was a *bad* move to kill Robin off. First of all they were a team—it would be like killing Dr. Watson off and leaving Sherlock Holmes by himself or Tonto and the Lone Ranger, Tarzan and Jane. It's the wrong move. And, of course, it *kills* the merchandizing on Robin. ..." ("Artist: Bob Kane," *Comics Interview* 70 (1989), p. 47).

45. "Spotlight: Dark Knight," *Comic's Interview* 31 (1986), p. 32.

46. Jim Starlin, *A Death in the Family* (New York: DC Comics, 1988).

47. Marv Wolfman, "A Lonely Place of Dying," part 1, *Batman* #440 (1989).

48. Letter from Malcolm Bourne, *Batman* #440 (1989).

49. Marv Wolfman, "A Lonely Place of Dying," *Batman* #442.

50. The quotation in the heading of this section is from "Frank Miller: Return of the Dark Knight," *The Comics Journal* 101 (August 1985), p. 64.

51. Sam Hamm, "Blind Justice" Part 3, *Detective Comics* #600 (1989).

52. Marv Wolfman, "The Coming Of Crimesmith," *Batman* #443 (January 1990).

53. Marv Wolfman, "Batman: Year Three (Part I)," *Batman* #436 (1989).

54. *Batman* #443 (January 1990).

55. Sam Hamm and Warren Skaaren, "*BATMAN*," unpublished screenplay, Oct. 6, 1988.

56. "Spotlight: Dark Knight," p. 37.

57. The quotation in the heading of this section is from Morrison.

58. Eric Van Lustbader, "Tribute," *Detective Comics* #600 (May 1989).

59. *Batman* #7 quoted in Mark Cotta Vaz, *Tales of the Dark Knight* p. 4.

60. Morrison.

61. Personal conversation, Dennis O'Neil, September 29, 1989.

62. Dean Husler, "Gotham Great Grows Grim," *Christianity Today*, May 12, 1989, p. 65.

63. *Batman* #443.

64. "Frank Miller: Return of the Dark Knight," *The Comics Journal* 101 (August 1985), p. 61.

65. Alan Grant, "Anarky in Gotham City," *Detective Comics* #608 (1989).

66. Sam Hamm, "Blind Justice," Part III, *Detective Comics* #600 (May 1989).

67. Neil Gaiman, "Original Sins," *Secret Origins* #1 (1989).